Power Tools

for

SYNTHESIZER PROGRAMMING

The Ultimate Reference for Sound Design

BY JIM AIKIN

Backbeat
Books

San Francisco

Published by Backbeat Books
600 Harrison Street, San Francisco, CA 94107
www.backbeatbooks.com
email: books@musicplayer.com

An imprint of the Music Player Network
Publishers of *Guitar Player*, *Bass Player*, *Keyboard*, and other magazines
United Entertainment Media, Inc.
A CMP Information company

CMP
United Business Media

Distributed to the book trade in the US and Canada by
Publishers Group West, 1700 Fourth Street, Berkeley, CA 94710

Distributed to the music trade in the US and Canada by
Hal Leonard Publishing, P.O. Box 13819, Milwaukee, WI 53213

Cover and text design by Doug Gordon

Library of Congress Cataloging-in-Publication Data

Aikin, Jim.
  Power tools for synthesizer programming : the ultimate reference for
    sound design / by Jim Aikin.
    p. cm.
  Includes index.
  ISBN 0-87930-773-0
  1. Synthesizer (Musical instrument) 2. Computer sound processing.
    I. Title.
  ML74.A53 2003
  786.7'419—dc22

                                                    2003063617

Printed in the United States of America

06 07 08   5 4 3 2

Contents

Foreword   v

Introduction   vii

Acknowledgments   viii

Chapter 1: The Map & the Territory   1

What Are the Power Tools?   3

Hardware vs. Software Synthesizers   8

Power Projects:

    Project 1-1: Research Your Instrument on the Internet 10

    Project 1-2: Learn About Your Synth's MIDI

        Implementation   10

Chapter 2: The Nature of Sound   13

Sound Waves   14

Frequency   16

Amplitude   18

Transducers   19

Digital Audio   20

Sampling Rate   21

Bit Resolution   22

Phase Cancellation   26

Power Projects:

    Project 2-1: Listen & Sample   29

    Project 2-2: Evaluate Your Monitoring Setup   29

Chapter 3: Operating Systems,

Edit Modes & Memory   31

Digital vs. Analog   32

Operating Systems   33

Memory   35

Pages, Menus & Soft Keys   40

Data Entry   42

Modes   43

Editing Presets   49

Program Changes   49

Power Projects:

    Project 3-1: Organize Your RAM   50

    Project 3-2: Big Multi   50

Chapter 4: Oscillators   53

Analog Waveforms   54

Aliasing   56

Noise   57

Sound Programming Techniques

    with Analog Oscillators   58

Sample Playback   65

Single-Cycle Digital Waves   70

Wave Sequencing   71

Audio-Rate Modulation   71

Additive Synthesis   73

Granular Synthesis   74

Physical Modeling   74

Power Projects:

    Project 4-1: Listen to the Waveforms   75

    Project 4-2: Combine Waveforms   76

    Project 4-3: Discover the Waveforms

        in the Factory Patches   76

    Project 4-4: Swap Waveforms   77

Chapter 5: Filters   79

Types of Filters   83

Formant Filters   84

Cutoff Frequency & Rolloff Slope   85

Resonance   88

Overdrive   90

Filters & Polyphony   90

Filter Modulation 91

Signal Routing 95

Power Projects:

    Project 5-1: Filter Modes & Cutoff Frequency 98

    Project 5-2: Filter Envelope & Velocity 98

Chapter 6: **LFOs** 101

Waveforms 102

LFO Amount 106

LFO Rate 108

Delay & Ramp-Up 109

Trigger Modes 110

Phase 112

Synchronization 114

Power Projects:

    Project 6-1: Trill Chords 114

    Project 6-2: Synced Timbre Grooves 115

Chapter 7: **Envelope Generators** 117

Gates, Triggers & MIDI 118

The Shape of Things to Come 120

Rates vs. Times 124

More Stages 125

Inverted Output 127

Single & Multiple Triggering 127

Throwing a Few Curves 128

Modulating the Envelope 130

Looping Envelopes 133

X/Y Envelopes 133

Envelope Followers 135

Unusual Contour Generators 135

Power Projects:

    Project 7-1: Snappy Segments 136

    Project 7-2: Reverse Staccato 136

Chapter 8: **Modulation** 139

Control Rate & Data Resolution 139

Modulation Signal Routing 143

Secondary Modulation 145

Modulation Signal Processing 146

Velocity Response Curves 147

MIDI Control Sources 149

Audio Signals as Control Signals 155

Power Projects:

    Project 8-1: Learn the Routings 156

    Project 8-2: The Bends 156

Chapter 9: **Effects Processing** 157

Processors & Algorithms 158

Signal Routing 160

Multitimbral Setups & Physical Outputs 163

External Audio Inputs 163

Reverb & Delay 164

Chorus, Flanger & Phaser 169

Rotary Speaker 170

Distortion 171

Pitch-Shifting 173

Filter & Envelope Follower 173

Equalization 174

Compressor, Limiter & Gate 177

Vocoder 179

Ring Modulator 181

Real-Time Control of Effects 182

Power Projects:

    Project 9-1: Dry vs. Wet 182

    Project 9-2: Effects Chaining 183

Appendix: CD Track Listing 185

Index 193

Foreword

I have been involved with this electronic music stuff for over 40 years, since the mid-1960s. I sort of took a left turn at doo-wop and ended up on the corner of Stockhausen and Varese. My involvement has been as a composer and educator, but the most exciting hat I've worn has been that of performer. The earliest gigs with this new medium were with black boxes connected with alligator clips and an occasional break-through innovation such as a battery-operated mixer from Radio Shack. Most of the instruments were homemade, and what audiences heard was, as often as not, the result of blown out op-amps and not really knowing what we were doing.

Then came the synthesizer. The Buchla boxes, Moog cabinets, and ARP racks were an easy transition. They were not much more than the circuits we were familiar with, except that the alligator clips were replaced with patch cords — and the term "patch" has been with us ever since! The real difference was in the playing and in the music. I'm still not convinced that a piano-type keyboard is the most efficient thing to put between the performer and an unlimited world of sonic ideas, but it did change the music. We could actually play predetermined notes and calculated rhythms. This electronic music stuff was no longer a genre of music — the instruments were crossing over into the mainstream of European music history, and musicians who used electronics could work in any area from Gabrieli to Subotnick. The "electronic" and "computer" music bins at record stores were starting to disappear. Those that remained contained the expected experimental and avant-garde works, but also included electronic-nouveau arrangements of Bach, Debussy, Stravinsky, Christmas carols, and country tunes, and the roots of what would become European techo-rock.

By the '80s it was clear what this electronic music stuff was — it was simply *orchestration*. The instruments were sophisticated enough to be embraced by the various flavors of current rock and pop, new music groups, solo renegade performers, and even Hollywood. But then appeared the green-eyed monster, and its name was the Factory Patch. Technological advances made it possible to store what had previously been patchcord connections in the instrument's memory for immediate recall. This, of course, was a boon for the traditional forms of performance, and probably the most significant marketing advance in the history of the instrument. However, it did not encourage what these instruments were all about — the creation of new sounds — *synthesis*. It was very easy to get the standard string pad, Rhodes piano, B3 organ, or metal-rimboid sound — and to be satisfied going no further.

As a teacher I observed that learning electronic music now meant mastering the latest hardware/software sequencer and tweaking the final mix. Now, don't get me wrong — this is an essential part of every musician's training in the 21st century. But synthesizers had their genesis in the desire, if not the need, to play with sound. Then, lo and behold, came the computer revolution (evolution), and all of 30 years of black boxes, cables, knobs, and racks turned to zeroes and ones behind a spiffy computer screen interface. The software synthesizer was born. What a concept — you could build it yourself, just the way we did in the '60s.

This has led a new generation of musicians back to the art of sound programming, thanks to low-cost and often free software, and has brought a renewed interest in retro-tech. Hardware, software, analog, digital — it makes no difference. Programming and electronic sound design use the same concepts, basically the same terms, and certainly the same creative logic that they have from the beginning. We've come full circle, returning once more to the task of innovative sound creation, and this brings me to the subject of this book.

Jim Aikin has been involved with this electronic music stuff as a player, composer, writer, consultant, and educator for many years. His work with *Keyboard* magazine provided him with an ideal hands-on history of the development of synthesis tools and techniques. His previous book, *Software Synthesizers*, provided a survey of the terrain of on-screen sound design. *Power Tools for Synthesizer Programming* is a comprehensive look at the concepts of sound programming as applied in either hardware or software instruments, focusing on and demystifying the more technical details of the craft. I anticipate that this book will provide a new generation of explorers the guidance, encouragement, and enthusiasm to explore the resources of electronic music for another 40 years.

—*Allen Strange*

Allen Strange is a composer and performer who works extensively with electronic media. He is the author of Electronic Music: Systems, Techniques, and Controls, *first published in 1972 and used for many years as a textbook and reference source. With Patricia Strange, he has more recently written* The Contemporary Violin [*University of California Press*].

Introduction

The reasons why a book on synthesizer programming is needed are discussed pretty thoroughly in Chapter One. Not much remains to be said by way of an introduction. Well, perhaps one or two things.

Power Tools for Synthesizer Programming is an uneasy blend of two distinct approaches to authorship. On the one hand, it's designed for a mainstream music market, where it will be (I hope) purchased and read by musicians who need to know — urgently, in many cases — how to make better music with their synthesizers, and who have found themselves floundering through badly written manuals or baffled by the jargon spouted by slick salespeople. On the other hand, I wanted to provide a solid enough discussion of technical details that the book could be used as a textbook in introductory courses on electronic music at the high-school and college level.

The mainstream market, it has to be admitted, has a bias against the paraphernalia of textbooks. Footnotes are taboo, and a rigorous discussion of minutiae sometimes has to give way before the need to rein in the page count. In any event, while I have quite a lot of practical experience in the electronic music field, which I've tried to compress into these pages, I have no academic credentials that would impress a textbook publisher. What you hold in your hands, then, is a pop music book that tries (perhaps, at times, a little too hard) to provide accurate detail about technical subjects.

Whether the book succeeds in meeting the needs of its readers remains to be seen. But since it's very possible that within a few years the publishers will want to bring out a second edition (synthesizers are *not* going to go away any time soon), I'd like to ask each and every one of you to help make the next edition as useful as possible. If there are topics you would have liked to see covered in the book that were omitted, or if the coverage of certain topics left you scratching your head, please let me know! I can be reached at synth1@musicwords.net. Also, in the event that you spot a technical error, I'd very much like to know about it.

—*Jim Aikin*
Livermore, California

Acknowledgments

I'd like to express my heartfelt thanks to Richard Johnston and Backbeat Books for making it possible for me to write *Power Tools for Synthesizer Programming*. Thanks also to Tom Darter, Dominic Milano, Greg Rule, and the rest of the folks at *Keyboard* for giving me the opportunity, over the course of many years, to spend so much time working with and writing about a wide assortment of synthesizers. A number of engineers throughout the industry have freely shared their time and expertise with me over the years; Bob Moog is at the very top of the list. Thanks, Bob!

Numerous manufacturers, developers, marketing directors, and product managers have generously provided software and hardware for my use, in some cases loaning expensive items to *Keyboard* for many years. (I certainly couldn't have afforded to buy all the stuff you'll read about in these pages.) Thanks, in no particular order, to Jerry Kovarsky of Korg, Chris Martirano of Kurzweil, Paul Youngblood of Roland, Avery Burdette and the team at Yamaha, Omar Torres and Tom Bolton at Native Instruments, Marsha Vdovin for providing a liaison with Propellerhead and other companies, and several other people whose names escape me at the moment. (You know who you are!)

Thanks to the readers of *Keyboard* for years of positive feedback and insightful questions, to the participants in various newsgroups and email lists I've been part of for putting up with my dumb questions and cranky attitude, and to Daniel Fisher and Gino Robair for their many helpful editing suggestions.

Finally, thanks to David Zicarelli of Cycling '74 for first pointing me in the direction of a new book on synthesizer programming. Needless to say, David is not responsible for the final shape or choice of contents in the finished work. Nor is anyone mentioned above responsible for any technical errors that may have eluded detection. Responsibility for the errors (I'm sure there are a few) is entirely my own.

—JA

Chapter 1
The Map & the Territory

What does a synthesizer sound like?

Like anything you can imagine, and like nothing in particular. And that fact is both more remarkable and more difficult to come to grips with than might at first appear.

Until the middle of the 20th century, each type of musical instrument could generate only a relatively small, fixed repertoire of closely related tone colors. Though there was some overlap (a piccolo sounds a lot like a flute, and a viola not unlike a cello when the two are played in the same range), each instrument stamped the sounds it made with its own identity. Few listeners will ever mistake a trumpet for an electric guitar.

Once electronic technology got into the act, however, the lid flew off. Sound itself has become a plastic medium — and the family of instruments that allows musicians to command the infinitely malleable palette of electronic sounds has come to be called synthesizers.

This is not the place for a complete history of electronic musical instruments. Which is a shame, because it's a fascinating story. Though it might come as a surprise to some readers, the synthesizer didn't spring full-grown from the forehead of Bob Moog in Trumansburg, New York, in 1964. The precursors of today's instruments stretch back at least as far as Thaddeus Cahill's mammoth Telharmonium, which he patented in 1897, several years before the invention of the vacuum tube. Between 1920 and the late 1950s, numerous electronic instruments were built and used. Most, however visionary, were mere curiosities; but a few, such as the Theremin, the Ondes Martenot, and the Hammond organ, were embraced by musicians and, in the case of the Hammond organ, manufactured in large numbers.

The instruments developed in the early 1960s by Moog on the East Coast and Don Buchla on the West Coast were groundbreaking in two ways: first because of the sheer range of tones they could produce, and second because they put the tone color under the control of the performer in a direct way via arrays of knobs and switches. (The RCA Synthesizer, which was developed in the mid-1950s and was the direct antecedent of Moog's early instruments, was "played" by punching holes in spools of paper tape — not exactly a spontaneous process.) Add to the picture the cultural ferment of the late 1960s, which produced a new kind of pop music, and the stage was set for the emergence of the synthesizer as an instrument in its own right.

Today synthesizers are heard everywhere, from mainstream pop to symphony concerts and the furthest reaches of the avant-garde. Yet the question immediately arises: *Is* the synthesizer an instrument in its own right? Its sound is undefined. The variety of instruments sold as synthesizers is so broad as to render the term "synthesizer" almost meaningless. Just about every model built by every manufacturer has a different array of controls (wheels, buttons, levers, knobs, ribbons, pedals, sliders), which makes it difficult for musicians to develop the kind of standardized performance techniques associated with traditional instruments. And given the rapid pace with which new technologies develop, it seems clear tomorrow's synthesizers will differ, perhaps radically, from today's and yesterday's.

Yet beneath the welter of confusion — feature sets, terminology, types of synthesis, and the fact that instrument builders sometimes go to great lengths to give listeners the illusion that they're hearing something else (an electric piano or violin section, for instance) — strong threads link the various instruments called synthesizers. What's more, there *is* a common body of performance technique that accomplished synthesizer players know and use, no matter what specific instrument they may be playing.

As a new kind of instrument, the synthesizer requires that we redefine the phrase "performance technique." On conventional instruments, technique is mostly about moving your fingers, plus maybe your arms and legs or your lips and tongue. Because the sound of the synthesizer is undefined, a significant part — perhaps the most important part — of synthesizer performance takes place *before* the performer goes onstage or enters the studio. A synthesizer player has to start by defining (or at least choosing) the sounds that he or she will use in a particular piece or set of pieces. A synthesizer player is, inevitably, a sound designer.

This book is about the tools that synthesizers provide for designing sounds, and about how to use those tools to create specific musical effects. Though you might not think it when you look at the front panels of two or three instruments built by different manufacturers, there's a surprising amount of commonality among synths. Every manufacturer tries to add a few wrinkles or widgets that will set their instrument apart, but good ideas tend to stick around. The ADSR envelope generator, for instance, has been a staple of synthesizer design since the late 1960s, and new instruments with unadorned ADSRs are still being built today. (For an explanation of this terminology, see Chapter Seven.)

If you own a synthesizer or are asked to play one at a rehearsal or recording session, you'll need to know about the tools the instrument provides. At the simplest level, you may need only to choose from among the presets found in the instrument's memory. Even this is not quite as simple a process as you might think; for details, turn to Chapter Three, "Operating Systems, Edit Modes & Memory." But what if you can't find the sound you need, or if you find a sound that's almost right, but not quite? In order to customize an instrument's existing sounds, you'll need a clear understanding of its features.

Sad to say, not all owner's manuals will tell you what you need to know. Ultimately, you'll need to read the manual, or at least consult it from time to time. This book couldn't possibly include all of the instrument-specific operations and obscure options found on hundreds of models, nor is it designed to. But most manuals are at least adequate when it comes to instrument-specific features. What's generally missing from manuals, I've found, is an overview that would put the features in some sort of musical context. The manual may list the parameters of the instrument's LFO (low-frequency oscillator), for instance, but provide not a glimmer about why or when you would want to use an LFO. Nor is the manual likely to tell you about features that might be musically important to you in a given situation, but that are *not* found in this particular instrument's LFO, filter, or whatever. Sometimes, the solution to a problem in sound design is to use a different synthesizer — or even to use something other than a synthesizer.

By providing an overview of the features found in many different instruments, this book will put the features of your instrument(s) in a musical context. Along the way, you may learn about some sound design possibilities that you might not have considered, either because your synth doesn't allow for them, or because it *does* allow for them but buries them deep in a sub-sub-sub-menu where only power users dare to tread.

If what you're looking for is a cookbook that will tell you how to get a great string or Clavinet sound, this book may not quite meet your needs. While a number of recipes, or at least key ingredients, are discussed, musicians' needs are too varied for a cookbook approach to be of much lasting value. Once you're familiar with the ingredients in the spice rack, you'll be able to develop your own recipes. Where synthesizers are concerned, cooking up your own sounds is part of the creative process.

What Are the Power Tools?

Since *Synthesizer Programming* is part of Backbeat's Power Tools series, the question naturally arises, what exactly *are* the "power tools" for synthesizer programming? Also, doesn't that term imply that the book will skip lightly over the basics?

As far as I'm concerned, every feature of every synthesizer is potentially a power tool. If it does what you want it to do musically, and if you aren't aware of what it will do until you learn about it and spend some time exploring what it will do, it's a power tool. All of the basics are included in these pages; nothing was skipped in an effort to appeal to folks who already know a thing or two; but the field is wide enough that few of us (myself included) can claim to know everything there is to know. Even if you're a power user already, you'll probably pick up a few new facts as you go along, or at least get a few new ideas on how to use the tools you're already familiar with.

Beyond that, however, there are some specialized tools that can make your life as a synthesizer player a bit more pleasant and productive.

Editor/Librarian Software. If you have a computer, you may want to look into acquiring an editor/librarian. An editor/librarian is a piece of software that works in conjunction with your hardware synthesizer, specifically to aid in the process of creating sounds and managing and storing them. An editor/librarian doesn't make any sound by itself, nor (with two or three exceptions that can safely be ignored) does it give your hardware synth any features that the synth doesn't have on its own. What an editor/librarian does, first and foremost, is to replace your synth's front panel controls, which may be fairly cramped and cryptic, with a nice big computer screen. It does this by communicating with your synth over MIDI using a type of MIDI data called *system-exclusive*.

Secondarily, an editor/librarian allows you to store an unlimited number of sound banks from your synth's memory on the computer's hard drive, and to reshuffle the data in those sound banks in ways that may be convenient for a particular project. For instance, if you're going to be playing a session where you know the producer will need string sounds, you can pre-load your synth's memory with dozens or hundreds of string programs, so as to be ready when the producer says, "Do you have something warmer?"

As of this writing (mid-2003) there are three main editor/librarian programs. Emagic SoundDiver (www.emagic.de) is Macintosh-only. Mark of the Unicorn Unisyn (www.motu.com) has always been a Mac program, but a Windows version appears imminent. Sound Quest Midi Quest (www.squest.com) is primarily Windows-only, but an earlier version for obsolete Macs is still available. Each program supports a long list of synths, which is why they're sometimes called "universal" editor/librarians. Because the universe of synthesizers is constantly expanding,

---

JARGON BUSTER: System-exclusive MIDI data is the one type of MIDI communication whose meaning isn't defined in the MIDI Specification. Instead, each manufacturer is allowed to define the sys-ex messages that will be sent and received by their own instruments. The mechanics of this process are simple: Each sys-ex data packet begins with hexadecimal number F0 and ends with F7. (To learn more about hexadecimal, see page 6.) In between, the manufacturer can stuff any number of data bytes. A sys-ex packet that changes the value of a single synth parameter might only be five or six bytes in length, but sys-ex packets containing thousands of bytes are used for some purposes, such as sending the entire contents of a synthesizer's memory from one place to another.

Most manufacturers publish the sys-ex implementations of their instruments. It's not too likely you'll ever need to refer to this documentation, however. Just follow the instructions in the manual and let the synth itself worry about the details of the sys-ex communications.

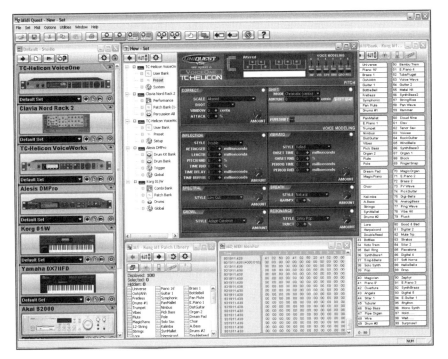

Figure 1-1.
Midi Quest editor/librarian software running in Windows XP. Installed instruments are in the column at left, an editor window for the TC Helicon is open in the center, and a patch bank for a Korg M1 is visible at right.

however, it's not easy for the software manufacturers to keep up, so you can't safely assume that your instrument will be supported by any of the programs: Ask before you buy. Each of them has tools with which you can write a template for an instrument that's not in the list, but this time-consuming exercise is not for the faint of heart. It requires the ability to decipher strings of MIDI system-exclusive data in hexadecimal format.

A few synths are sold with special one-instrument versions of SoundDiver already in the box. In addition, Yamaha has started creating dedicated editor/librarians for their own instruments, which again are included when you buy the synth. While more limited in some ways than universal ed/libs (Yamaha, for instance, provides no technical support for their software), bundled software is a valuable enhancement for a product.

Editor/librarians are arguably a less important type of support product today than they were ten or fifteen years ago. This is because newer synths have more memory for storing programs than earlier models, as well as better operating systems, larger displays, and more physical controls. Even so, if you're serious about using synthesizers, you may find an editor/librarian a worthwhile investment. All three programs have another useful feature: If you have a sequencer that's compatible with the editor/librarian, you can make parameter changes from the

I PUT A HEX ON YOU: Two-digit hexadecimal numbers are often used in technical descriptions of MIDI data. Hexadecimal (familiarly known as "hex") is base-16, which means that it has six more digits than our usual base-10 (decimal) system. In hexadecimal, the digits are 0, 1, 2, 3, 4, 5, 6, 7, 8, 9, A, B, C, D, E, and F. If you keep counting, the single digit F (equivalent to 15 in base-10 arithmetic) is followed by 10 (equivalent to 16 in base-10). The second digit is the "sixteens place" rather than the "tens place."

Hexadecimal numbers are sometimes indicated in print with an 'H' following the number or a '$' or '0x' preceding it. So the number 0BH is equivalent to decimal 11. An eight-bit byte can be written as a two-digit hex number. It's customary to indicate the first digit, even when it's 0 (0B rather than just B).

A MIDI *status byte* is a two-digit hex number whose first digit is 8 or higher. For instance, a program change message begins with the status byte C*n*, where *n* is the channel number. And while we humans think of MIDI as having channels 1 through 16, in hexadecimal they're numbered 0 through 15. So the program change status byte CA is on channel 11, not channel 10.

MIDI *data bytes* are in the range between 00 and 7F. A normal MIDI message consists of a status byte followed by zero or more data bytes. Each status byte is unique, and has a meaning that's defined in the MIDI Specification, but the meanings of the data bytes depend entirely on the value of the preceding status byte.

editor/librarian while a sequence plays and record them into the sequencer. This makes it possible to automate sound changes in ways that your synth may not be able to manage on its own.

If all you need to do is make computer backups of the sound banks in your synth's memory, you can do so without an editor/librarian. Most synths can transmit their memory contents as system-exclusive data. (A chunk of data containing an entire sound bank is sometimes known as a MIDI bulk dump.) This data can be recorded into a computer sequencer. You won't be able to edit it in the sequencer, but you'll be able to store it to hard disk as a song file, reload it at a later date, and play the song file into the synth so as to restore the sound bank. When saving this type of song file, it's advisable to take notes. Your synth may have an *instrument ID* number in its global or system area. If you should change this number after storing the sys-ex data, the synth will probably refuse to recognize the data.

MIDI. By any definition of the term, MIDI is a power tool for those who want to get the most out of their synthesizers. True, there still are a few analog synths around that don't use MIDI. For that matter, a few computer-based synthesis programs, such as Csound, can operate entirely outside the MIDI realm. Nonetheless, an understanding of MIDI is essential.

This is not the place for a full-fledged MIDI tutorial, but if you're new to using MIDI, a few basic concepts are well worth knowing.

MIDI (the Musical Instrument Digital Interface) is a communications protocol that allows synthesizers, sequencers, and other similar devices to talk to one another. MIDI signals don't carry sound: MIDI is strictly a way of encoding performance information, such as which key has just been struck on a MIDI keyboard and how hard it was struck, or which knob has been turned and how far.

Many types of messages are defined in the MIDI Specification. However, very few synthesizers make use of all of the types of messages. Each synth will be able to transmit certain message types and understand them when they're received. It may even be able to understand a few types of messages that it can't transmit.

The MIDI features of a synth are known, collectively, as its MIDI implementation. It's up to the manufacturer to decide which MIDI features to put in the MIDI implementation; as a user, you can't do anything to expand or enhance the implementation. The MIDI implementation of a given instrument will probably be explained in the owner's manual, but in most cases this part of the manual is cryptic in the extreme, printed in tiny, light gray type, or both.

MIDI messages are of two types: channel messages and system messages. Channel messages contain the actual music performance information — note-on and note-off messages, pitch-bend, and so on. System messages are used for everything else. For the most part, when you're playing a synthesizer you'll be concerned with sending and receiving channel messages. Only in a few cases, such as when you're synchronizing an LFO to MIDI clock signals (a type of system message), will you be using non-channel messages for musical purposes.

Aspects of synths' MIDI implementations are discussed throughout this book where it seemed appropriate to do so.

Your Ears. The ultimate power tool in synthesizer programming is your sensitivity to sound. As you spend more time customizing existing sounds and designing your own, you'll begin to develop a far greater awareness of phenomena like attack transients and beating (both of which are defined in these pages). This can be both a blessing and a curse. On the plus side, you'll find yourself getting excited about sounds that you hear, imagining ways to use them musically or make them your own. On the minus side, it's easy to waste half an hour trying to nail down the filter envelope settings or some other aspect of a sound, only to realize at the end of the process that the sound wasn't worth all that trouble to begin with.

When synthesizer players talk about sound, a certain amount of voodoo, or at least mystification, can creep into the discussion. Does real analog truly sound different from digital simulations thereof? Maybe. Does it make a significant difference in the music? Maybe not.

If you're convinced a particular instrument or patch sounds warmer or fatter in a subtle way that you can't quite put your finger on, but that you *know* is real because you can hear it, check how you're monitoring the sound. The human ear is fairly sensitive to subtle differences in loudness level, but they may be perceived subjectively as something other than loudness. I've read that in blind listening tests, sounds that were 1dB louder were sometimes perceived as being warmer or fuller or having more presence.

Other aspects of monitoring are important as well. Trying to program a synth in a room with poor acoustics or background noise, or while listening through inadequate speakers, is an invitation to frustration and dissatisfaction. Headphones can be useful for helping you focus on sonic details, detect subtle distortion or

TIP: If your synth can be set to transmit MIDI system-exclusive in response to the changes you make in front panel parameter settings, switch this feature on when you're doing any extensive sound design work. Put your sequencer in record mode (making sure to set its input filter so that it will record sys-ex data but not pass it through to the MIDI out) and leave the sequencer running in the background while you edit sounds in the synth.

At any point where you realize you've lost the magic sound you were aiming at — that you had it five minutes ago, but then you did something wrong and now you don't know how to get back to where you were — the sequencer will save the day. Stop recording, recall the stored sound (the one you started with at the beginning of the editing session) from the synth's memory, and then play back the sequence. When you reach the point where you're hearing the magic sound again, stop the sequencer and store the patch. (Thanks to Michael Marans, former Technical Editor of *Keyboard* and now Vice President of Event Electronics, who first suggested this idea to me.)

clicking noises, and so on, but they can also cause aural fatigue, provide an unrealistic stereo image, and mislead you by magnifying details that aren't important.

Hardware vs. Software Synthesizers

The synthesizer market has been transformed in the past few years by the development of synthesizers that exist only in the form of programs that run on general-purpose computers. These instruments offer significant advantages in terms of cost and ease of use, along with some undeniable disadvantages. While they're often referred to as software synthesizers (indeed, I recently produced a book with that title), it's more correct to refer to them as computer-based synthesizers. There are two reasons for this. First, most dedicated-hardware synths are all-digital on the inside, which means they require software in order to make their sounds. They're as much "software synths" as any instrument that runs on a computer. Second, a computer is itself an expensive piece of hardware, so pretending that one type of instrument is "hardware" while another exists in a realm that's free of hardware is just silly.

Having said all that, though, using the term "softsynth" to refer to a computer-based instrument and "hardware" to refer to one that exists only in a dedicated piece of hardware is easy, and will be easily understood. When insisting on a pedantic distinction would make the writing clumsy, I've taken the easy way out.

With respect to many of the topics discussed in this book, there are few or no significant differences between hardware and software instruments. A single section can cover them both without referring explicitly to either. In situations where the two types of instruments operate differently, I've noted the differences. (See, for instance, the discussion of memory in Chapter Three.)

If you're considering which type of instrument to buy, you may find the discussion below, which is adapted from the first chapter of my book *Software Synthesizers* [Backbeat, 2003], helpful:

■ Nine times out of ten, the software in a "hardware" synth will be more stable and reliable than its computer-based counterpart. This is because the manufacturer designed the operating system (OS) and also designed or at least chose the chips on which the instrument runs. The manufacturer doesn't have to write code that can survive in the often hostile environment of a multitasking computer OS. At the very least, if the software in the hardware synth is bug-ridden, it won't wipe out a half-written, unsaved email message when it crashes.

■ If well cared for, a hardware synth will last for many years. Before too much longer, obsolescence is going to become a real and painful problem in the world of software synths, because a given synth can only run on computer operating systems that were in existence when it was created. When you upgrade to a new OS from Microsoft or Apple, which you may want or need to do in order to get access to other features, your favorite softsynth may no longer be usable. This is especially likely if the softsynth developer has gone out of business. If the developer is still in business and still supporting that particular synth, many months may pass before a version compatible with the new OS is released. The long-term picture is fairly bleak: No matter how much you may love Absynth, Reason, or Stylus, the probability that it will still be usable 20 years from now is small.

■ With a hardware synth, you almost always get a guaranteed voice count. Synths that can play 32, 64, or even 128 notes at once are common and affordable. Most computer-based synths choke at far fewer than 128 voices, even on a blazingly fast computer. As computers get faster, softsynth developers seem to respond not by adding more polyphony but by designing ever more complex synthesis processes, so that the total voice count stays low.

■ A hardware synth has a fixed amount of memory. You may be able to store 128 of your own sounds, or 512, but no more. The hard drive on a computer can store gazillions of synthesizer patches.

■ Hardware synths often have keyboards and/or front panels studded with knobs. In a single box you get both the tone-producing circuitry and a responsive user interface. The mouse and the QWERTY keyboard were never intended for music performance. On the other hand, the big screen in a computer is a huge advantage when it comes to programming your own sounds, or even seeing what's going on in an existing sound.

■ If you already have a fast computer equipped with a decent audio interface, a softsynth will be considerably cheaper than its hardware counterpart. And because the manufacturing and shipping costs are far lower, softsynth developers have more freedom to innovate. For the foreseeable future, the frontiers of sound design are likely to be in the computer realm, not in dedicated hardware.

■ A hardware synth doesn't require a separate audio or MIDI interface, with all of the attendant installation hassles — all of the basic connectivity is built in. The convenience factor is hard to knock. If you're starting from scratch, a computer-based synth is *not* necessarily cheaper than its dedicated-hardware counterpart, because you'll have to buy not only the computer but several accessories, including a MIDI keyboard, to assemble an equivalent instrument. The cost savings occur later, as you buy programs that add new types of synthesis to your existing hardware — something that at this date is possible with very few dedicated-hardware instruments (for example, CreamWare Noah and the Symbolic Sound Capybara).

■ Computers are not notoriously easy to take on a gig. Granted, a hardware synth is fragile too. It's not something you want to see a drunken roadie toss into the back of a van at 2:00 in the morning. But for the most part, hardware synths are built to survive the normal rigors of the road. Most computers aren't.

■ Many developers of computer-based synths offer free downloadable demos, with which you can try out the instrument for a limited time before buying it. Very few stores provide loaner hardware to prospective customers.

■ Softsynths can be updated with new features and bugfixes somewhat more easily than their hardware counterparts. This is less true than it used to be. As discussed in Chapter Three, OS updates for many hardware synths can be downloaded and transmitted to the synth via MIDI. But even so, softsynths still have an edge when it comes to updates.

■ You can use an effect plug-in from a different manufacturer pretty easily with a softsynth. I don't know of any current hardware synth that allows third-party effects to be installed.

■ Hardware synths are always *low-latency*. That is, when you press a key, the synth will start producing sound within a few milliseconds. While low-latency computer audio interfaces are a lot more common than they used to be, you may have to spend a little time fine-tuning your computer system, or buy a more expensive audio interface, so that the softsynth can respond to a MIDI performance without out perceptible time lags.

 ## Power Projects for Chapter 1

Project 1-1: Research Your Instrument on the Internet. The online resources for synthesizer players are well worth investigating. A good place to start your search is the Synth Zone (www.synthzone.com). They have pages of links for all of the major synth manufacturers, as well as links for support products.

Visit the manufacturer's website to learn about possible operating system updates, accessories, and so on. Some manufacturers (Roland, for instance) sell user-installable add-on boards that increase the sound palette by expanding the memory of the synth. Others (such as Yamaha) offer boards that expand the instrument's polyphony and provide additional types of synthesis.

If you have access to newsgroups, add rec.music.makers.synth to your list of subscribed groups. While a lot of the messages posted there are for-sale notices, you'll also find technical discussions and debates about the desirability of particular instruments. The forums on sites like Music Player (www.musicplayer.com) are another good resource, whether you're looking for information on synth programming or some other topic. The manufacturer of your synth may also have a forum where you can communicate with other owners.

Project 1-2: Learn About Your Synth's MIDI Implementation. Somewhere near the back of your synthesizer's owner's manual, you'll probably find a page, or perhaps several pages, providing cryptic data on the instrument's MIDI implementation. Spend a little time perusing this information. Even if you don't memorize all the details (nobody ever does), figuring out the format of the charts and listings will pay dividends when you need to look up something in the future.

A MIDI implementation chart typically has an 'X' for data types that are not transmitted or received, and an 'O' for types that are. Some manuals also provide byte-by-byte descriptions (in hexadecimal) of the instrument's bank select, control change, and system-exclusive implementation. If you ever need to reset the pitch-bend depth on the fly in the middle of a sequence, this is where you'll find out how to do it.

Chapter 2
The Nature of Sound

Synthesizers are designed to produce sound. A synth that doesn't perform this function with reasonable reliability is, at best, an expensive doorstop. In order to get the most out of your synth, then, you'll need to start by developing a basic understanding of the physics of sound.

Mere physics won't quite do the job, however. The study of sound is separated, with some overlap, into two areas — acoustics (what's actually going on in the air) and psychoacoustics (what happens when the sound waves reach your ears and brain). The ear is pretty good at reporting to the brain on the waves of sound that reach it, but it has some built-in biases and limitations.

A quick practical example, before we go on: The ear gives the brain fairly reliable information about the frequencies of sounds when they're in the middle of the frequency spectrum. (We'll define the term "frequency" in a minute.) But the frequencies of extremely high and extremely low sounds are not perceived with as much accuracy. This is why it's so hard to hear the pitch of a sub-bass patch (whose foundation is a sine or triangle wave — something with few or no overtones). The sub-bass can be out of tune, yet you may not notice until after you've finished mixing and sent the master off to the duplicating plant, which would be somewhat unfortunate.

In order to talk intelligently about what happens to sounds inside a synthesizer, we need to start by looking at how sound behaves in the air. In this chapter we'll nail down some other vital concepts as well — things like the overtone series and digital sampling technology. If some of this seems pretty abstract, when all you want to do is crank the knob on a filter and get down with your bad self, feel free to spin forward to Chapter Three or Four. This chapter will still be here whenever you need to refer back to it.

Sound Waves

Our senses screen out information that wasn't important to our ancestors' survival. One of the things that wasn't terribly important until we began building high-altitude airliners is that we live at the bottom of a thick blanket of air called the atmosphere. The reason the air doesn't fly away into space is because of gravity. Above your head at this moment (unless you're reading this on a spaceship) are several miles of air, all of it being pulled downward by gravity. The result: At sea level, the atmosphere exerts a constant pressure of about 14.7 pounds per square inch. We never notice this pressure, because our bodies evolved in such a way that we're perfectly at home in it.

The air pressure isn't entirely constant. It's always increasing and decreasing — not very much, but some. The phenomenon we call sound consists of changes in air pressure. To qualify as sound, the changes have to be fairly rapid; a change in barometric pressure over the course of a day wouldn't usually be called sound, though in some sense it's a form of low-frequency sound.

To take a practical example, let's suppose that the fluctuations in air pressure originate at some point — perhaps the stretched skin of a drumhead when a conga player smacks it with his or her hand. When first struck, the drumhead moves downward. This creates a zone of slightly lower than normal air pressure on the upper surface (and a zone of slightly higher than normal pressure on the underside of the surface, but let's ignore that for now). Because all of the air is under a lot of pressure, air molecules will rush in from the surrounding area to fill the low-pressure zone and bring it back to normal pressure. As a result, the air pressure in the surrounding area drops momentarily, and molecules from still further out have to rush in (in fact, they're pushed in by the molecules beyond them) to restore the normal pressure. As a result, the zone of low pressure moves rapidly outward, away from the drumhead.

Meanwhile, the drumhead, which is somewhat elastic and was stretched downward, has rebounded upward. It's now pushing *up* on the air just above it, creating a zone of slightly higher than normal air pressure. The air molecules, which a moment ago were slightly further apart than average, are now jammed slightly closer together than they usually are. Since there's nothing holding them together, however, they spread out. As they enter the nearby region, they increase the pressure there for a moment.

The result of all this hectic activity is fairly simple: Zones of higher and lower pressure, which are called *sound waves*, propagate outward in all directions from

PROGRAMMING TIP: When recording a bass synth part, especially one from a genuine analog synth, (1) switch to a sawtooth wave temporarily, (2) open up the filter, and (3) check to make sure the bass is in tune with the other instruments. The oscillators in genuine analog instruments can drift slightly (change frequency) due to temperature and other factors. Also, the tuning knobs on some analog oscillators can be varied in a continuous fashion. There may not be a notch or detent on the knob where you can be sure the oscillator is perfectly in tune, so you may have to nudge it carefully.

the drumhead. This process continues for as long as the drumhead keeps wobbling up and down. When it stops, the air pressure stabilizes and the sound stops.

"Wobbling up and down" is a loose way of saying "vibrating." Sounds are produced by the vibration of physical objects, and we can also refer to the sound waves themselves as vibrations. Exactly the same thing happens in the air, whether the vibrations are coming from a drumhead, a guitar string, a trumpeter's lips, or a speaker cone.

The speed with which the pressure waves travel through a medium (the speed of sound) depends on the density of the medium. Sound travels more quickly through denser materials. At normal air pressure — at sea level, in other words — sound travels at a little more than 1,000 feet per second.

Even though we can't observe it directly in its travel, this fact has some practical consequences. In a large symphony orchestra, for instance, the players at one side of the stage may be more than 100 feet from those at the other side. Thus the sound of the woodblock will reach the violinists at the back of the violin section 1/10 second after the woodblock was struck. If the violinists play in perfect time with the woodblock as they hear it, from the audience the violins will sound 1/10 second late.

To return to the earlier example, the harder our imaginary conga drum is struck, the further up and down the drumhead will travel. This will increase the *pressure differential* between the highest and lowest pressures in the sound. The technical term for a change in the amount of air pressure (or, for that matter, a change in the amount of an electrical signal) is *amplitude*. The wider the swings in pressure, the greater the amplitude of the sound. Our ears interpret amplitude as *loudness*. A light tap of the drumhead produces only very slight pressure changes, and thus a quiet sound. Smack the drum smartly and the pressure differences will be much greater, thus the sound will be much louder.

If you spend any time reading about audio, before long you'll surely run into a diagram that looks more or less like **Figure 2-1**. This shows what sound would look like if we could see it. In this type of diagram, the amplitude of a sound is shown as the distance away from the center line that the waveform travels: Quiet sounds are close to the line, and loud sounds are shown as wide sweeps. (Amplitude is not quite the same thing as loudness, but for the moment we'll consider the two terms interchangeable.) The frequency of the sound can be judged, at least in a general way, by looking at how close together or far apart the peaks and dips are.

On a computer audio editor, you'll be able to zoom in, either vertically or horizontally, in order to inspect the waveform more closely. If you've zoomed in vertically, a waveform whose amplitude is low can fill the entire vertical range of the window, so it's not easy to get any exact information about loudness (or, for that matter, frequency) simply by looking at the display. However, the X (horizontal) and Y (vertical) axes of the diagram will usually be marked off in units of measurement.

16   Power Tools for Synthesizer Programming

Figure 2-1.
This graph shows what a
sound (in this case, a kick
drum hit) looks like when
displayed on a computer
screen. The horizontal line
down the center indicates
the normal background air
pressure, and time moves
from left to right. The
wiggly line is called a
waveform. Places where
the waveform rises above
the center line indicate
times when the air
pressure is higher than
normal. In places where
the waveform dips below
the center line, the air
pressure is less than
normal.

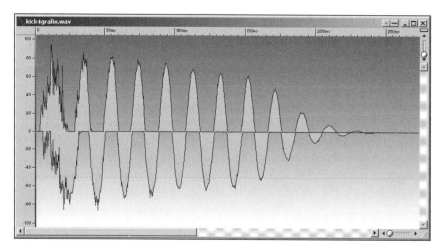

The markings are often called rulers. Glancing at the rulers will give you a better idea of what's going on in the waveform.

Amplitude and frequency are the two primary characteristics of sound. In order to talk intelligently about sound, we need to lay out a bit of terminology for both.

Frequency

Frequency is measured in cycles per second. The unit of measurement used to describe cycles per second is *Hertz* (abbreviated Hz). If the pressure wave of a sound increases and decreases three times each second, we can say it has a frequency of three cycles per second, or 3Hz. If it increases and decreases 3,000 times per second, the frequency is 3,000Hz. The prefix "kilo-" means "thousand," so 3,000 Hertz is the same as 3 kiloHertz, which is abbreviated 3kHz.

Sounds whose frequencies are less than 20Hz are not generally perceptible by the human ear, though you may be able to feel them in your gut. Sounds whose frequencies are greater than 20kHz are so high that, again, your ear simply isn't built to pick them up. The range of frequencies that the human ear can hear is generally considered to be 20Hz–20kHz. As people get older, however, their ability to hear high frequencies generally diminishes.

Very few sounds in nature consist entirely of vibrations at a single frequency. This is because a real physical object, such as a drumhead, vibrates in a complex way. Depending on how the drum is constructed, some portions of the head may be moving upward while others are moving downward, and some of them may be moving quickly while others move more slowly. As a result, the sound of a drum will contain vibrations at many different frequencies at once.

An 18th Century French mathematician named Jean-Baptiste Fourier (pronounced "Four-yay") developed a procedure that allows any complex vibration to be described as the sum of one or more *sine waves*. This procedure is called *Fourier analysis*. Fourier analysis is a complex mathematical process; fortunately, you don't need to be able to do the math to program sounds on a synthesizer. But having at least an intuitive understanding of what Fourier analysis reveals about sound is highly useful.

Each of the sine waves in a complex, real-world sound has its own frequency and loudness characteristics. To give an overly simple example, a sound might consist of a relatively loud, sustained sine wave at 100Hz, a slightly quieter sine wave, also sustaining, at 200Hz, and a third sine wave at 783Hz that started very loud but died away quickly. If you look at the waveform of this sound, you won't necessarily see the three sine waves as separate parts of the display (though they're there if you know how to look for them), because the sine waves are blended together into a composite waveform.

For more on what can happen when sine waves are combined, see "Phase Cancellation," near the end of this chapter.

In many musical sounds, the frequencies of the sine wave components are whole-number multiples of one another (or close approximations thereof). For instance, a sound whose lowest sine wave has a frequency of 125Hz will quite likely have other sine wave components at frequencies of 250Hz, 375Hz, 500Hz, and so on. (These frequencies are whole-number multiples because 125 x 2 = 250, 125 x 3 = 375, and so on. Multiplying by the integers 2, 3, and so on gives us the frequencies of the higher sine waves.) In other types of sounds, especially percussive sounds and bell-like sounds, the frequencies of the sine waves are not whole-number multiples of one another. Bell-like sounds are referred to as *clangorous*, and percussive sounds often contain quasi-random frequency components called *noise*.

The sine waves that make up a composite sound are known as *partials*. If they're related to one another in whole-number ratios, they're called *harmonics*. The lowest partial in a sound whose partials are harmonically related is called the *fundamental*, and the harmonics above the fundamental are called *overtones*.

If this seems like a lot of jargon to absorb at once, read the paragraph again and think about it for a moment. All sounds have one or more partials. Not all partials are harmonics — that is, they're not all related by whole-number harmonic ratios — but all harmonics are partials. The fundamental is the lowest harmonic in a sound whose partials are harmonically related. Overtones are also harmonics, but the fundamental is not an overtone, because it isn't "over" anything. Here's where it gets a bit confusing: The first overtone is the second harmonic. In other words, if the fundamental of a sound (the first harmonic) is at 100Hz, the first overtone (the second harmonic) is at 200Hz. The prefix "over-" means "above the fundamental"; bearing that in mind might make the distinction easier to remember.

The human ear is quite good at perceiving and interpreting partials, even when they last only a fraction of a second. The presence or absence of specific partials is, in fact, a large part of what enables us to distinguish one sound from another. A trumpet, an oboe, and a violin playing the same note sound dissimilar enough that most listeners can tell them apart without a moment's conscious thought. The differences between the *timbre* (tone color) of the trumpet, oboe, and violin are entirely a matter of which partials are present in the tone of each instrument and how loud they are. (By the way, it's pronounced "tam-br," not "tim-br.")

Amplitude

Earlier, I indicated that amplitude and loudness are not quite the same thing, though they're similar concepts. Loudness is a subjective phenomenon, while amplitude can be measured scientifically. Also, we can use "amplitude" as a synonym for *amount*. We can say that an electrical signal has a high or low amplitude, even when it's not an audio signal — that is, not something we could conceivably listen to.

The perceived loudness of a sound depends not only on its amplitude but on its frequency and other factors. According to *Computer Music* by Charles Dodge and Thomas A. Jerse [Schirmer, 1997], a book I'll refer to from time to time in these pages, our ears are most sensitive to sounds in the frequency range between 250Hz and 3kHz. It's not hard to see why: That's the frequency range of human speech, and also the range in which most of the natural sounds that would have been important to our ancestors' survival — rustling leaves, animal growls, and so on — are heard. Our ears evolved to be useful, not to be scientifically accurate. As a result, a sine wave at 75Hz (which is well below the "survival" range) has to have a lot more amplitude than a sine wave at 750Hz for them to be perceived subjectively as equally loud.

One musical result of this is that as we add higher overtones to a sound — by raising the cutoff frequency of a lowpass filter, for instance — the sound will appear to get louder, even if it has the same amplitude as before.

For musical purposes, it's seldom necessary to describe amplitude with quite the degree of scientific rigor needed to describe frequency. If one sound, or one partial within a sound, is "a little louder" than another, and needs to be turned down a little, that may be enough information. Nevertheless, it's possible to describe amplitude with more precision.

Amplitude is measured in *decibels* (abbreviated dB — and in case you're wondering why the "B" is capitalized, it's because this unit of measurement is named after Alexander Graham Bell, who invented the telephone). Dodge and Jerse define decibels this way: "The decibel is a logarithmic unit of relative measurement used to compare the ratio of the intensities of two signals." The key words in that sentence are "relative" and "logarithmic."

Because decibels are a relative measurement, it's not possible to say that a given signal has a level of, say, 85dB in an absolute sense. It has a level of 85dB only in relation to some other signal that is used as a point of reference. This is why spec sheets describing mixers and other audio gear give measurements in dBu, dBm, and dBV. The third letter indicates the type of signal that's being used as a reference.

Even so, you'll see sounds being described as having an amplitude in dB. In such a case, the reference level is considered to be the threshold of audibility. An 85dB sound is 85dB above the softest sound that the human ear can hear.

Because decibels are measured logarithmically, it's not the case that an 80dB signal has twice the amplitude of a 40dB signal. The formula, in case you're curious (you absolutely don't need to know this in order to make music with a synthesizer), is that the ratio R of two signals with amplitudes A1 and A2 is as follows:

$$R = 20 * \log10 (A1/A2)$$

If your pocket calculator will do logarithms, you can discover for yourself that when A1 has twice the amplitude of A2, R is just slightly more than 6. This means that when the amplitude of a signal doubles, it has increased by about 6dB.

Transducers

Up to this point, we've been talking (explicitly or implicitly) about sounds flying through the air. A synthesizer is not made of air, however. So we need to say a little about how sounds get in and out of the box.

Changes in air pressure (momentary increases or decreases in the normal background pressure) are a form of energy. A device that changes energy from one form to another is called a *transducer*. The transducers you may be most familiar with are our old friends the microphone and the loudspeaker.

Without getting into the complexities of microphone design, about which whole books have been written, we can oversimplify what a microphone does by describing it like this: A small, lightweight piece of plastic called a diaphragm or ribbon is suspended in air. It's connected to a lightweight coil of wire, which is located within a magnetic field. When air pressure waves hit the diaphragm, it moves back and forth, and causes the coil of wire to move. The movement of the coil within the magnetic field produces an electrical signal. This signal can then be sent to a mixer or whatever electronic device we happen to be using.

A loudspeaker does the same thing in reverse. An electrical signal is applied to a metal coil that's situated within the field of a powerful magnet. The signal causes the coil to move back and forth. A stiff piece of paper called the speaker cone is attached to the metal coil, so the cone moves in and out as well, producing changes in air pressure.

The conversion of sound to an electrical signal and back again is never perfect; various kinds of distortion are introduced by microphones and loudspeakers. But if the hardware is well designed, if you take good care of it, and if you're using it as it was intended to be used, the distortion won't be objectionable. If you notice the distortion at all, you may even like it.

The signal coming from a microphone is at a fairly low level. It needs to be boosted by an amplifier (sometimes called a mic preamp, or simply a "mic pre") before it will match the level of other signals in a music system. An amplifier is also needed to boost the signal coming from a synth or mixer up to a level where the speaker cone will move much air.

If you're using an all-analog synthesizer, you may not need to know much more than that. You can plug a mic into a mic preamp, plug the preamp's output into your synth's external audio input, and thereby run the signal through the synth's filter or whatever. With a patchable synth, the output from any module can be connected directly to an amp and speaker. With a digital synth, however, the audio signal has to go through another conversion process.

Digital Audio

The signal coming from a microphone is called an *analog* electrical signal (or "analogue" if you're in Great Britain) because the pattern of changes in voltage is directly *analogous* to the pattern of changes in air pressure. If we map the voltage level of the signal on the Y axis of Figure 2-1 instead of air pressure, the diagram will look exactly the same. Both in the air and when converted into analog voltages, sound waves fluctuate in a smooth, continuous manner.

As noted in Chapter One, however, everything that happens in a digital device comes down to strings of 1's and 0's. To represent sound digitally, then, it has to be translated somehow into numerical form.

This neat trick is accomplished with a device called an *analog-to-digital converter* (ADC or A/D for short). The A/D converter, which is typically built into a computer soundcard or some other type of audio interface, measures the incoming voltage, which is being sent by a microphone, mixer, or some other analog device. It measures the voltage over and over at a very rapid rate, each measurement being in the form of a number. After taking each measurement, it sends the number down the line to the computer (or, for that matter, to a digital sampler or hard disk recorder), then takes another measurement, sends it on to the digital audio device, takes another measurement, and so on.

Once inside the digital audio device, the stream of numbers representing the sound can be processed in an almost infinite variety of ways. In order to listen to the numbers, though, we'll have to translate them back into an analog voltage. If we send the numbers to an amp and loudspeaker without translating them, they'll sound like a burst of very unpleasant noise.

The translation from a stream of numbers to a continuously varying voltage is handled by a *digital-to-analog converter* (D/A, D-to-A, or DAC, often pronounced "dack"). Once the digital signal has passed through the DAC, it can safely be sent to an amp and speaker, and we'll hear it as sound.

A digital audio recorder, whether it's in a computer or in a stand-alone desktop unit, operates on exactly this principle. Incoming sounds (in the form of analog voltages) are translated by the analog-to-digital converter — a process called *sampling* — and then stored in the recorder as streams of numbers. On playback, each stream of numbers is translated back into voltages by a DAC.

If all goes well, and if the person operating the recorder hasn't been too creative about processing the streams of numbers, we'll recognize the sound coming from the recorder as being identical to the sound — be it a conga drum, a human voice, or an entire orchestral concert — that first entered the microphone. But alas, all may not go well. Any number of problems can get in the way, causing the sound to be distorted and mangled — perhaps subtly, perhaps so radically that it's rendered unrecognizable. In order to ensure that the recorder reproduces the desired sounds, the ADC and DAC (to say nothing of the mic and speakers) have to represent the sound waves in an accurate way.

The key question, then, is this: How accurate does the digital representation of a sound have to be in order for human listeners to find it not only recognizable but musically acceptable?

Now we're ready to talk specs. The two most important factors in producing good-quality digital audio are *bit resolution* and *sampling rate*. These terms both refer to the accuracy with which the audio is represented in the form of numbers.

Sampling Rate

You probably know that a movie or a TV picture doesn't actually consist of moving images. It consists of a sequence of still photos. The photos are projected on the screen one by one, but because one photo follows another so rapidly, our brains blend them together into the illusion of a single moving image. A similar process is used to represent a continuous stream of audio as a stream of discrete numbers.

A typical movie runs at a rate of 24, 25, or 30 images (called "frames") per second. But the ear is a lot more discriminating than the eye. In order to create a good-sounding digital representation of a sound, we have to take "snapshots" of the fluctuating voltage at least 40,000 times per second. Each snapshot is referred to as a *sample* or *sample word*. (The term "sample" has two separate but related meanings.

It can refer either to a single number representing the voltage level at a particular moment, or to the stream of numbers that represents an entire sound. In the discussion below, it's used mostly to refer to a single number, not to a complete digital sound recording.) The rate at which samples are taken is known as the *sampling rate*.

The sampling rate used in music CDs is 44,100 sample words per second, or 44.1kHz. This rate is used by many digital synthesizers as well as by other types of music gear. These days it's a minimum standard: Many software synths can run at higher rates, such as 48kHz, 96kHz, or even 192kHz. Some older hardware synths run at a lower sampling rate, such as 32kHz. And if you're running music software on an old, slow computer, you may want to take advantage of the possibility of running at a lower sampling rate, such as 22,050 or even 11,025 samples per second. With a lower sampling rate, the fidelity of the sound will be somewhat degraded, but the digital device won't have to work as hard and may also be less expensive to build.

For technical reasons, the highest frequency that can be represented in a digital audio signal is half of the sampling rate. With a 48kHz sampling rate, for instance, the signal can contain no overtones higher than 24kHz. This frequency (half the sampling rate) is called the *Nyquist frequency*, and the math behind it is called the *Nyquist theorem*.

Since the human ear can only perceive overtones up to 20kHz, you'd expect that a 48kHz sampling rate would provide plenty of frequency range. There's some debate about this, however. Some listeners report that sounds recorded at a 96kHz sampling rate sound superior; other listeners are unable to hear any difference at all.

For now, let's forget about about microphones and digital recording. A digital synthesizer generates its tones from scratch as strings of numbers, and sends the numbers to the DAC so we can listen to the results. Each and every second, then, a synth has to generate 44,100 discrete sample words (if not more). And that's *per note*. Play a five-note chord, and the synth has to churn out 220,500 samples every second. That's a lot of number-crunching. Hardware-based digital keyboards have existed since the 1970s, but the early instruments relied on specially engineered chips that could streamline the number-crunching. Affordable general-purpose computers only became fast enough to do real-time digital synthesis in the early 1990s.

On a slow computer, a software synth can *render* its audio output to a disk file, in which case it can take as long as it needs to calculate the stream of numbers. But while rendering is a powerful technique that works fine even on a slow computer, you can't play a renderer from a keyboard and hear the music. That's what "real-time" means. For the most part, rendering synths are beyond the scope of this book.

Bit Resolution

Let's go back to what happens at the ADC, when the signal from the mic is first being turned into numbers. We're measuring the signal 44,100 times per second — but how accurate are those individual measurements?

When you're measuring how tall your children are, you probably use a yardstick. The yardstick is most likely marked off in 16ths of an inch. (In the backwoods USA, that is. In most of the modern world, it's a meter stick, not a yardstick, and it's marked off in millimeters, but we'll go with the yardstick.) If your yardstick were marked off only in feet, with no marks in between, you'd have to record your children as all being two feet tall, three feet tall, four feet tall, or five feet tall. A child whose actual height was between three feet and four feet would have to be recorded as being either three feet or four feet tall, because your measuring system would provide no information more precise than that.

Being human, you're a lot smarter than a computer, so if you were using such a stupid yardstick you'd probably record Suzy's height as "a little more than three feet" or "not quite four feet." But a computer can't do that. For a computer, those in-between measurements *don't exist*. The computer can only record whole, exact numbers. So it needs to use a yardstick that's as precise as possible — a yardstick marked off into a lot of tiny increments.

The yardstick for measuring sound is described in terms of the number of *bits* that can be used to store each sample word. The more bits, the more precise the measurement.

It turns out that eight bits are just about the minimum you need to represent sound acceptably. With an 8-bit ADC, the sound "yardstick" is marked off with 256 small increments. This is because an 8-bit value is always between 0 and 255. In binary arithmetic, we'd say that a value of zero is 0000 0000, while a value of 255 is 1111 1111.

First-generation sampling instruments such as the Fairlight CMI, E-mu Emulator, and Ensoniq Mirage recorded and played back sound as streams of 8-bit numbers. Eight-bit sound is noticeably harsh and grainy, because the measurements of the sound pressure level are often slightly inaccurate. When inaccuracy creeps into the system, we perceive it as added noise. The noise can't be filtered out: Once it's recorded into the sample, it's there forever.

BINARY NUMBERS: In Chapter One, hexadecimal notation was introduced. Hexadecimal is a convenient way to write the values of bytes because it's not too difficult for humans to read. Inside the digital device, however, each byte consists not of a two-digit hexadecimal number but of eight *bits* (binary digits). Each bit is either a 1 or a 0. When it's necessary to write out strings of bits, a space is usually put between bits four and five, like this: 0110 1011.

Sound is stored on standard music CDs as 16-bit numbers. Sixteen-bit audio has a much cleaner sound (less inherent noise), because the sound waves can be represented much more precisely. The 16-bit "yardstick" is marked off into 65,536 tiny increments. This is enough precision for many musical purposes, and indeed 16-bit recording at 44.1kHz is the industry standard. It's often referred to as "CD-quality." Beware, though: Advertisers often apply this term to lower-quality audio in a deliberate, cynical attempt to mislead consumers.

Each time a bit is added to the digital audio data, the number of marks on the yardstick doubles. This cuts the amount of residual noise in the signal in half. In other words, the *signal-to-noise ratio* (often abbreviated "s/n ratio") improves by 6dB. As a rule of thumb, the s/n ratio of 8-bit recording can be no better than 48dB (not quite as good as a turntable), while a 16-bit recording can have an s/n ratio of 96dB. In the real world, an ADC may not perform quite this well, so these figures are approximate.

But why stop there? If 16-bit sound is good, why not use 24-bit sound, or 32-bit sound, or 64-bit?

Modern digital audio software, running on a fast computer, often uses 24-bit or 32-bit numbers to represent sound waves. But the computer has to work harder to process larger numbers. When the computer is forced to work too hard, one of two things happens: Either the program refuses to add any more audio channels — for instance, a software synth might be unable to play new notes when you try to add them to an existing sonority — or the audio output abruptly fills up with ugly pops, clicks, and stuttering noises. The audio output might even shut down entirely.

When the audio engine in your computer stutters or chokes because it can't spit out enough numbers quickly enough, we say you're hearing *dropouts*. Asking a softsynth to play too many notes or a computer-based recorder to use too many effects plug-ins at once is just one possible source of audio dropouts; there are others. On a PC, for instance, your soundcard may be sharing an IRQ (interrupt request) with other devices. To prevent dropouts, you may need to move the soundcard physically to a different slot in the computer. (This operation requires some care, however. If you're encountering dropouts, don't just start fooling around in the guts of the machine. If you're not sure what you're doing, phone your soundcard manufacturer's technical support hotline and ask for their help.) Hardware digital synths are usually engineered well enough that you won't hear dropouts in the audio; this is mainly an issue for computer users.

> **JARGON BUSTER:** The *signal-to-noise ratio* (s/n) of an electrical system, which is expressed in dB, is a measurement of the difference between the signal (the stuff we want to listen to) and the background noise that exists in the system. There are many ways of measuring the s/n ratio. Also, there may be more noise in a digital system when a signal is present than when there's no signal. You can expect a decent piece of music gear to have a s/n ratio above 80dB — unless it's a turntable. The inherent noise of a stylus on vinyl reduces the s/n ratio to between 50 and 60dB at best.

Each time the manufacturer of a new synth decides to improve the instrument's audio quality by using a higher sampling rate or bit resolution, the audio software (or the OS in the hardware synth) can accomplish less before it uses up all of the available bandwidth in the CPU. Sooner or later, we reach a point of diminishing returns: Improving the audio quality further by increasing the sample resolution and bit rate isn't useful, because the difference to human ears will be very, very subtle, while the degradation in performance caused by the amount of arithmetic the software has to execute in real time becomes overwhelming.

If the sampling rate is too low, the high frequencies in the sound will get lost.

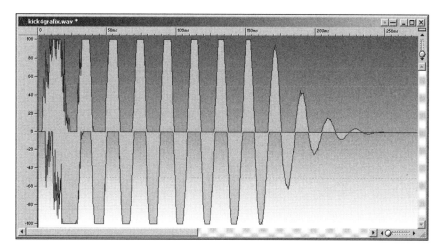

Figure 2-2.
When you do something, such as push a volume fader up to 11, that would require a digital audio signal to go past the maximum dynamic range of a component or module anywhere in the system, the signal clips. When viewed in an audio editor, a clipped signal has a flat top and/or bottom rather than a rounded shape. Clipping adds buzzy, high-pitched partials to the sound.

If the bit resolution (also called word length, because each sample is stored as an 8-bit, 16-bit, or 24-bit numerical "word") is too low, the sound will be noisy. That's pretty much all you need to know.

Most likely, your digital synthesizer will support at least a 16-bit, 44.1kHz data stream, so if you're hearing a poor-quality signal, the source of your problems will probably lie elsewhere. Other forms of digital audio nastiness include:

■ *Clipping.* There's an absolute limit on how large the numbers in a digital audio system can be. (With floating-point math, this isn't precisely true, but clipping can still become a problem at various points in the signal path.) If your audio software tries to make or use a number that's too big, the waveform will reach the maximum possible level and then "clip." In an audio editing program, clipping looks like **Figure 2-2**. If it's brief, clipping sounds like a pop or click. If it goes on for more than a few milliseconds, it sounds as if the audio is being mangled with a buzz saw.

■ *Aliasing.* If a digital synth tries to make a sound that contains any overtones higher than the Nyquist frequency, new partials will be introduced. The new partials will not be harmonically related to the fundamental. This phenomenon is called aliasing or *foldover*. A detailed discussion of aliasing would take several pages and several diagrams. Suffice it to say that if a high-pitched tone sounds bell-like when you don't expect it to, or if a tone with vibrato has an unexpected up-and-down whooshing quality, you've got aliasing. It may help if you choose a waveform that has fewer overtones (such as a triangle wave instead of a sawtooth).

In a computer-based synth, you may also want to check whether the output is set to a 44.1kHz sampling rate. If the synth lets you choose this value, and if it's currently set to 22.05kHz or 32kHz, increasing the value to 44.1kHz will quite likely reduce or eliminate aliasing.

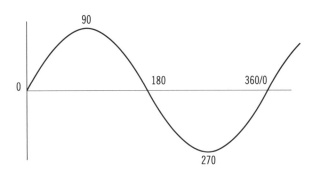

Figure 2-3.
The phase of a sine wave
is measured in degrees.
Each cycle of the wave
goes through 360 degrees.
360 is the same as zero.

Phase Cancellation

A sine wave has another important characteristic besides frequency and amplitude: It has *phase*. The phase changes from moment to moment as the waveform moves up and down. If you'd like to know more about phase, consult a good book on trigonometry. Without getting too technical, we can say that a single cycle of a waveform goes through 360 degrees of phase, as shown in **Figure 2-3**.

When two sine waves are added together — mixed, to use the musical term — the result depends on their phase relationship. If their phase is the same, they're said to be "in phase." Basically, two waves are in phase when their peaks occur at the same moment in time. If the peaks of one wave occur at the same moment as the dips in the other wave, they're said to be "out of phase." These relationships are shown in **Figure 2-4**.

The human ear is not good at distinguishing the phase of individual sine waves. Because of this, strange as it may seem, two waveforms that appear quite different on a computer screen can sound identical, if their partials all have the same frequencies and amplitudes. But when two tones are sounding at once, their phase relationship can become not only perceptible but a crucial element in sound design. This is because of the phenomenon called *phase cancellation*. If two sine waves have the same amplitude but are 180 degrees out of phase, when they're mixed the result is silence. If they're in phase, however, mixing will produce a louder sound.

This is true whether or not the sine waves have the same frequency. If their frequencies are far apart, it doesn't make much sense to talk about their relative phase, because the phase relationship will change quite rapidly. If their frequencies are close but not iden-

KICK ME: Although the ear is not good at detecting the phase of individual sine waves, I've read that some listeners can distinguish the polarity of extremely low-pitched, percussive sounds — kick drum samples, in other words. When a drummer hits the kick drum head with the beater, the head begins its vibration by moving toward the listener, so the waveform begins with a peak. If the polarity of the sample is flipped, the speaker cone begins the kick sound by moving away from the listener, which results in a dip rather than a peak. If a kick sample feels hollow or unsatisfying to you even though it has plenty of bottom, try reversing its polarity.

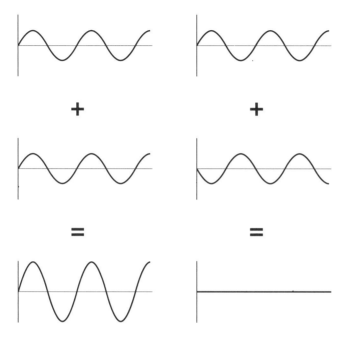

Figure 2-4.
When two sine waves that have the same frequency and amplitude are added together (mixed), the result depends on their relative phase. If they're in phase (left), the peaks and dips in the wave reinforce one another, so the result of mixing is a wave with twice the amplitude of either source wave. If they're 180 degrees out of phase, however (right), the peaks and dips cancel out, and the result is silence.

tical, however, the phase relationship will change slowly. At this point, our ears will perceive the changes in phase as *beating*. As two sine waves of equal amplitude and slightly different frequencies are mixed, the amplitude of the mixed signal will fluctuate between zero and twice the amplitude of the individual waves. This effect is shown in **Figure 2-5**. The frequency of the fluctuations in amplitude will equal the *difference* between the frequencies of the two sine waves. For instance, if one sine wave has a frequency of 250Hz and the other a frequency of 252Hz, when they're mixed they'll beat at a frequency of 2Hz.

If the beating is below 20Hz, as in this example, it will be perceived as a rhythm or pulse within the mixed sound. If it's above 20Hz, it's perceived as a new frequency component, which is called a *difference tone*. For instance, if we mix a 500Hz sine wave with a 600Hz sine wave, the mix will include a difference tone at 100Hz.

The musical result of beating depends very largely on the context. If you mix two bass synth sounds that are slightly out of tune with one another, phase cancellation will cause some of the bass notes to be much lower in volume than others. This is most likely a bad thing. But in a higher frequency range, detuning two oscillators to produce beating is a common and useful technique, as discussed in Chapter Four.

CD TRACK 3

Figure 2-5.
If two sine waves have
slightly different frequencies, they will move in and
out of phase. When they're
mixed, the result will be a
series of peaks and dips.
The frequency of the peaks
and dips will be the
difference between the two
waves. This phenomenon is
called beating.

Figure 2-5.
If two sine waves have slightly different frequencies, they will move in and out of phase. When they're mixed, the result will be a series of peaks and dips. The frequency of the peaks and dips will be the difference between the two waves. This phenomenon is called beating.

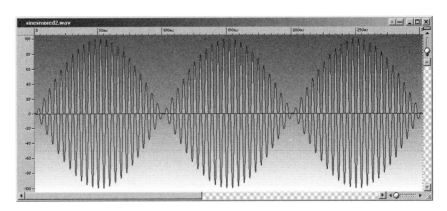

Up to now, we've been discussing beating between sine waves. Most sounds, however, are not simple sine waves. When each sound has a number of partials (all of which are sine waves, as discussed above), beating will occur between *each* pair of partials. To give a simple example, let's suppose that one sound has partials at 100Hz, 200Hz, 300Hz, and 400Hz, while the other has partials at 102Hz, 204Hz, 306Hz, and 408Hz. The mix will contain a number of difference tones, as Table 2-1 shows.

Table 2-1. Difference tones produced by two tones each of which comprises four partials.

	102	204	306	408
100	2	104	206	308
200	98	4	106	208
300	198	96	6	108
400	298	196	94	8

The amplitudes of the difference tones will depend on the relative amplitudes of the various partials. Most of them will be soft enough that you won't perceive them directly. What you'll perceive is a kind of spreading of the pitch. In addition to the clear sine waves at 100Hz and 102Hz, you'll also hear quieter sine waves at 94, 96, 98, 104, 106, and 108Hz. And with complex tones like these, it's unlikely that all of the partials will be 180 degrees out of phase at the same time. Thus, even though phase cancellation is causing individual partials to fade in and out, the tone as a whole won't fade in and out. Instead, you'll hear a kind of animation in the tone that can be quite pleasing.

Phase vs. Polarity. One way to put a sine wave 180 degrees out of phase is to flip it upside down, so that the peaks in the waveform become dips and vice-versa.

This is easy to do electrically. In fact, if you look at a good mixer you'll probably find switches labelled "phase," which do exactly that to the signals passing through mixer channels. Technically, however, such a switch doesn't reverse the phase of the signal; it reverses its *polarity*. This distinction may or may not matter. In effect, the switch is changing the phase of all of the partials at the same time. But if you like nice academic distinctions, you might want to know that phase and polarity are not the same thing.

 ## Power Projects for Chapter 2

Project 2-1: Listen & Sample. If you have access to any sort of device that will do digital recording, take the time to sample some of the sounds in your natural environment (birdsong, the motor in the refrigerator, etc.). Before sampling, listen carefully to the harmonic spectrum of the sound: Overall, is it high in frequency, or low? Is it rich in overtones, or relatively simple and dull? After recording the sound, use the filter or equalizer features of your sampler to emphasize or remove certain frequency components. (For more on filtering and equalization, see Chapters Five and Nine, respectively.) Then listen to the sound in its original form again, and try to hear the frequency spectrum more clearly.

If your recorder or sampler allows it, try sampling at a lower sampling rate, such as 22.05kHz, and/or at a lower bit resolution, such as 8-bit. Compare this lower-fidelity recording with a recording made at 16-bit, 44.1kHz, and see if you can hear the subtle differences in sound quality.

Project 2-2: Evaluate Your Monitoring Setup. What you hear coming from your speakers depends not only on the sound source and the quality of the speakers, but on the room in which the speakers are operating. The surfaces in rooms absorb certain sound frequencies while reflecting others, and the room itself operates as a resonant cavity (not unlike the body of an acoustic guitar or bass, but larger).

While playing a short segment of sound over and over, move around your studio and listen to how it sounds at different places in the room. Try this with various sounds containing different frequencies (basses, cymbals, and so on).

Research your amplifier and speakers to learn what their frequency response characteristics are. The details of such specifications are beyond the scope of this book, but using the information in this chapter on frequency and amplitude, you should be able to read the specs intelligently. Compare the specs of your monitoring system with those of other systems that are more expensive or less expensive.

Chapter 3
Operating Systems, Edit Modes & Memory

In the beginning was the front panel. And musicians looked upon the front panel, and saw that it was good. Each knob, slider, and switch did a single thing, and what it did was labeled on the panel. There were no hidden functions, no menus, no downloadable updates with bug-fixes, and the words "operating system" were not heard in the land.

But then, in the late 1970s, synthesizer manufacturers started putting microprocessors in their instruments. Digital chips, in other words. Everyone welcomed this development (well, almost everyone), because microprocessors allowed the instruments to do lots of new and useful things without hugely inflating the price tag. Before long, just about any synth you could buy had digital "smarts" of one sort or another to augment the functionality of the traditional analog circuits. In 1983, with the introduction of the Yamaha DX7, fully digital synthesizers started to take over the market.

The most popular first-generation microprocessor-equipped instrument, the Sequential Circuits Prophet-5 (introduced in 1978) still operated pretty much like an earlier analog synth: In the first Prophets, each knob was tied to one function, and each switch did one thing. The microprocessor simply looked at the positions of the knobs. (It also scanned the keys to determine which keys were being played.) But before long, manufacturers figured out that they could cut costs dramatically by having each piece of front-panel hardware do several different things. The Oberheim OB-8 had a shift key called "Page 2," which allowed the knobs to do double duty. Some Page 2 functions weren't labeled on the panel, however, which meant you had to haul out the manual to figure out what you were doing.

That was the start of a trend. For most of the 1980s, musicians who bought new synths were forced to contend with data entry systems of one sort or another. A typical data entry synth (the pre-MIDI Korg Poly-61 was one of the earliest) had a single knob or slider that was used for data entry, together with some method of choosing which parameter the data entry device would affect at any given moment. The spontaneity with which sound designers had created synth patches swirled down the drain. What's worse, controlling the sound during performance (if it was possible at all) was no longer intuitive and tactile, but required forethought and didn't always sound good, due to the limited resolution of the digital controller hardware. At almost every recording session, the keyboard player could be spotted flipping frantically through a manual. If the instruments hadn't been more powerful and less expensive than ever before, nobody would have put up with the inconveniences.

> **JARGON BUSTER:** A *parameter* is a setting that can be changed by the user. For instance, changing the value of the the filter cutoff parameter has the effect of changing the filter's cutoff frequency. Some parameters are in the form of on/off switches, but others can be set to many different values.

In the years since, synthesizers have continued to get more complex. But in order to stay competitive, manufacturers have had to figure out ways to make their instruments easier to use. Today, even modestly priced synths are likely to have a few knobs for real-time control, and some of the more expensive units have both banks of knobs and large, high-resolution liquid crystal displays (LCDs) in which related parameters can all be seen at a glance. This is a lovely trend, but it doesn't make my job — writing about the instruments — any easier. While there's some degree of uniformity among instruments, at least at a conceptual level, the user interfaces in the current crop of synths diverge widely. As we explore the underlying concepts in the pages that follow, don't be surprised if you see more pedantic phrasing of the "in some instruments, but by no means all" variety than elsewhere in this book.

As usual, there's no substitute for reading the manual. The specific features of your instrument may or may not be alluded to in the discussion below, and the features that *are* discussed may or may not be found in your instrument. Unless it was built on Mars, however, there's a good chance it will be similar to other instruments in ways that can be described and explained.

Digital vs. Analog

The transition from discrete front panel controls to data entry systems was made possible by the switch from analog to digital electronics. The differences between the two, and their relevance for synthesizer operations, are discussed at several points in this book (see, for instance, "Control Rate & Data Resolution" in Chapter Eight).

To oversimplify slightly, analog circuits are built of discrete components — capacitors, transistors, resistors, and so on — and the signals passing through the circuits can meaningfully take on many different values. In an analog synth, a control voltage of 2.3 volts will produce a different sound than a control voltage at 2.6 volts, assuming the voltage is patched into a destination somewhere. What a given circuit does when it receives a certain voltage at an input depends on what components are used and how they're wired together. As a result, each circuit typically does only one thing.

Voltages (and for that matter transistors) are also used in digital circuits, but a given voltage can have only one or the other of two meaningful values. We might think of these as high and low, or off and on; in digital terms, they're referred to as the numbers 0 and 1. Digital circuits operate by reshuffling these two numbers very rapidly and in sophisticated ways. All of the operations of digital technology are based on numbers and mathematics. The higher math that takes place in a microprocessor is handled by long strings of 0's and 1's, but that underlying fact is not usually of much importance to musicians. Nevertheless, the fact that digital synths use math and logic to represent and manipulate sound is extremely important.

Unlike analog circuits, digital circuits tend to be general-purpose devices. Your computer, for instance, can be a word processor, a graphic design tool, a spreadsheet, or a video game. Its function at any given moment depends entirely on what instructions it has been given, and all of the instructions — and thus, the distinction between a synthesizer and a word processor — boil down to strings of 1's and 0's.

In a computer, the instructions are provided by programs (also known as applications). A computer has both programs that do specific things and a master program called the *operating system*, which provides the environment in which other programs function. Today Windows, Unix/Linux, and the MacOS (in all their respective flavors) are the best known examples of operating systems.

Operating Systems

A hardware synthesizer is not a general-purpose device, so most synths are not designed to run a variety of programs. However, every digital synth has an operating system. The operating system is the set of instructions that tells the synth how to respond when you press a button or move a slider, what text to display in the LCD, and so on. In the absence of an operating system, the knob labeled Filter Cutoff wouldn't do anything, because it isn't physically connected to a filter. (For that matter, an all-digital instrument doesn't actually *have* audio filters in the voicing circuitry. What it has is a way of simulating analog voice filters digitally.)

The operating system (OS) is stored on a memory chip. These days the chip is often an EEPROM (electrically erasable, programmable read-only memory). Since you can't open the case of the synth without voiding the warranty, and would probably

FACT FILE: To my knowledge, there has only been one hardware-based electronic instrument that could run programs supplied by third parties. The Ensoniq Mirage sampler, which was popular in the mid-1980s, had to load its operating system from floppy disk each time it was turned on. This allowed one or two outside programmers (who happened to be Ensoniq employees) to enhance the Mirage OS in various ways. The CreamWare Noah, released in 2003, can load and run various types of digital synthesis algorithms, but thus far all of them are sold by CreamWare, not by third parties.

Several computer-based instruments, including Cycling '74 Max/MSP, allow users to write their own objects in a computer language called C. These objects can then be loaded into and used in Max. Max externals, as they're called, are available from independent programmers in the Max community.

have no way of figuring out which chip holds the OS even if you did so, the fact that the chip is an EEPROM may not seem significant. But it is. Here's why:

All software programs except the very simplest ones contain bugs. A bug is an error in the instruction set, an error that causes the software to do something that its designers didn't intend. The error could be so trivial that you'll never notice it, or it could be so serious as to cause your synth to lock up and refuse to make a sound. Most likely it will be somewhere in between.

CAVEAT EMPTOR: This resonant phrase is Latin for "let the buyer beware." Things that one should beware of (or at least be aware of) are often called *caveats*. In the case of a synthesizer or other electronic device, an important caveat is that it's almost always a bad idea to purchase the product based on the manufacturer's promises about features that will be added to the next version of the operating system.

Even major, reputable manufacturers are notoriously optimistic about how quickly they'll be able to finish and release an OS update. Features that are promised "in a few weeks" may not appear for six months, a year, or even longer. In a few heartbreaking cases, products have been orphaned: The promised features *never* appeared. To avoid this nightmare, it's a good idea to base all of your purchasing decisions on features that are already included in the instrument you'll download or take home from the store. Don't buy promises.

When bugs are found, especially serious ones, the manufacturer needs to provide an *update* for the operating system — a new version of the OS in which the bugs are fixed. OS updates sometimes contain new features as well as bugfixes. This exciting possibility opens the door to abuses, however: Once in a while, a manufacturer will start selling a synth in a slightly unfinished state. Features that are promised or advertised may not be included in the initial OS.

For the first decade or so after digital synths became common, updates were generally provided in the form of new memory chips. In order to get the OS update, you would have to take your synth to an authorized repair shop and pay a hefty bench charge for the repair technician to open the case, pull the old OS chip out of its socket, and insert the new one. This is not actually a difficult job — I've done it many times, and I can't even solder a guitar cord without making a mess. But it has to be done carefully, because the chip has two rows of thin metal pins, which insert into holes in the socket, and if one of the pins breaks off, the chip is useless.

With the proliferation of personal computers and the evolution of the Internet, a cheaper and more convenient way to provide OS updates was soon found. Today, most synths allow their operating systems to be updated over MIDI. The OS data itself is downloaded from the manufacturer's website in the form of a Standard MIDI File (SMF) containing system-exclusive data. The SMF can be loaded into and played back from any software sequencer. The synth generally has to be switched into a special "OS receive" mode before the new version can be installed. This is sometimes done by switching it on while pressing some unlikely combination of front-panel buttons. The software sequencer then transmits the sys-ex data to the synth. The synth erases the old OS from its EEPROM and then burns the new OS into the EEPROM.

This process can be a little finicky. You need to follow the manufacturer's instructions with care. But I've never seen a case where it actually failed to work.

Some manufacturers use slightly different methods for installing updates. If the synth has a floppy disk drive, for instance, you might be able to download the update into your PC, copy it to a floppy, and then put the floppy in the synth. Some instruments with SmartMedia slots can be updated from SmartMedia cards, which you might be able to burn yourself (assuming your computer has a peripheral that can do this), buy from a music retailer, or receive in the mail direct from the manufacturer.

Traditionally, the released versions of operating systems, like other software, are numbered. The version included in the first instruments shipped is usually numbered 1.0. Later releases will have correspondingly higher numbers. Your instrument may display its OS version number each time it's switched on, it may display this information only when powered up in a special way, or there may be a page buried somewhere in a submenu that will show the number. Small updates are indicated by small changes in the number — for instance, from 1.00.003 to 1.00.005. Larger, more significant updates are indicated by larger number changes. The most significant updates typically change the leftmost number — for instance, an update from 1.2 to 2.0. Significant updates are sometimes referred to as *upgrades*. By checking the version number and comparing it to the version number of the update offered on the manufacturer's website, you can tell whether you need to download and install the update.

With synthesizers that run on computers, the business of installing an update will probably be a lot easier: Just download the update, double-click on the icon, and the computer will do the rest. Before installing the update, though, it's a good idea to do a little research. The manufacturer's website should provide a list of the new features, and responsible manufacturers also provide a list of known problems that remain (or have been introduced) in the new version. Most new software versions add features and fix bugs without introducing problems, but this is not guaranteed. For instance, a new version of a software synth might be unable to read program files created and stored using the older version, or it might no longer be compatible with an older audio interface. If you've done significant creative work with one version of a program, you need to make sure you won't lose your work when you install the update.

Memory

The advent of synthesizers with user-programmable preset memory was one of the great advances in the history of musical instrument design. Prior to this, the best way to keep track of synth sounds that you figured you might want to use again was to write down all of the front panel settings with a pencil and paper. Not only was this time-consuming, but the results were, at best, approximate. (Pencil and paper weren't the only possible solution. In the early '70s, it was rumored that a certain rock star had bought a whole stack of Minimoogs, set each one up to produce a certain sound, and then taped the front panels with duct tape so the sounds wouldn't be lost.)

In an instrument with digital memory, all of the settings for the parameters that affect a given sound can be stored and later recalled with only a few button-presses. Storing is also called *writing* or *saving*. Your instrument will probably have a prominent write/store/save button.

Before we go on, let's clear up a bit of nomenclature. The blocks of data that instruct the synth about what settings to use for all of the parameters needed to generate a sound are variously known as patches, programs, presets, and voices. "Voices" is a Yamaha-specific term, and rather confusing, because the rest of the world tends to use the same word to refer to an audio channel that produces one note of polyphony. For most of us, an "eight-voice synthesizer" is a synth that can play eight notes at once, not one that has eight memory locations for storing sound programs. Yamaha's usage of the term derives from the fact that the act of creating sound programs for a synth can be referred to as *voicing*. From time to time in this book, I've also referred to programs/presets/patches simply as sounds. This is just as confusing, because a sound is what you hear, not the settings that are used to generate it.

Some people prefer to reserve the word "presets" for sound programs that can't be altered by the user. And at least one manufacturer (Ensoniq) used "presets" to refer to a higher level of data structure that others refer to as multis or combis (see below). From here on, I'll use "programs," "patches," and "presets" indiscriminately to refer to the same thing, namely, the blocks of data containing all of the parameter settings needed to produce a particular sound in a particular synth. When discussing all-analog synths — those with no memory — the word "patches" is probably more appropriate, even when the instrument doesn't use patch cords.

In case it's not obvious, the preset data from one type of synthesizer can almost never be loaded into a different model. Some musicians naively assume that by loading, let's say, the preset data from a Novation Supernova into a Korg Triton, they can get the Triton to play Supernova-style modeled analog sounds. This is a complete misunderstanding of what a sound program actually is. If a synth can load *samples* (actual digital recordings), as the Triton can, you can sample the output of the Supernova and then create a preset in the Triton that plays the samples, but in this case the Supernova's sounds are no different from a dog bark or a car horn to the Triton. The Supernova's preset data will have no meaning to the Triton, and if the Triton's panel controls are able to duplicate the functions of the Supernova's, it will be purely a coincidence.

A few instruments can use preset data from other instruments. Usually they come from the same manufacturer. Roland JV-80 sounds, for instance, could be played by certain other Roland synths. And the Native Instruments FM7 software synth can load voices (presets, in other words) created on various Yamaha FM instruments, including the DX7 and TX81Z. But this type of compatibility is very much the exception, not the rule.

One more note, before we proceed: Most of the discussion below is specific to hardware-based synthesizers. With a software synthesizer that runs on a general-purpose computer, memory is handled a bit differently.

Okay, now back to the subject at hand.

It's hard to overstate the convenience of being able to design exactly the sound programs you need for a given gig and then access the programs as needed onstage or in the studio. A few all-analog instruments are still built with no memory, but for most musicians, having programmable memory is essential.

Most hardware synths provide two types of memory for sound programs: ROM and RAM. In the ROM (read-only memory) are the factory presets — sounds designed by professionals to address the needs of a wide variety of musicians. Often, the factory presets may be all you'll need for a given project. On the other hand, you may need to customize the presets. After doing so, you'll store your new version in RAM (random-access memory). These days, it's not unusual to see instruments with 512 ROM presets and 128 or more RAM locations.

If you use a computer, you'll already be familiar with RAM. Synthesizer RAM is not exactly the same as computer RAM, however. In a computer, the contents of RAM are lost when the computer is switched off. The data in a synth's RAM (at least, in most portions of its RAM) is retained when the instrument is powered down or unplugged. This neat trick is accomplished by means of a small, long-life battery, which is installed somewhere in the instrument. The battery trickles a small amount of power into the RAM, assuring that it's never wiped out.

It's worth noting, however, that the battery in a synth has a finite lifespan. After eight or ten years, you may see a low-battery warning when you power up the synth. Take this warning seriously. When it appears, you need to store the RAM contents in some other manner (such as on a disk, if the synth has its own disk drive) before replacing the battery. When the old battery is pulled out, whatever is in RAM will be gone forever, unless you've stored it somewhere else.

A few instruments, such as the Kurzweil K2500 rack, use ordinary flashlight batteries, and allow you to replace them yourself. This is a brilliant feature. More often, it's necessary that the case be opened up and a special battery installed. If you're not comfortable doing this, you may need to take the instrument to a qualified technician to replace the battery. I've even seen one unit (not a synthesizer — it was an Ensoniq effects processor) in which the original battery was soldered onto the circuit board, a hideous design that left me no alternative but to take the unit to a service shop and pay the shop charge for the battery replacement.

In addition to ROM and RAM, most instruments have a special area of memory called the *edit buffer*. When you're editing a sound, you're not actually fiddling with the data stored in ROM or RAM. Instead, when you enter edit mode (see below), the contents of the ROM or RAM location you've chosen are copied into the edit buffer. When you're finished editing the sound, you can either copy the contents of the edit buffer back into RAM using the save/store operation, or abandon your work.

In most synths (though not all of them), the contents of the edit buffer will be lost when you switch off the power. Also, in many but not all synths, the contents of the edit buffer will be lost when you leave edit mode and select a different sound.

It's not possible to store a sound to ROM. When you press the store button, the OS will prompt you for a RAM location in which to store the sound. When you store a new sound to a given RAM slot, whatever was in that slot before will be gone forever. So you need to think carefully about where to store your new sounds. When you're prompted for a memory location in which to store the sound, you may be given an opportunity to listen to the sound that's already in that location, so that you can make sure it's not something you want to keep.

This is one of the ways in which a *compare* feature can be implemented. If your synth has a compare button, you can press it during a sound editing session to hear the original version of the sound (the one stored in ROM or RAM). When you press the compare button again, you'll be whisked back to the version of the sound that's in the edit buffer.

Your instrument may have a command with which the contents of the edit buffer can be *initialized*. Initialization loads the buffer with a basic, dry, useless sound. This is useful because it guarantees that the sound won't have any obscure settings, such as effects or modulation routings, that will confuse you or just take up extra time when you're creating a new sound from scratch.

On the surface, some instruments appear to have only RAM for storing patches, not ROM. Typically, the memory locations will be loaded at the factory with useful presets, but all of the memory can be overwritten with your own sounds. In such an instrument, however, you may be able to restore the factory sounds. The factory sounds are actually in the box, stored in ROM pretty much the way they are in any other synth. But the only way to get at the ROM data is to copy it (one patch or an entire bank at a time) into RAM.

In computer-based synths, the RAM/ROM distinction is irrelevant. Banks of patches are stored on the computer's hard drive between sessions, and the data in all of the banks can be overwritten by the user. The number of banks (or, for that matter, individual patches) that can be stored is essentially unlimited. Your synth may automatically load the bank that was being used in your last session, and when you quit the synth program, the software *should* ask (though it may not) whether you want to save any changes you've made in the current sound bank.

START FROM SCRATCH: If your synth lacks a command for initializing the sound edit buffer, create your own init sound and store it somewhere convenient (such as in RAM location 128). Shut off all of the effects and modulation routings, open up the filter, create organ-style on/off envelopes, use only a single oscillator, and so on. You may want to include a few settings, such as a modest amount of velocity response, that you know you'll generally want to include in new patches.

Some computer synths also lack an edit buffer: Any changes you make in a given patch will become part of the data in the currently loaded bank. This is convenient, in that it saves you the trouble of saving a sound twice — first to the loaded bank and then to the hard drive. But it also opens the door to trouble. If you've fiddled with a few patches and later want to save the bank to the hard drive, your fiddling will be saved for posterity. It's always a good idea to make backups of computer files, and files containing synthesizer sound programs are no exception.

Categories. A few synths provide some means of classifying patches into types. Because space in the LCD is limited, the types tend to be given short abbreviations — ep (electric piano), gtr (guitar), bas (bass), and so on. In instruments where patches can be categorized, some method is provided with which you can scan through the patches in a particular category. This feature speeds up the process of developing an arrangement in the studio: Most often, you'll know you want a string-type sound, for instance, so it's handy to be able to audition just the strings. When you create your own patches, you'll have an opportunity to choose the appropriate category. Some instruments even have a few user-definable categories, or allow you to list your favorite patches in a Favorites category.

Waveform Memory. Up to this point, we've been talking about the memory that synths use to store patches. This is not the only type of memory in a typical digital instrument, however. As you'll learn in Chapter Four, many synthesizers use a type of synthesis called *sample playback*. These instruments provide a palette of sampled digital waveforms, which form the raw material out of which sound programs are synthesized.

Waveform memory also comes in the form of ROM and RAM. The ROM waveforms are sculpted and tweezed at the factory, and there's generally not much you can do with them except select one of them for playback by each oscillator. In RAM waveform memory, you can store and use waveforms you've created yourself.

When it comes to memory, more is better. But how much is enough? The memory in which presets are stored is usually measured in terms of the number of presets (for instance, you may see it listed as "256 ROM, 128 RAM"). Waveform memory, on the other hand, is usually measured just the way computer memory is — in megabytes. A megabyte (abbreviated MB) is a million bytes. Actually, it may be a bit more than a million; that's a round number.

During the last 20 years, as memory has become more affordable, the amount of ROM waveform storage in sample-playback synths has steadily increased. Today (2003), instruments with 32MB or more of waveform

TERMINOLOGY: For the most part, waveform RAM is found in instruments called *samplers*, not in synthesizers. In recent years, however, the distinction has become more than a bit blurred. A number of instruments have been marketed that include both ROM waveforms and waveform RAM with which you can do your own sampling. Simultaneously (and perhaps in consequence), the market for dedicated hardware samplers has declined. In any case, all but the very earliest samplers had a decent array of synthesizer features of the sort discussed in this book. Maybe it makes sense to reserve the term "sampler" for a synthesizer that has no waveform ROM.

To add to the confusion, computer-based instruments that play back sampled waveforms chosen by the user are universally called samplers, even though none of them can actually sample— *i.e.*, record external sounds. All hardware samplers can sample, as can most hardware synth/samplers that have both ROM and RAM for waveforms.

BYTE SIZE: Digital memory, including the type used in a synthesizer, handles data in the form of bytes. A byte normally contains eight bits (binary digits), each bit consisting of either a 1 or a 0. So 16-bit audio, which is more or less an industry standard, requires two bytes to store each *sample word*. If the digital recording was made at a sampling rate of 44,100 samples per second (another industry standard, more or less), each second of sound occupies 88,200 bytes of memory. If the sound is stereo, make that 176,400 bytes. If the sampling rate is higher, and if 24-bit recording is used instead of 16-bit, the amount of storage space needed will increase accordingly.

ROM are not uncommon. Into that 32MB, the manufacturer has to pack all of the waveforms that you're likely to need, from electric piano and string samples to acoustic basses, drums, and so on.

Using various forms of data compression, manufacturers are able to fit more waveforms into less memory without significantly compromising audio quality. While it's true that an instrument with 32MB of waveforms will probably give you more choices than an instrument with 8MB, it's not very meaningful to whip out a calculator and try to figure out how many seconds of audio are actually present in an instrument's ROM. Data compression is not usually used with waveforms in sample RAM, however. If your instrument includes RAM waveform memory, you can safely assume that each second of monaural, 16-bit audio whose sampling rate is 44.1kHz will occupy 88,200 bytes.

Here again, more is better. Your synth may arrive from the factory with only 8MB of RAM, but you'll probably be able to expand that to 128MB or more by installing additional memory chips. For specifics on how far the memory of a particular instrument can be expanded and what type of chips can be used, consult the owner's manual or the manufacturer's website.

Pages, Menus & Soft Keys

A few synths are still being built that are either simple enough, or have enough front panel controls, that they use only a 2- or 3-digit LED (light-emitting diode) for displaying numerical information to the user. Most instruments, however, have LCDs in which quite a few numbers or letters can be displayed at once. But of course, no LCD is large enough to display all of a synth's user-editable parameters at once. So some method of organization is required with which to allow the user to choose which parameters will be displayed at any given moment.

The most widely used system organizes the parameters into what are called "pages" (a metaphor closely related to the "windows" displayed on a computer screen). A page contains a few closely related parameters — on a small LCD, perhaps only a single parameter. The two most common methods of arranging and providing access to the pages are what might be termed the grid system and the function/menu system.

In a grid system, the pages are organized in a geometrical matrix of some sort. Only one page in the grid is displayed at a time, but it's easy and natural, when working in such a system, to visualize the entire grid at once. The grid may be arranged horizontally, as a row of pages; vertically, as a column of pages; or in a rectangular grid with both rows and columns, as shown in **Figure 3-1**. The user moves from page to page using up/down buttons, left/right buttons, or both.

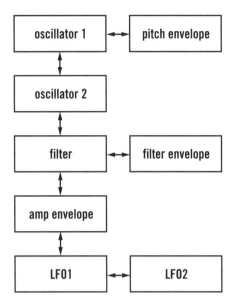

Figure 3-1.
The pages displayed in a synth's LCD will most likely be organized in a conceptual grid like this one. Only one page is displayed at a time. Either pairs of page left/right and up/down buttons or a system of function keys will be used to move from one page to another.

A row or column of pages is sometimes referred to as a menu. Like a drop-down menu in a computer program, it provides access to a related set of options. Unlike a drop-down menu, however, you won't see the entire menu at once. The menu metaphor tends to be used in synths that have smaller LCDs, while the page metaphor is used when more information can be displayed at once. A few synths with large LCDs also have drop-down menus, which operate pretty much the way computer menus do.

In a function/menu system, a row of buttons along the bottom of the LCD provides access to various pages. In a few instruments, the buttons are positioned at the left and right sides of the LCD rather than at the bottom. Typically, the labels of the buttons are displayed in the LCD itself (sometimes called "menu tabs"), not marked on the panel. Thus, the functions of the buttons are controlled by software (the synth's OS). Because of this, some manufacturers have taken to calling the buttons "soft buttons" or "soft keys." They're also called function buttons or (by analogy with the row of keys along the top of a computer keyboard) F keys. The choice of pages provided by the F keys will most likely change depending on what page is currently displayed.

Within any page, some method is provided with which the user can select individual parameters. Some Korg synths, for example, have touch-sensing LCDs, with which you can select a parameter by tapping it with a fingernail. Generally, the currently selected parameter is highlighted in some way, either by being underlined or by being displayed in inverted colors (white numbers on a black background rather than the normal black characters on a white background). The highlighting is called the *cursor*. Cursor keys are often provided with which you can move the cursor up, down, left, or right within a page. In some synths, the same cursor keys are used for selecting parameters within a page and for moving from page to page. Cursoring to the right when the cursor is already in the rightmost data field in a given page, for instance, may move you to the next page to the right.

There are many variants on these concepts. In the E-mu Proteus 2000, for instance, you can cursor left or right within a given page, and the item at the top left corner of each page is a page selector. When the cursor is on the page selector, the data entry knob moves you to a new page rather than changing the value of a sound parameter. The Hartmann Neuron uses a two-dimensional grid of pages, but you can only move up or down when you're in a page at the left end of a given row. The Korg Wavestation SR, a rackmount synth with a small LCD, employs both page up/down buttons and a cursor left/right/up/down control, creating the equivalent of a three-dimensional grid.

As you might imagine, navigating around a complex system of pages sometimes requires a fair amount of button-pushing. To ease the pain, some manufacturers provide *mark* and *jump* buttons. By pressing the mark button, you can "mark" a particular parameter. After navigating to another page, you can then press the jump button to jump back to the marked parameter.

Data Entry

As you may have gathered from the foregoing discussion, digital synths deal with all of their parameters, both the parameters responsible for defining sound programs and those that control other aspects of the instrument's operation, in the form of numbers. In some cases the "number" will be merely a two-position on/off switch, but even in this case you're editing a number — the parameter will be set to either 1 or 0. In any case, you'll be changing the values of the parameters using some method of *data entry*. The device used for data entry in a hardware synth might be a knob, a slider, increment/decrement buttons, or a numeric keypad.

"Increment" is a fancy word for "increase." Likewise, "decrement" means "decrease." Sometimes these buttons are labeled "inc" and "dec," or simply "+" and "–".

In some instruments, two or more data entry systems can be used interchangeably. For instance, let's say a parameter can be set anywhere between 0 and 99, and that you want to set it to 87. You grab the data entry slider and push it up. When your finger comes to rest, the display indicates that you've set the parameter to 86. Rather than trying to nudge the slider up by a single value (which might be difficult, since the slider may not be engineered for such precise control), you tap the increment button once, increasing the value from 86 to 87. Instead of working this way, you may be able to select the parameter using the cursor keys and then tap the 8, 7, and Enter keys on the numeric keypad.

In a computer-based synth, you'll most likely choose the parameter you want to edit with the mouse. If it's displayed as a slider, clicking on the slider and holding the mouse button while dragging the mouse up or down will change the value. You may be able to move the slider by finer increments by holding down the shift key while dragging; check the owner's manual for details.

There's an unresolved controversy in the land of computer-based synths about whether on-screen knobs should be "turned" by moving the mouse up and down, or by moving it in a rotary fashion around the center point of the knob. Some synths let you choose the method you prefer.

Some computer synths let you select a parameter (either with the mouse or by navigating to it with the Tab key) and then type in a new value using the QWERTY keyboard. Sadly, many programs don't allow this. A few, in a misguided attempt to emulate analog hardware, don't even display the numerical value at which knobs are set.

Many computer synths implement a standard undo command, with which you can undo your most recent parameter edit (or a whole string of edits), and a redo command, with which you can undo the undo. A few hardware synths have undo buttons, but this feature is not common.

Some parameters are programmed in real-world units of measurement (seconds, Hz, dB, and so on); others are not. For instance, you may be able to program LFO rate in a range between 0.01Hz and 50Hz, or the parameter may provide arbitrary values. The range of the arbitrary values will differ from one instrument to another, and from one parameter to another within the same synth; ranges from 0 to 99, from 0 to 127, and from -64 to +63 are common. The arbitrary values will be mapped internally by the synth's OS to whatever range of LFO rates the manufacturer feels is appropriate. Real-world settings generally make programming a little easier, but your ears should always be the final arbiter of what setting is correct, not the number in the LCD. On occasion, you may find that the difference between two adjacent settings of a parameter — for instance, an envelope attack time of 0 vs. an attack time of 1 — may be larger than you'd like. Generally, little or nothing can be done about this.

Modes

Hardware-based digital synths can often operate in any of two or more different *modes*. A mode is simply a manner of operation — it's the way the synth is operating at any given time. After switching to edit mode, for instance, you'll

JUST IGNORE IT: When a synthesizer has been switched to MIDI *local off* mode, its keyboard, pitch-bender, and other performance controls are still active, but they're no longer connected to the instrument's internal sound-generating circuitry. The performance controls still send MIDI to the instrument's MIDI out jack, however. It's as if you have two separate pieces of hardware — a MIDI tone module (playable only via the MIDI in jack) and a master keyboard that transmits MIDI data but makes no sound of its own. The two just happen to reside in the same box. An instrument is usually switched to local off mode when being used in conjunction with a computer sequencer. The keyboard sends performance data to the sequencer, and the sequencer's MIDI output can be directed either back to the synth itself or to another MIDI module.

be able to edit sound programs. In multitimbral mode, the synth will operate multitimbrally. And so on.

The reason hardware synths have modes is primarily because the front-panel controls have to serve several different purposes. It makes sense to organize operations so that at any given time, the physical controls are all doing related things. Most computer-based synths, because they have a large screen to display parameters and settings but only two physical controls (the mouse and the QWERTY keyboard), don't divide their operations conceptually into discrete modes. You may need to switch back and forth between windows and open and close dialog boxes, which amounts to the same thing, but the word "modes" is seldom used.

So let's focus for a moment on hardware instruments. The modes you'll most likely encounter in your instrument, in one form or another, are these:

Global Mode. The parameters that affect the entire instrument, as opposed to any single preset, are found in global mode (also known as system mode, master mode, and so on). In global mode, you'll probably be able to choose the instrument's primary MIDI receive channel and use other MIDI features, such as a local off switch. There will probably be a master tuning parameter. If your instrument has any time-based features, such as an arpeggiator or syncable LFOs, there will probably be a switch in global mode for choosing either the instrument's internal clock or an external MIDI clock. Other features, such as a memory-protect switch, a utility for resetting the internal patch memory to the factory presets, or user-programmable tuning scales and velocity curves, may be available. You may be able to switch the operation of certain hardware controllers, such as footpedals, from a menu in global mode. Finally, manufacturers often put the commands for transmitting a MIDI system-exclusive data dump in the global mode menu.

Single Mode. In this mode, which is more or less the default on many instruments, a single sound program is assigned to the entire keyboard and the panel controls are configured so as to be ready for performance. It's sometimes called play mode.

Unison Mode. In unison mode, a polyphonic synth pretends it's monophonic: The keyboard plays only one note at any given time. In many instruments, all of the voice channels are sent to the output in unison mode, which results in a massively thick sound. You may have a *unison detune* parameter, which controls the amount of pitch spread between the voices. You may also be able to choose how many voices will be included in the unison.

Edit Mode. Edit mode is used for editing the parameters of individual presets.

In edit mode, some of the performance controls on the panel may be disabled, or may have special functions. If a synth allows you to program both single presets and multitimbral combinations, it will probably have an edit mode for each. For more, see "Editing Presets," below.

Disk Mode. If your synth has a disk drive, it probably has a disk mode or disk menu. In this mode you'll find all of the commands for disk operations — saving the instrument's internal memory contents to disk, loading files from disk into memory, deleting files from disk, and perhaps other utilities, such as creating disk directories.

Sequencer Mode. Instruments with built-in sequencers generally have a dedicated sequencer mode, also called song mode, in which the sequencer is active (whether or not it's playing or recording at the moment). The sequencer may interact with the instrument's multitimbral mode, in that sequences will play back using the presets in the currently selected multi. In other instruments, this is not the case, and in fact you may be able to assign an entire multitimbral setup to a single sequencer track. You may be able to program the synth's built-in effects processors for a given sequence rather than using the effects parameters stored with a single or multi program. Built-in sequencers are beyond the scope of this book.

Multitimbral Mode. When the instrument is in multitimbral mode (also called multi mode, combi mode, setup mode, performance mode, mix mode, and so on), several sound programs will be playable at the same time. The exact number of patches you'll be able to use at once depends on the instrument model: Four, eight, 16, and 32 are the most common upper limits. Some synths contain only a single multitimbral setup. Others have a separate memory bank for multis, which may contain 64 or 128 memory slots.

ONE IS THE LONELIEST NUMBER: Until the mid-1970s, most synthesizers were *monophonic*—capable of playing only one note at a time. These instruments were great at lead and bass lines, but recording chord parts required laborious multitracking: Each note in the chord had to be recorded to a separate tape track, and the results mixed. Technological advances led to the birth of the *polyphonic* synthesizer, which was capable of playing several notes at once. A few monophonic synths, mostly of the real analog variety, are still being manufactured today.

Depending on how the instrument is set up, operating in multitimbral mode can have one or both of two related results. First, the instrument will probably be able to respond to MIDI performance data arriving on more than one MIDI channel. Second, it will probably be able to assign two or more sounds to different regions of the keyboard — for example, a bass preset in the lower register and an electric piano preset in the upper register — and play all of these sounds on a single MIDI channel. A few synths make a distinction between these two modes: They may have both a performance mode, in which several sounds can be assigned to the keyboard but all will share one MIDI channel; and also a multi mode, in which several sounds, or for that matter several multi-preset performances, can be assigned to separate MIDI channels and will all be active at the same time.

A few early multitimbral synths, including the Yamaha TX802 and the Oberheim Xpander, had rotational voice assignment algorithms that could be used in multitimbral mode. With this algorithm, several patches could be active on a single MIDI channel, and the synth would step through the patches in order as new notes were played.

While each multitimbral setup contains two or more presets, it's important to understand that the data defining the presets (all of the parameter settings) is not usually included in the data that defines the multitimbral setup. A setup only contains *pointers* to the presets that are being used. A pointer is simply the number of the preset. If you store a different sound in that preset location, the sound of the multi will change. It might be nice if synthesizers alerted you when you were about to overwrite a preset that was being used in a multi, but I don't know of any instrument that does this.

Even though the multi doesn't contain all of the data for single-mode presets, you may be able to edit the single-mode presets in a multi without leaving multi edit mode. In this situation, the instrument may indeed alert you if you leave multi edit mode without saving the single preset. A few instruments have multiple edit buffers for single-mode presets — usually, the same number of buffers as there are parts in the multi. With this feature, you can freely edit the sounds in a number of parts in order to create the multi of your dreams, and not commit to any of the edits (saving them, in other words) until you're satisfied with the results. If there's only one edit buffer, creating a perfectly matched layered sound in a multi will take more time, because you'll have to guess about the correct settings for one single preset, save it to memory, and then start editing another. After saving the second preset, you may need to go back and edit the first one further.

In addition to letting you select several sound programs and assign them to keyboard regions and/or MIDI channels, a multi will have some parameters that give you more control over the musical results. The multi will be organized into *parts* (also called slots, timbres, and so on). A preset will be assigned to each part. The part will also contain settings for all of the other parameters that will be used when that preset plays as part of the multi. Part parameters typically include some or all of the following:

- MIDI channel
- key zone (top and bottom key)
- transpose (in half-steps)
- fine-tune
- loudness
- velocity range (highest and lowest velocity)
- response to various controllers, such as sustain pedal (on/off switchable)

• audio output
• effects busing

In the case of key zone and velocity range settings, notes that are on the correct MIDI channel but fall outside the zone or range will be ignored by the part.

A few synths, notably some Yamaha models, go further. Their multis include *offsets* for such sound parameters as filter cutoff and LFO rate. An offset raises or lowers the value of the parameter stored in the sound program, without actually changing the data stored in memory for that program. This feature is an efficient use of memory: It allows you to use a single preset in several different multis and achieve a better blend of sounds within the multi, without having to use up several memory locations to store variations on the preset — variations that are very similar except for their filter cutoff or whatever.

It's worth noting that all synthesizers have limited polyphony. That is, they'll play only so many notes at once. In modern synths the number of notes may be quite large (128-voice hardware instruments are now widely available), but it's still finite. And because each sound program may use as many as four voice channels to play each single note, when operating in multi mode you may run out of polyphony sooner than you expect. For instance, let's suppose your instrument is 32-voice polyphonic, and that you've created a multi in which three presets are layered. The first preset uses a two-oscillator electric piano sound, the second uses a three-oscillator string sound, and the third uses a two-oscillator chime sound. At this point, each note you play on the keyboard will use seven voice channels, so you'll be able to play only four notes at a time on the keyboard before you run out of voices (because 4 x 7 = 28, but 5 x 7 = 35, and 35 is larger than the 32-voice limit). When you run out of voices, you'll hear one of two things: Either some of the notes you play (or transmit from your sequencer) won't play at all because there are no voices left to play them, or new notes may cut off older notes prematurely, which can result in ugly chopped-up noises called "voice stealing."

Some instruments, especially older ones, dealt with this problem by including a *voice reserve* parameter for each part in the multi. A part whose voice reserve was set to 8 would be guaranteed eight voices (which might produce only two or four notes, as explained in the "Hearing Voices" sidebar). This system is called *fixed voice allocation*. The trend in newer instruments is toward *dynamic* voice allocation, a system in which the synth itself decides

HEARING VOICES: A *voice channel* is a software or hardware signal path capable of producing a single note of polyphony. Typically, a voice channel includes an oscillator, a filter, a couple of envelope generators, and perhaps one or two LFOs. Sample playback synths usually allow two or four voice channels to be layered within a single sound program. In modeled analog synths, it's more usual for two or three oscillators to be found within a single voice channel, and to be processed by a single filter (or perhaps a single filter section that includes two filters).

The number used in advertisements to describe a synth's total available polyphony (64 notes, for example) actually refers to its total number of voice channels. An instrument described as 64-note polyphonic may also allow four voice channels to be assigned to a single sound program. In this situation, the sound program will play only 16 notes polyphonically before the instrument runs out of voices.

how to assign its available voices to newly played notes. It may cut off the oldest notes or the quietest ones, for instance. Both types of allocation have musical advantages, but fixed voice allocation poses more musical problems on a synth with a limited number of voices, and also requires more forethought on the part of the musician, so it has fallen out of favor.

When a synth is operating in multitimbral mode and is being asked to play a lot of voices at once, you may start to notice some other audio problems besides missing or chopped-off notes.

First, the multi may simply be producing so much sound that the synth's audio output is clipping (overloading). Lowering the volume of some or all of the parts in the multi should cure this.

Second, when a number of notes are started at once, some of them may start a little late. The attack of a thick chord may sound smeared, for instance. This happens because a significant amount of processor time is required to get a new note ready to play. There's not much you can do about this except remove some of the notes from the chord or reprogram some of the single presets in the multi so they use fewer voices. The problem can become especially noticeable when the synth is playing a drum track on one MIDI channel, because the ear tends to be very sensitive to slight timing variations in the drums. Some synths address this issue by always giving priority to notes on channel 10, which has been designated the drum channel in General MIDI instruments. But this won't help if a note-on arrives on another MIDI channel a few milliseconds *before* the drum note. You may find it helpful to advance the drum tracks in your sequencer by a single clock tick. This should ensure that the drum notes are sent out before any other notes on the same beat.

A third, related problem occurs when a synth receives a program change message on one MIDI channel. This may cause the playback on other channels to "hang" briefly. New notes may start late, for instance, or an LFO may pause in mid-cycle. You may need to move the program change message a little earlier or later in the sequence, so that it's transmitted at a moment when the synth is less busy.

Effects in Multitimbral Mode. Most hardware synths have only a fixed amount of processing power available for producing effects (chorus, reverb, and so on). As a result, it's normal that when you select presets for the parts in a multi, the presets won't sound the way they do in single mode. This is because they won't have access to the effects settings that were programmed into the presets. Instead, they'll have to use whatever effects are available in the multi.

Various synths provide various workarounds for this problem. You may be able to select one part as the "effects part," for example, so that the multi will use whatever effects are defined in the program assigned to this part. For more on the effects options in multis, see Chapter Nine.

Editing Presets

Depending on how many front panel controls your synth has, you may be able to make some basic changes in your presets (and store the changes) without entering edit mode. Edit mode may contain additional parameters not available directly from the panel in play mode, however. For instance, the envelope generators may provide physical knobs for attack and decay times, but in edit mode you may be able to edit the sustain level and release time as well.

Analog-type instruments sometimes have no edit mode — or, to put it another way, they're always in edit mode. Turn a knob and you've edited the patch. Another type of design provides a number of edit menus in different areas of the panel — an oscillator menu, a filter menu, and so on — but no general-purpose edit mode.

One advantage of a dedicated edit mode is that the synth may ignore MIDI program changes when in edit mode. This allows you to tinker with a sound and listen to your edits in the context of an existing MIDI sequence without having to mute program changes already embedded in the sequence. Another advantage is that when you leave edit mode, the synth may ask whether you want to save your edits. This reminder helps ensure that you don't inadvertently lose creative work.

Irrespective of how your instrument is set up for editing, you'll be able to make changes in the parameters somehow. If you can't, it isn't much of a synthesizer.

Program Changes

Assuming you haven't disabled program change reception in the global area, when your synth receives a MIDI program change message it will switch to a new program. This seemingly simple operation can be handled in various ways, however, depending on the instrument. Some synths cut off any sounding notes on a given channel when they receive a new program change on that channel. Others allow already-sounding notes to sustain and release with their original sounds — but inevitably, the old notes have to be routed through the new effects settings, so the sound may change in undesirable ways as the notes are dying away.

Responding to a program change message always takes the synth a little time. When recording and editing sequencer data, it's always a good idea to send the program change a few beats before you want the new program to become available.

Many instruments have a "multi receive channel." In multitimbral mode, program changes on this MIDI channel will switch to a new multi, while program changes on other channels will choose new presets for individual parts within the multi.

Because many synths are equipped with multiple banks of presets, most of them have some way of responding to MIDI bank select messages. There's very little uniformity in this area, however, and a full discussion of bank select is beyond the scope of this book. In addition to consulting your owner's manual, you may need to try a few experiments in order to determine exactly what data your sequencer will need to transmit.

 Power Projects for Chapter 3

Project 3-1: Organize Your RAM. Go through all of the sounds in your synth's RAM patch memory, listening to them and making notes about which ones you want to use, perhaps for specific musical projects, and which you can live without. If the RAM sounds are a jumble, you may want to organize them into groups, so that related sounds — basses, for instance — are together.

Moving sound programs around in memory requires at least one unused (temporary) memory location: To swap two sounds, you need to write the first sound into the temporary slot, then write the second sound into the slot where the first sound started, and then grab the first sound from its temporary location and write it to the slot where the second sound started.

To ensure that you never inadvertently overwrite a sound that you need, create a silent sound, and name it Nothing. Save this to each memory location where there's a sound you're sure you're never going to use. Next time you create a new sound that you want to keep, you can safely save it to any memory location that currently contains Nothing.

If you have access to an editor/librarian, however, you should save the synth's RAM contents to your computer before starting this process. (Editor/librarians are discussed in Chapter One.) Doing so offers an added level of protection, and also ensures that if your tastes or musical needs change, you'll be able to restore those sounds you thought you'd never use.

Project 3-2: Big Multi. To explore your instrument's multitimbral mode, try these experiments:

■ Assign the same sound to four parts, and detune the parts from one another using their coarse or fine-tune parameters. Try fine-tuning part 1 about 6 cents sharp, part 2 about 2 cents sharp, part 3 about 2 cents flat, and part 4 about 6 cents flat. With sustained sounds, this detuning will give the sound a rich chorused quality. By panning the opposite-tuned parts hard left and hard right, you'll add space to the chorusing. With coarse (half-step) detuning, try programming the four parts so that you can play various chords with one finger — a dominant 7th or 9th, stacked fourths, and so on.

■ Edit the one-finger-chord multi so that each note in the chord is played by a different but closely related sound. Try using four brass-type presets, or four plucked presets. If necessary, adjust the loudness of the various parts so that the chord is voiced in a balanced way. If your instrument has a start delay parameter for individual parts within a multi, program the multi so that the voices play an arpeggio rather than a block chord.

■ Stack (layer) two different sounds on one channel or zone. Assign a chord-type preset to one part and a monophonic lead preset to the other part. Set the lead preset to high-note priority, so that it will always play the top note in a chord.

Chapter 4
Oscillators

All synthesizers have a way (or perhaps two or three different ways) to generate sounds. The devices that generate the sounds are called oscillators. The sounds coming from the synth's oscillators are the building blocks out of which all of your finished synth programs will be made. You'll seldom listen to the raw sound of an oscillator by itself. Usually its sound will be massaged and sculpted by the other components of the instrument — filters, effects, and so on — before being sent to the instrument's audio output. But without the oscillators, these other components would have nothing to chew on.

Actually, that's not strictly true. Many synthesizers have external audio inputs. After patching an audio signal (from a microphone or a previously recorded audio track, for example) to the synth's audio input, if the synth has one, you'll be able to shape the external signal in most of the same ways you could if it were coming from an oscillator. Synths with external audio inputs open up a lot of musical possibilities, but in essence they're functioning as effects processors on steroids, not as synthesizers. The details of external audio processing are beyond the scope of this book, but you'll find a bit more information in Chapter Nine.

The two types of oscillators you'll see most often are analog-style (in which category I'll include both real analog and digital simulations thereof) and sample playback. There's also an in-between category. And a few synths sport additive oscillators and other clever designs. In this chapter we'll take a close look at all of them. We'll also cover an assortment of features you'll often see associated with oscillators, including oscillator sync and intermodulation.

The sound of one oscillator by itself tends to be a little naked — one-oscillator patches are the tool of choice for pointed, in-your-face sounds such as bass, but not for rich, swirling colors — so most synths offer at least two. Designs with three or four oscillators are common. One of the most important ways to create new sounds is to blend the sounds coming from several oscillators into unique combinations.

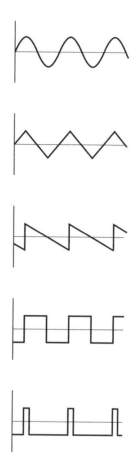

Figure 4-1.
The basic analog
waveforms (top to bottom):
sine, triangle, sawtooth,
square, and pulse.

Analog Waveforms

The first generation of analog synthesizers, which appeared in the 1960s, was built using real analog circuits — resistors, capacitors, diodes, and so on. Fortunately, it's not difficult to build musically useful tone generators with such circuits. An analog oscillator outputs a signal (a voltage) that fluctuates in a simple repeating pattern. The pattern is called the *waveshape* or *waveform*, and the rapidity with which the waveform repeats determines the frequency, as explained in Chapter Two. The two most important controls on such an oscillator are the waveform selector and a frequency knob. The waveform selector is often a switch with several discrete positions, but some synths have a continuous waveshape knob, with which you can morph smoothly from one waveshape to another.

TRACK 4   The waveforms found most often in analog oscillators are the *sine wave*, the *triangle wave*, the *sawtooth wave*, and the *square* or *pulse wave*. These waveforms are shown in **Figure 4-1**.

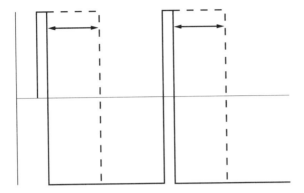

Figure 4-2.
Changing the width of a pulse (square) wave changes its harmonic content without changing its frequency.

The sine wave, as explained in Chapter Two, is a pure tone with no overtones. On its own, it has an extremely dull, muted quality. Once in a while you can do something useful with a sine wave by itself, but more often it's blended with other waves to make a composite sound. In fact, additive synthesis (see below) is usually done by combining handfuls of sine waves. Tuned to a low pitch, a sine wave can reinforce the bass frequencies in a tone (though there's some danger of phase cancellation, as explained in Chapter Two). Tuned to a high pitch, a sine wave can add a ringing overtone to spice up a sound.

The triangle wave also has a muted sound, but it has a few weak overtones. You can make a nice new age lead tone with a triangle wave, and it's also good for discreet, understated basses. Like the sine wave, it's often blended with other waves.

As you might expect from its shape, the sawtooth wave has a bright, buzzy sound. It contains all of the overtones in the harmonic series, though the higher overtones are progressively weaker than the lower ones. Its rich harmonic content makes the sawtooth a good choice as an input for a lowpass filter: You can easily control the strength of the harmonics by changing the filter's cutoff frequency. Sawtooth waves can be used for most types of sounds, including leads, basses, and pads.

The square wave also has plenty of energy in the higher harmonics, but its spectrum contains only the odd-numbered harmonics (1, 3, 5, 7, and so on), not the even-numbered ones. Because of this, it has a rich but hollow sound. In the midrange, a square wave can sound somewhat like a clarinet.

Pulse Width. The square wave has another useful property, which explains why it's often called a pulse wave. On many synths, the pulse width (also known as the *duty cycle*) of the square wave can be changed, as shown in **Figure 4-2**. An analog-style synth will provide a knob for this purpose. Sample playback synths don't allow the pulse width to be changed in real time, but they almost always provide several sampled pulse waves with different widths.

Changing the pulse width doesn't change the fundamental frequency of the pulse wave. What changes is the percentage of time the wave spends in the "up" portion of its cycle as opposed to the percentage in the "down" portion of the cycle. As the pulse becomes narrower (less time in the "up" portion of the cycle), the wave acquires a thinner, more biting character. A thin pulse wave is good for synthesizing Clavinet sounds.

If you modulate the width of a pulse/square wave from an LFO, as the LFO rate speeds up the pitch of the oscillator will sound as if it's changing, even though it's not. In other words, rapid pulse width modulation takes on some of the character of vibrato. This is because the phase of the overtones is changing rapidly.

Also worth noting: Wide swings in the pulse width can cause the width to become effectively zero or 100%. When this happens, the pulse wave oscillator will "choke off" and fall silent. This effect can be put to good use. If you don't want it, you have two options: Reduce the amount of pulse width modulation, or turn the pulse width knob (not the PW mod amount knob) so that the modulation sweeps the pulse width from a different starting point — for example, from 10% to 80% rather than from 30% to 100%.

> ## ■ Recipe 1
>
> **Clavinet:** In the Hohner Clavinet, often used in funk and R&B in the '60s and '70s, the characteristic twangy sound was created by the striking of strings inside the body of the instrument. To synthesize a Clavinet tone, start with a thin pulse wave. Use plucked envelopes (instant attack, steady decay to silence) for both the lowpass filter and the amplitude. Use very little or no filter resonance. To add realism, you may want to try adding the smallest possible amount of pitch envelope so that the sound begins slightly sharp and falls back to concert pitch as it decays.

Aliasing

The waveforms shown in Figure 4-1 are abstract ideals, not real-world waves. If you look at a square or sawtooth wave in a digital audio editing program, you may be surprised to find that the real waveform doesn't look quite the way you expected. There can be several reasons for this — and it may or may not matter musically. Oddly enough, two waveforms that look very different may sound exactly the same, as explained in Chapter Two.

What's more significant, when it comes to digital simulations of analog waveforms, is the problem of *aliasing*. As mentioned in Chapter Two, if a digital sound has frequency components whose frequencies are more than half the sampling rate, the digital audio process will cause these high frequencies to *fold over*. They'll be audible in the output as lower frequencies at non-harmonic (out-of-tune) intervals. That's aliasing.

If you dial up a sawtooth wave, which is rich in harmonics, on a digital synth, and if you then play a scale up the keyboard, as you get into the upper register you may hear aliasing. The tone will acquire non-harmonic overtones. As you continue to play upward, all semblance of a scale may disappear, leaving you with nothing but a series of abstract, clangorous beeping noises. This can be useful musically, but more often it's a nuisance, and renders an otherwise gorgeous sound unplayable in the high register.

In some digital synthesizers, the oscillators are *anti-aliased*. This means that the waveform being generated changes as you play up the keyboard: Overtones are removed in some manner in order to prevent or minimize aliasing. Note that filtering the waveform with a conventional lowpass filter won't prevent aliasing, because the aliasing occurs in the oscillator waveform itself, before the signal is sent to the filter. If you hear aliasing in a patch you're editing, the best way to minimize it, assuming you're working with a multi-oscillator patch, is by using the oscillator's keyboard amplitude tracking parameter to reduce the amplitude of the offending oscillator at the upper end of the keyboard.

Noise

Many analog-type and sample playback oscillators let you choose *noise* as the oscillator waveform. In other synths, noise may be available (in the mixer module, for instance) as a separate sound source, not associated with any of the oscillators. Noise is very useful for programming gunshots, snare drums, wind, surf, and other special effects.

Noise is also useful as a modulation source. By modulating the pitch of an oscillator with low-pitched noise, for instance, you can lend the pitch a gargly, unstable quality.

The definition of "noise" is that it's a signal that exhibits no periodicity — in which the frequency varies constantly in a random way. Another way of looking at it is that a noise signal contains energy at *all* frequencies. This fact has some practical consequences. First, if you're using a true analog noise source, modulating its pitch (assuming this is even allowed by the synth) will probably have no audible effect. Think about it: If the signal contains energy at all frequencies, and if you double the average frequency, you'll still hear energy at all frequencies. On the other hand, if your synth relies on sample playback to produce noise, by definition the noise sample will be of a finite length. It will loop. As you play up the keyboard, then, the loop will get shorter and shorter, and you'll probably hear it rising in pitch as well. A good sample playback synth has a noise sample that's long enough that you won't hear it looping, but don't be surprised if you hear a rapid "swsh-swsh-swsh" when you play a noise note in the top octave.

Noise comes in several flavors. The most common are *white noise* and *pink noise*.

White noise is defined as noise that has equal energy per unit bandwidth. In other words, given that the noise signal contains energy at all frequencies, white noise will contain the same amount of energy between 100Hz and 200Hz that it contains between 1,100Hz and 1,200Hz.

Pink noise is defined as noise that has equal energy *per octave*. In other words, it will contain the same amount of energy between 100Hz and 200Hz as between 1,100Hz and 2,200Hz. The result: Pink noise sounds subjectively lower in pitch than white noise, because it concentrates a higher percentage of its energy in the low part of the frequency spectrum.

When programming sounds that use noise, you'll often find it helpful to shape the noise with a lowpass or bandpass filter. By modulating the filter cutoff, you can control the apparent pitch of the noise. Adding filter resonance will give the noise a more focused pitch, because more of its energy will be concentrated in a narrow band.

Giving the noise its own amplitude envelope is also a useful technique. By adding a short burst of noise to the attack portion of sound with an envelope that quickly decays to zero, you can simulate the unstable (*i.e.*, noisy) behavior of an acoustic instrument during the first few milliseconds of its tone. When the musician adds energy to a vibrating element such as a string, membrane, or air column, the vibration doesn't start up from zero with a nice smooth waveform: It's chaotic for a brief period of time before it stabilizes, and adding noise is one of several ways to simulate the instability of the attack transient.

Sound Programming Techniques with Analog Oscillators

Several programming techniques are commonly used with analog-type oscillators. Some of these techniques are equally applicable to sample playback, which is discussed in the next section, but let's take a break and do a little programming before we dive into the next chunk of theory.

Detuning. One oscillator, by itself, tends to produce a tone that's static — rigid and unmoving. Sometimes that's what you want, but often a richer, more animated tone is called for. A classic solution is to have two oscillators play the same waveform and then *detune* one from the other using the *fine-tune* parameter. (An example can be heard in CD track 3, tone 2.)

When two oscillators playing sustained tones are detuned from one another, their combined tone will have a chorused type of sound. This effect is called beating. Beating is caused by phase cancellation, which is discussed in Chapter Two.

The speed of the beating is dependent on the frequency difference between the two oscillators. For instance, if one oscillator has a frequency of 800Hz and the other a frequency of 802Hz, the difference between them is 2Hz (two cycles per second), so you'll hear two beats per second. As the two oscillators are detuned further, the beats will speed up.

Both slow beating and rapid beating can be musically useful. But if your synth's detuning parameter is designed to change the frequency of an oscillator by some fraction of a half-step, as most detuning parameters are, the speed of the beating will increase as you play up the keyboard. This is because the half-steps are much closer together in frequency at the low end of the key-

CD TRACK 5

■ Recipe 2

Synth Strings: For a classic synth string sound, use the following settings:

■ Two or three sawtooth wave oscillators, slightly detuned from one another.

■ A lowpass filter with a low to moderate cutoff frequency, a shallow rolloff slope (6dB per octave if possible), and no resonance.

■ Little or no envelope modulation of the filter cutoff frequency.

■ An amplitude envelope with moderate attack and release times and full sustain.

■ If desired, modulate amplitude and/or filter cutoff from aftertouch so you can play swells.

■ Try substituting a pulse wave for one of the sawtooth waves, and add some pulse width modulation from a slow LFO.

board than at the upper end, because we perceive pitch in a logarithmic rather than a linear manner. The distance between the low C and C♯ on a five-octave MIDI keyboard (assuming the keyboard is tuned to concert pitch) is less than 3.9Hz. The distance between the high B and C on the same five-octave keyboard is almost 117.5Hz. So if we detune two oscillators from one another by 5 cents (1/20 of a semitone), when we play the low C on the keyboard we'll hear beating at a rate slower than 0.2Hz, while at the top of the keyboard it will be about 5.9Hz.

TRACK 6

If your synth offers a parameter with which an oscillator can be detuned in *constant Hz*, you can avoid this discrepancy. Detuning an oscillator by a constant 2Hz, for example, will cause it to beat against a non-detuned oscillator at a rate of 2Hz from the low end of the keyboard to the high end. The disadvantage of this technique is that at the low end of the keyboard, 2Hz is a fairly large fraction of a half-step. The detuned oscillators may sound as if they're playing different pitches, and the sense of a unified center pitch may be lost.

MAKES CENTS TO ME: On some synths, the fine-tuning parameter for each oscillator is calibrated in *cents*. A cent is 1/100 of an equal-tempered semitone (half-step).

Detuning is most often used with oscillators whose coarse tuning is set to a unison. When two tones an octave or two apart are detuned from one another, they tend simply to sound out of tune. Detuning is also useful, however, when the coarse tuning is set to an interval of a third, fifth, or sixth. These intervals produce beats in equal temperament — the beating of thirds is quite severe — and the detune parameter can be used to slow or eliminate the beats.

In some two-oscillator synths, only oscillator 2 has a fine-tune parameter, because the manufacturer assumes that oscillator 1 provides the unvarying base pitch of the sound, from which oscillator 2 can deviate. This is a poor assumption. When two oscillators are detuned from one another by a few cents, the perceived center frequency of the sound will tend to be halfway between them. In other words, the composite tone will sound "in tune" when one oscillator is tuned a few cents sharp and the other oscillator a few cents flat. If you're forced to detune oscillator 2 while leaving oscillator 1 at concert pitch, the tone will tend to be perceived as either flat or sharp. You may be able to compensate by adjusting the instrument's global tuning parameter — but if you're using the instrument in live performance, this is not an efficient workaround, because the setting of the global tuning parameter can't be stored in a patch.

Using three or more detuned oscillators rather than two will add to the thickness of the sound. In fact, a few analog-type digital synths include a "waveform" in which three or more detuned signals, usually sawtooth waves, are produced by a single oscillator. If your synth has one of these "triple saw" or "six saws" waves, you'll also find a detune amount parameter. The larger the detuning amount, the thicker the sound. Synths in which several voices can double one another in unison mode tend to have a unison detune parameter, which does much the same thing.

Oscillator Sync. Oscillator sync has been used since the early days of analog synthesis to add more tone colors to the synthesist's palette. I'm not aware of any sample playback synths that do true oscillator sync (at least, not with their sampled waveforms; the Kurzweil K2000 series does both sample playback and oscillator sync, but not with the same voice at the same time). You may find a sampled "osc sync" waveform in a sample playback synth, however. True oscillator sync is available only in analog-type oscillators and those that play single-cycle digital waves.

Please don't confuse oscillator sync with timing synchronization. Except for a brief discussion in Chapter Six, timing sync is not covered in this book. In oscillator sync, one oscillator (often called the *master*) is used as a timing reference for the waveform of another oscillator (often called the *slave*). In essence, the slave oscillator is forced to restart its waveform from the beginning each time the master oscillator starts a new waveform. The result is that their frequencies will always be the same.

Described this way, oscillator sync may not seem too useful. After all, if you want oscillator 2 to be tuned to the same frequency as oscillator 1, you can just tune it. Why sync it?

To see why, take a look at **Figure 4-3**. When the slave oscillator's frequency is modulated (often from an envelope or LFO, though driving it from the mod wheel is also a useful expressive technique), its base frequency can't change. Instead, its waveform changes. For instance, if the slave oscillator is trying to produce a tone a perfect fifth above the master oscillator, it will play through 1½ cycles of its waveform and then have to restart. If it's trying to produce a tone an octave and a fifth above the master, it will play through 2½ cycles before restarting.

The tone of a synced oscillator has a prominent overtone at or near the pitch it would produce if it weren't synced. As we attempt to increase its pitch, either from modulation or simply by adjusting its coarse tune parameter, this overtone will become more prominent. Tuning a synced oscillator below the frequency of the master, by contrast, does nothing very interesting to the sound.

A synced oscillator often has a biting, metallic tone color. Moving its pitch rapidly through a couple of octaves with an envelope generator will produce a dramatic sweep. If your synth allows oscillators to be synced, try a few experiments. It may not be clear from the panel which oscillator is the master and which is the slave; you may simply have a button labelled "sync." To hear the effect of oscillator sync, the slave oscillator must be turned up in the mixer. The effect will be more dramatic if the master oscillator is turned down in the mixer, but there are times when you want to hear the master oscillator, because it will add more fundamental.

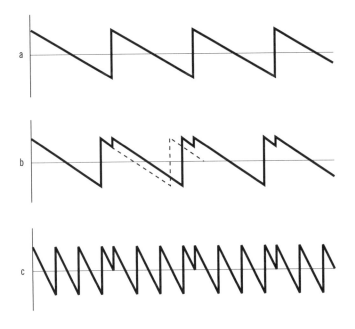

Figure 4-3.
When oscillator 2 (b and c) is synced to oscillator 1 (a), oscillator 2's waveform has to start over each time oscillator 1 starts a new waveform cycle. Thus their fundamental frequencies will always be the same. By modulating the frequency of oscillator 2, however, we can change its waveform. In (b), the frequency of oscillator 2 is only slightly higher than that of oscillator 1, so their waveforms are similar. (The dotted line shows what the waveform of oscillator 2 would be if it weren't synced.) In (c), the frequency of oscillator 2 is more than an octave higher than that of oscillator 1, so the synced waveform has many more peaks.

Pitch Modulation. Most synths provide some method for modulating the pitch of an oscillator while it is sounding. (For details on various types of modulation routings, see Chapter Eight.) The most common types of pitch modulation use an LFO (see Chapter Six), an envelope generator, or MIDI pitch-bend data as a source. In almost all synths, the amount of LFO modulation can be controlled from a secondary modulation source, such as a MIDI modulation wheel/lever. Such a lever normally sends MIDI continuous controller 1 (CC1) messages. By controlling the amount of LFO modulation from CC1, you can add vibrato to a note. Vibrato can also be pre-programmed, so that it is applied to every note. In this case, the secondary modulation from CC1 is bypassed, and the LFO's output modulates pitch directly.

Pitch-bend. MIDI pitch-bend is one of several types of channel messages. Pitch-bend is unusual in the MIDI world in that it's a *bidirectional* message: The zero value is in the center of the control range rather than at the lower end. As a result, a pitch-bender can either raise or lower the pitch of the oscillators.

The raw value of a pitch-bend message (which can range from –8192 to +8191) says nothing about the amount of pitch change that will be produced by a given pitch-bend message. The maximum pitch-bend depth is set within the receiving synthesizer, either in the global area or in a particular patch. Typically, the depth is set as a number of equal-tempered half-steps. (If you're a devotee of alternate

MERCEDES BENDS: MIDI pitch-bend messages can be transmitted and responded to with 14-bit precision, which means that the maximum range of the data is from −8192 to +8191. However, not all pitch-bend hardware actually transmits data with 14-bit precision — nor are all synthesizers equipped to respond with 14-bit precision. In practice, you may find that your pitch-bends are restricted to a range from −64 to +63. Strange as it may seem, this range is not any narrower than the −8192/+8191 range; it simply has less resolution. The −64/+63 range is defined by the seven most significant bits of the pitch-bend message. In a synth that uses the more restricted −64/+63 range, the seven least significant bits, which are present in all pitch-bend messages, are simply ignored. A low-precision hardware pitch-bender will most likely transmit the seven least significant bits as a string of zeroes. (In fact, not all hardware pitch-benders are even this sensitive. Some of them can only sense between 32 and 64 discrete positions.)

tunings, you may find this fact somewhat irksome. I'm not aware of any commercially available synth that allows its pitch-bend depth to be set as a number of scale steps in the currently selected tuning scale. It's not terribly difficult to create your own pitch-bend algorithm, however, in a software-based modular synth such as Native Instruments Reaktor.)

In some instruments, both the maximum range of an upward bend and the maximum range of a downward bend are set with a single parameter. For instance, if you set the pitch-bend depth to two half-steps, you'll be able to bend the pitch upward by two half-steps by pushing the pitch-bend wheel or lever forward (or to the right), and downward by two half-steps by pulling the wheel or lever back toward you (or to the left). In other instruments, upward and downward bend depth can be programmed separately.

If your instrument allows pitch-bend depth to be programmed in individual oscillators, you can program a sound so that the oscillators play in unison when the pitch-bender is centered and some interval (or, with three oscillators, a chord) when the bender is pushed forward or pulled back. This technique can be especially effective if the patch uses a distortion effect, because the distortion will magnify the beating between the oscillators as they go out of tune with one another.

Using a Pitch Envelope. Several musical effects can be achieved by modulating the pitch of an oscillator with an envelope generator (EG). Your synth may allow any envelope to be used as a pitch modulation source, or it may have an envelope generator dedicated to pitch modulation (or one for each oscillator). The features of envelope generators are covered in detail in Chapter Seven. The most significant fact at the moment is that a dedicated pitch EG may have fewer stages than a multi-purpose EG. Pitch envelopes with only two parameters — starting pitch and decay time — are fairly common.

This is because pitch EGs are most often used to add pitch changes to the attack of each note. A simple pitch EG will let you program the starting pitch (which may be above or below the oscillator's base pitch) and the amount of time required for the pitch to rise or fall from this starting value back to the base pitch.

When the decay time of the pitch EG is quick (in the 1–50ms range), you'll hear a quick "blip" on the attack of each note. The exact timbre of the blip will depend on the starting pitch and on what the other envelopes are doing during the attack of the note. If your amplitude envelope takes 100ms to open, you'll never hear a 5ms pitch envelope. Another factor you may have to work with is how often your synth allows its oscillator pitch to be updated. If the oscillator pitch can be changed only in blocks of 20ms or so, as was fairly common on older digital synths, a quick pitch envelope will produce a "chirp" rather than a click.

Slower pitch envelopes are useful for modulating a synced oscillator (see above) and for special effects such as spacey sighing noises.

Controlling the depth of the pitch envelope from velocity is a useful technique, as it lets you add a more percussive attack when you play harder.

Fractional Scaling. Normally, the pitch of an oscillator will track the keyboard. That is, the pitch will increase by one equal-tempered half-step per key as you play up the keyboard. Many synths give you some form of control over the oscillator's keyboard tracking, however.

The simplest way to control keyboard tracking is to switch it off. The Minimoog, for instance, had a switch for choosing whether oscillator 3 would track the keyboard or would have a fixed pitch. The fixed pitch was controlled by the oscillator's tuning knob and switch, but it was not affected by the key you played. Turning off keyboard tracking entirely is mainly useful for creating drones (in programming a bagpipe patch, for instance) and when the oscillator is being used as a modulation source rather than being listened to directly.

An oscillator that is programmed to track the keyboard at less or more than 100% (100% being one equal-tempered half-step per key) is sometimes said to be using *fractional keyboard scaling*. If the scaling parameter is set to 50%, for example, the oscillator will respond to the keyboard by playing a scale of equal-tempered quarter-tones. If the scaling parameter is set to –100%, the keyboard will be *inverted*. Low keys will produce high pitches and vice-versa.

Using fractional scaling for one oscillator in a multi-oscillator synth is an important programming technique. Typically, the fractionally scaled oscillator is programmed to play only a brief, percussive attack transient. This transient will typically become only slightly higher in pitch as you play up the keyboard. This mimics the way attack transients behave in acoustic instruments such as piano and guitar. (For more on how the sound of a piano hammer varies across the keyboard, see below under "Multisampling.")

Tuning Tables. Many synthesizers, though by no means all of them, are equipped with tuning tables. When a tuning table is active, the oscillator(s) to which it is applied will respond to the keyboard by playing whatever set of pitches is stored in the tuning table. Some tuning tables are pre-programmed at the factory, usually with historical tunings (also called *temperaments*) used in Medieval, Renaissance, and Baroque music. Others are user-programmable.

JUST FOR KICKS: *Just intonation* is not a single tuning. It's a system of tunings in which the frequencies chosen are based on intervals that can be expressed as whole-number fractions (such as 3/2 for a perfect fifth) rather than on intervals based on irrational numbers. All intervals in the familiar 12-note equal-tempered tuning are based on the 12th root of 2, which is about 1.059463.

In many instruments, tuning tables are chosen at the global level. When a tuning is selected, it will be used by any sound the synth plays. In other instruments, you may be able to select a tuning table for a given patch, or even for a single oscillator within a patch.

Most user-programmable tuning tables consist of a set of 12 pitch offsets (typically ± 50 cents), which are applied to the notes in each octave of the keyboard. You may also see a parameter for choosing the starting key of the tuning — very useful if you've programmed a scale in just intonation in order to play a piece in the key of C, and later want to play a piece in A, B♭, or some other key using the same tuning.

A few instruments, such as the long-obsolete Yamaha TX802 and the E-mu Proteus 2000 series, provide full-range tuning tables. With such a tuning table, you can tune each MIDI key to any pitch. Full-range tuning tables are good for creating microtonal tunings in which you need more than 12 notes per octave, such as 19-tone equal temperament. Playing the keyboard after setting up such a tuning is not easy, however.

The frequency resolution of most tuning tables is limited. For instance, if you can tune a MIDI note up or down by a half-step using a parameter whose range is –64/+63, the nominal resolution of the tuning table is about 0.78 cent. With some modular software synths, such as Native Instruments Reaktor, you can create tuning tables that have finer resolution, but both the process of doing so and the reasons why you might want to are beyond the scope of this book.

Random Pitch. In early analog synths, the oscillator pitch was somewhat unstable — not by design, but because analog components respond somewhat differently as they heat up. In an effort to mimic this effect, some manufacturers (Roland, for instance) include a parameter with which the pitch can vary randomly from note to note. This parameter doesn't produce random fluctuations within a single note, though you may be able to do so by using a noise-type LFO waveform as a modulation source. Instead, each note will randomly be a few cents sharp or flat compared to its expected pitch. If the random pitch parameter is set to a high value, each note may fall anywhere within a fairly wide pitch range.

Whether this parameter is useful for emulating analog synths is open to debate. Slight amounts of random detuning can cause the amount of beating in intervals (or the amount of beating caused by detuning in unisons) to vary in speed, which may be useful but can also be quite distracting, because some of the notes or intervals you play will have no detuning at all, causing them to stand out.

You may want to try random detuning with a realistic brass patch, on the assumption that the players in your "brass section" don't play perfectly in tune with one another. The best use of the parameter, though, may be in conjunction with percussive sounds. A snare drum, for instance, will vary considerably in timbre from note to note depending on where the drumhead is struck by the stick.

Random detuning doesn't really mimic this effect very well, but it may be preferable to hearing exactly the same snare sound over and over. If your snare is synthesized by layering two or more samples, randomly detuning one or all of the samples can be even more effective.

Sample Playback

Beginning in the mid-1980s with the Roland D-50 and the Korg M1, sample playback synthesizers became an important instrument category. For a number of years, sample playback eclipsed all competing technologies. It's still a vital technology, found in millions of instruments — but as the speed of digital chips has increased, it has become practical to build synths that can create complex, musically useful tones using other methods. Today, sample playback is only one color in a well-rounded musical palette.

The basics of digital sampling were covered in Chapter Two. To recap, in sampling an actual sound is recorded digitally. The sound could be anything: a single note on a clarinet, a two-bar beat played on a drum kit, a guitar playing a distorted power chord, a human voice saying "doh!," or you name it. After recording, the sample is stored in memory and assigned to the keyboard. When you play a key, the sample is played back. To be a little more technical, the oscillator reads the sample from memory and sends it on to the rest of the synth (the filter and so on).

The advantages of sample playback over traditional analog synthesis are considerable. With sampling, we can create complex and realistic sounds with the greatest of ease. Simply replace the clarinet sample with a bassoon sample (which you can do by selecting the bassoon waveform on the oscillator's edit page), and your synth will sound like a bassoon rather than a clarinet. Sounds like an unbeatable deal — but there are limitations to sample playback technology, as we'll see.

In order to be musically useful, a sample playback oscillator has to be able to change the frequency of the sound as you play up and down the keyboard. This is not a trivial issue, but fortunately it isn't anything you need to worry about as a musician and synth programmer. The details of how a sample playback oscillator changes the frequency of the sample are beyond the scope of this book, but a brief detour might be useful. An analogy that's often used (not quite correctly) is that a sample playback oscillator changes the frequency of the sample by playing the sample faster or slower. In this analogy, sample playback works much like an analog tape deck or turntable. The latter devices change the frequency of playback by passing the recording (tape or vinyl groove) across the playback device (tape head or stylus) faster or slower.

The tricky bit is, in a sample playback synth you can't actually speed up or slow down the rate of playback. The entire synth always operates at one fixed clock speed — for example, 44.1kHz. All of the samples will always be played back at that speed. In order to create the illusion that the playback of a given sample has been sped up or slowed down, a sample playback oscillator uses *interpolation*. If the sample needs to be slowed down in order to sound at a lower pitch, the oscillator actually adds new sample words between the existing sample words. Conversely, if the sample needs to be sped up, the oscillator will drop some of the sample words so that it takes less time to play through the whole sample.

Interpolation, however, changes the shape of the waveform. In other words, it introduces distortion. In first-generation digital samplers, such as the Ensoniq Mirage, this distortion was quite audible. (In fact, it's one of the reasons why these instruments are sometimes prized for their distinctive sound.) But in general, uncontrolled distortion is a bad thing. So software engineers have developed some clever mathematical operations to perform better interpolation, thereby reducing the distortion. I'm not aware of any instrument in which the interpolation algorithm is a user-programmable choice.

Interpolation can become a sonic issue when a sample is assigned to a wide keyboard range and is then played several octaves below the frequency at which it was recorded. All sounds change character radically when transposed down by several octaves, but poor interpolation can give the sample a grainy, chirpy, breathy quality. Which might be exactly what you want, of course.

Because of technical limitations in their interpolation algorithms, some instruments limit the amount of upward transposition of samples to an octave or so.

Multisampling. As you might have gathered from the foregoing, the character of a sampled sound will usually change as its pitch is raised or lowered. When the pitch is raised or lowered by more than a few half-steps, the change can become musically objectionable. This happens because some of the components of the sound will no longer be realistic.

For instance, when a sample of an acoustic piano is transposed up or down, the "thwock" of the hammer striking the strings is transposed along with the string tone itself. But in in a real piano, this percussive attack is always at pretty much the same pitch, no matter what key you strike (it's a little higher in the upper register, because the hammers in the piano's upper register are smaller, but the change from key to key is much less than a half-step). If you take a sample of a piano playing a single note and transpose it up by an octave, it will sound as if the strings are being struck with a tiny aluminum hammer.

Another example: If a violinist is sampled playing a note with vibrato, when the note is transpose upward more than two or three half-steps, the vibrato gets fast and twittery. When the note is transposed down, the vibrato gets slow and seasick — good for a special effect, but not good for playing conventional violin sounds.

In order to make sampled instrument sounds such as guitar and electric piano playable over a wide range of the keyboard, manufacturers use a technique called *multisampling*.

In multisampling, the manufacturer or sound designer records a number of samples from the same source, such as an acoustic instrument, at various pitches. These samples are then assigned to various zones of the keyboard. With an electric piano, for instance, there might be two or more samples in every octave, each assigned to a range of keys (a zone) spanning only four or five half-steps. In this case each sample only needs to be transposed up or down by a few half-steps, so the sonic changes caused by transposition are less apparent.

When you choose a sampled "waveform" for a synth patch, quite often what you're really choosing is not a single waveform but a multisample — a group of related samples that are already mapped to the keyboard in an appropriate way. In some synths, such as the Kurzweil K2000 series, it's possible to change the way the samples in a factory (ROM-based) multisample are assigned to the keyboard, but in many instruments this mapping is not user-programmable.

Multisampling can give a good approximation of the sound of an acoustic instrument across its whole range. By editing the MIDI data in a sequencer track with care, you may be able to give listeners the impression that they're hearing a performance on the original instrument. (The tricks involved in editing the sequencer data are well beyond the scope of this book.) But not all multisamples lend themselves to realistic performance.

The biggest problem with multisampling is that quite often the individual samples in the multisample don't match one another very well. When you play a scale up or down the keyboard, the places where one sample stops and another begins (called *multisample split points*) can be distressingly obvious. This can happen because the person doing the sampling is unable to find samples that match one another, or because he or she isn't listening to the samples closely enough. But when samples are assigned to zones that are a number of keys wide, the note just below the split point plays a sample that has been transposed up by a number of half-steps, while the note just above the split point plays a sample that has been transposed *down* by a number of half-steps. The change in sound quality due to transposition exaggerates even tiny differences between the samples.

One solution to the latter problem would be a multisample in which each key on the keyboard plays a different sample. If the samples were reasonably well matched, such a multisample would minimize the problems of both split points and transposition artifacts. Unfortunately, such a multisample takes up a lot of memory.

Synthesizer manufacturers naturally want to provide their customers with a wide array of sampled sounds. But no instrument has an unlimited amount of memory. So compromises are necessary. Manufacturers have to compromise: If they dedicate twice as much memory to an electric piano multisample, the instrument will have room for fewer multisamples overall. Also, developing a good multisample takes time. As memory gets cheaper, a manufacturer may elect to use an existing piano or woodwind multisample from one of their older instruments and spend their limited R&D budget on entirely new samples.

Velocity Cross-Switching. Many — indeed, most — acoustic instruments sound quite different when played softly than when played hard. Typically, a loudly played note will be brighter. In the case of plucked and percussive instruments, louder notes will also have more prominent attack transients, and the sound will last longer. This fact poses a problem for sample playback instruments.

If we sample a single note on a snare drum, for instance, by playing the drum at a medium loudness level, we can simulate some of the characteristic dynamic differences of a real drum by using a lowpass filter to filter out some of the high overtones at low MIDI velocities. (Filters are discussed in Chapter Five.) But such a snare drum preset won't sound completely realistic at either low or high velocities.

This problem is addressed in many sample playback synths by means of *velocity cross-switching*. Instead of providing one sample of a given snare drum, the manufacturer or sound designer records two or more samples of the same drum. The drum is sampled being tapped lightly, being hit very hard, and perhaps at a number of levels in between. These samples are then assigned to the multisample in *velocity zones*, so that low MIDI velocities cause the light tap sample to be played and so on.

I'd love to be able to tell you that this type of multisampling guarantees that the multisample will respond to a MIDI performance in a realistic way, but real life is messier than that. Some velocity cross-switched multisamples are very good indeed, but many of them are offensively bad. Electric piano multisamples seem to be among the worst offenders. Quite often, a synthesizer's electric piano sound will be beautiful and smooth if you play at moderate velocities, but if you spank the keys hard enough that the high-velocity samples kick in, you'll hear a radically different timbre. Controlling your keyboard performance so as to get smooth transitions between moderate and high velocities may well be impossible.

As with other types of multisampling, the problems are due to cost and limited memory. In order to provide enough samples at different velocities to allow the instrument to be played in a musically satisfying fashion, the manufacturer would have to spend far more time developing the multisample, and dedicate more memory space to it in the synth.

Actually, the real problem is a little deeper than that. Sample playback is not, in the end, a very good technology for creating synthesizers that can respond to a musician's performance in a satisfying way. The early promise of sampling — "Hey, you can sound exactly like any instrument!" — has proven gloriously optimistic. Sampling is very good for some musical tasks, but if you want the sound of a real acoustic instrument, the best solution (though not the cheapest or easiest one) is still to hire someone who plays the instrument well and record them playing the entire part, not single notes.

Sample Playback Modulation. The sound of sample playback is made a little more musically responsive in some instruments by the inclusion of features for modifying the sample data before or during playback. The most common parameter for this purpose, found in E-mu synths among others, is the *sample start point*. Normally, sample playback starts at the beginning of the sample. But when the sample start point has been set to some value other than zero, playback will start at some other point in memory — presumably at some point after the beginning of the sample.

This is useful because the sounds made by acoustic instruments usually change most rapidly during their first 50ms or so. The changes that take place during this period are called the *attack transients*. The attack transients give listeners important aural clues about what they're hearing. Once the instrument has settled down to produce a steady tone, it has less individual character.

By modulating the sample start point from velocity, you can program a sound so that the full portion of the sample containing the attack transients will be heard only at high velocities. At low velocities, some or all of the attack transients will be skipped. This will make the sound less percussive at low velocities, mimicking (to some extent) the behavior of an acoustic instrument. Used with care, this technique can produce fairly realistic results.

In some synths, you may be given a choice of waveforms with or without the attack transients. Since the sample will typically go into a loop after the attack, you may see waveforms with names like "EP1" and "EP1(loop)." The two waveforms will most likely use exactly the same wave data, but the first will contain the attack transients followed by the sustaining loop, and the second will contain only the loop.

Another type of control over the sample start, found on some instruments, works in exactly the opposite way. Instead of starting the sample playback immediately when the note is played, the synth waits for some period of time (from a few milliseconds to a couple of seconds) and then starts the sample — from the beginning, but late. A start delay parameter is useful mainly for special effects. Usually it's used only on multi-oscillator instruments, and one oscillator is programmed for no delay so as to define the start of the note. Small amounts of delay can smear the attacks of the notes by spreading out the attack transients. Larger amounts can be used for harmonic effects. On a three-oscillator synth, for instance, you may be able to tune the three oscillators to a triad, delay the third of the triad by some amount, and delay the fifth by twice as much, producing an arpeggiation on each note.

Drum Kit Multisamples. Many sample playback synths provide special multisamples in which many of the instruments in a percussion setup can be played from the keyboard at the same time. In some instruments these drum kit multi-samples can be edited by the user so as to use a different snare or hi-hat, or to bring together all of the samples that will be needed for a given musical project.

In many synths, drum kit editing goes far beyond selecting drum samples for individual notes on the keyboard. You may also be able to tune the samples individually, give each key its own filter settings and panning, send specific drums to specific effects buses, and so on. (Effects busing is covered in Chapter Nine.)

Hi-hat groups are an important feature in drum kit programming. Other terms used for the same feature include "exclusive channels" and "mute groups," but the feature dates back to early drum machines, when it was used exclusively for the hi-hat voices. In a real trap set, the hi-hat (a pair of cymbals on a pedal-operated stand) can be open or closed, and can be either struck with a drumstick or brought closed by pressing the pedal. If the hi-hat is struck while open and is then closed with the pedal, the open sound, in which the cymbals ring for some period of time, is abruptly cut off. To simulate this, synthesizers and drum machines allow two or more keys playing separate hi-hat samples to be assigned to the same voice channel. (Voice channels are discussed in Chapter Three.) When the musician triggers the closed hi-hat sample, it will cut off the playback of the open hi-hat sample.

Your synth may provide several independent hi-hat groups. If it does, try assigning other types of semi-sustained percussion sounds to these groups and experiment with the kinds of rhythmic effects you can create.

Single-Cycle Digital Waves

Early in the history of synthesis, musicians concluded that there was only so much that could be done timbrally with standard analog waveforms (sawtooth, pulse, etc.) and lowpass filters. In order to provide a broader sound palette, several manufacturers developed hybrid instruments that combined digital oscillators with analog filters. (At the time, computer chips were too slow to allow resonant filters to be implemented digitally.) The best-known of these instruments were the PPG Wave 2.2 and the Ensoniq ESQ-1.

Due to the limited memory available in these instruments, the digital oscillators didn't play full-length samples. Instead, they played *single-cycle waves*. Only a few hundred bytes of memory were needed to encode a waveform that had an interesting harmonic content — for example, the fundamental together with the fourth and sixth harmonics, but no other harmonics. Mixing and filtering these waveforms within the synth opened up new types of sound.

The PPG had a number of wavetables, each of which included 64 of these single-cycle waves. Instead of selecting a single wave for playback, the sound programmer could direct the instrument to sweep through the wavetable under the control of an envelope or LFO. If the waves adjacent to one another in the wavetable were closely related to one another harmonically, the wavetable sweep could sound fairly smooth. If the waves were more disparate, the sweep would sound quite gargly and gritty. The sound most often associated with the PPG was precisely the gargly sound of the wavetable sweeps. This technique isn't found on many current synthesizers, but Waldorf has released a faithful clone of the Wave 2.2 in software. Called the Wave 2.V, this softsynth includes the original PPG wavetables, and is faithful to the design of the original in other ways as well. Single-cycle waves are also used effectively in the Malström synth in Propellerhead Reason.

Wave Sequencing

When it became practical to store longer waveforms in ROM, a few synths expanded on the PPG's wavetable sweep concept by introducing various forms of *wave sequencing*. The most primitive form of this technique was found in Roland's first sample playback synth, the D-50. The D-50 included a set of "waveforms" each of which was a chunk of wave memory in which several of the standard waveforms were stored. When one of these chunks of memory was selected for playback, a comical and uncontrollable rhythmic loop consisting of an ill-matched assortment of tones would be heard. Kurzweil K2000/2500 series instruments can do the same trick, but the user can choose any chunk of memory as the wave sequence.

Korg took this idea and ran with it in the Wavestation. The Wavestation allowed the user to line up short ROM waveforms (samples, in other words) in any order and play them back with any rhythm. The Wavestation quickly became known for its distinctive one-finger rhythm patterns. When the samples in the wave sequence crossfade with one another rather than being separate, the result of wave-sequencing can be a smooth blend from one timbre into another. This technique uses twices as many voice channels, however.

As of early 2003, there were no current instruments on the market that used wave sequencing, but it was only a matter of time until the technique resurfaced. Just before sending this book off to press, I received a copy of Steinberg Xphrase, a new software synth with a full wave sequencing implementation. If the idea intrigues you, you can build your own wave sequences in any sampler by splicing samples together, but some of the more advanced features of Xphrase and the Wavestation will be difficult to duplicate in this manner.

Audio-Rate Modulation

Modulating the frequency or amplitude of one oscillator with a signal coming from another oscillator is an important technique for creating interesting timbres.

Modulating the amplitude of the oscillator's signal is called, naturally enough, *amplitude modulation*, while modulating the frequency is called *frequency modulation*. Some synths provide both in their oscillator sections.

Frequency Modulation (FM). FM is such a versatile way of generating musically useful tones that some successful synths have used only FM. The Yamaha DX7, which was manufactured in the mid-1980s, is probably the best-known FM synth, and FM is still part of Yamaha's product line. More recently, Native Instruments' FM7 software has made FM synthesis available to computer users. Today, pure FM synths like the DX7 are rare: Most FM synthesizers combine FM with other synthesis techniques, such as filtering. In addition, many synths that are primarily oriented toward other types of synthesis, such as analog emulation, provide limited implementations of FM.

At a basic level, FM synthesis is nothing but vibrato on steroids. To create vibrato in a synthesizer, the frequency of an oscillator is modulated by an LFO (a low-frequency oscillator). In vibrato, the modulating signal coming from the LFO typically has a frequency between 3Hz and 6Hz, so the frequency of the oscillator we're actually listening to will increase and decrease at this rate. In FM, the LFO is replaced with an oscillator whose frequency is in the audio range (above 20Hz).

FM synthesis requires at least two oscillators. The oscillator whose signal is sent to the synth's output so we can listen to it is called the *carrier*. The oscillator whose signal is used to modulate the frequency of the carrier is called, naturally enough, the *modulator*. In classic DX7-style FM synthesis, both the carrier and the modulator would be producing sine waves, but in synths that give you a little FM along with other synthesis methods, you'll probably be able to choose any of the available waveforms for both the carrier and the modulator — even a sample or noise (though it would be meaningless for a true noise source to be an FM carrier, because modulating a random frequency can only produce another random frequency). In the discussion that follows we'll assume that the modulator is producing not noise but a periodic wave; that is, one that repeats in a cyclic way.

When the frequency of the modulator is in the audio range, something extremely interesting happens: The carrier is still changing frequency, but our ears no longer perceive the modulation as changes in frequency. Instead, the modulation is perceived as adding new overtones to the sound of the carrier. FM changes the tone color of the carrier by adding overtones.

The frequencies and amplitudes of the new overtones depend in a complex mathematical way on the relative frequencies of the two oscillators and on the amplitude of the modulator. If you're curious to learn the details, I can recommend the discussion of FM in *Computer Music*. If you just want to program some sounds, here are a couple of quick guidelines:

Tuning the carrier and the modulator to a whole-number ratio such as 1:1 or 1:4 produces a tone that's harmonically related to the original frequency of the carrier. Tuning the two to a non-whole-number ratio produces a more complex, clangorous timbre.

Increasing the amplitude of the modulator distributes more energy among the higher overtones. Because of this, using an envelope generator to shape the amplitude of the modulator is a very effective way to shape the tone color of the carrier's output.

A few analog-style synths implement FM in an extremely limited way — either with an on/off switch or with a simple level knob for controlling the amplitude of the modulator. If your synth lets the FM amount (the amplitude of the modulator, in other words) be controlled by an envelope, you'll find FM extremely useful for adding bright attack transients, growling sub-octaves, and everything in between.

I've been describing FM as a two-oscillator process. If your synth makes more oscillators available for FM, you may be able to make composite sounds using two carrier/modulator pairs, drive a single carrier from two modulators, create a "stack" in which oscillator 1 modulates oscillator 2 and oscillator 2 modulates oscillator 3 (the carrier), and so on. These configurations are known collectively as FM *algorithms*.

Amplitude Modulation (AM). Broadly speaking, any change in the loudness (amplitude) of a synthesizer's tone is a form of amplitude modulation. The term is generally used, however, to refer to a synthesis technique in which both the signal being modulated and the signal that does the modulating are in the audio frequency range. AM sounds somewhat similar to FM, and is used for some of the same musical purposes. *Ring modulation*, also seen in a lot of instruments, is a type of AM. Ring modulation is discussed in Chapter Nine.

Additive Synthesis

Since any sound can be described as the sum of one or more sine waves, each with its own frequency, amplitude, and phase characteristics, it's natural to wonder whether one might be able to build a synthesizer that generates complex sounds by summing (mixing) sine waves. This technique is called *additive synthesis*.

Additive synthesis has been implemented in a few commercial instruments, most notably the Kawai K5 and K5000, and it's available as a tool in computer-based synthesis systems such as Csound, but it has not proven an extremely fruitful technique conceptually, nor has it been extremely successful in the market. This is because defining the frequencies and amplitude envelopes of the large numbers of sine waves needed to create musically useful sounds is a fairly laborious and not always intuitive process. The VirSyn Cube software synth, just released at this writing (mid-2003), provides, for the first time, a workable user interface for real-time additive synthesis. U&I Software's Metasynth also makes additive synthesis accessible, but Metasynth is a rendering program, not a real-time instrument. As computers become more powerful, we can expect to see more additive synthesizers.

Granular Synthesis

Granular synthesis is an experimental technique, and is not found in many commercially available synths. You'll find it most often in software for experimental types, such as Native Instruments Reaktor, Cycling '74 MaxMSP, and Csound.

In granular synthesis, a source waveform (usually a sample) is chopped up into a number of smaller "grains." A new sound is synthesized by recombining these grains in various ways. You may be given control over the grain size, the tuning of individual grains, the amount of overlap, the order in which the grains will be played back, the density of the playback, the amount of randomness in any of the above, and so on. By modulating these parameters during the course of a single "note" (though the concept of what's a note can get pretty vague, once a granular process gets under way), you can create effects like having a spoken voice emerge from a swirling cloud of seemingly random hash.

Granular synthesis is well suited to producing hazy clouds of sound, but it wouldn't be my first choice for a sound that needs pinpoint clarity, such as a melodic synthesizer patch. It's sometimes used for time-stretching and pitch-shifting complex sampled sounds, such as drum loops, but in my experience the results tend not to be very convincing.

Physical Modeling

Yet another approach to generating sounds is to start with a mathematical description of the behavior of a physical object (such as a saxophone with its vibrating reed, conical bore, and array of keys) — a mathematical model, in other words. Some models are designed to be used as sound sources (oscillators), and others are implemented as sound processor/resonators with which certain characteristics can be imparted to a signal. This technique is called *physical modeling synthesis*.

Various manufacturers have implemented physical modeling in various ways. In fact, the term has become somewhat puffy. I've seen it used as a buzzword to describe a fast delay line used as a resonator, which is a physical model only in the broadest sense. I've also seen it used to describe what happens in a straight sample playback synth when samples taken from various physical parts of an instrument (such as a piano's hammers and the acoustic reverberation of its harp and soundboard) are made available for performance.

In true physical modeling, many of the aspects of the model are likely to be hidden from the user. The user is likely to be presented with high-level controls over such elements as the amount of breath or the stiffness of the reed in a saxophone model, or the material of which a drum head is made. Varying these elements, especially in real time during the course of a note, can result in extremely interesting, animated sounds. A physical model of a trumpet or flute can "overblow" in a realistic way in response to velocity or pitch-bend data. This effect is difficult to simulate with any other type of synthesis.

The performance techniques required to play a physical modeling synth are not always easy to learn, however. Yamaha's breath controller, used with their groundbreaking VL-1 physical modeling synth, required keyboard players to learn to think and play like wind players. This fact may account for the limited success physical modeling has had in the market. If you're interested in experimenting with physical modeling, Applied Acoustic Systems' Tassman modular software synth would be a good tool, as it includes a number of modules that implement physical models in various ways.

A new (as of mid-2003) synth called the Hartmann Neuron takes an approach that might be termed reverse physical modeling or analysis/resynthesis. The Neuron's resynthesizing oscillators, which are called resynators, make use of models created in a software program called ModelMaker. This program "deconstructs" samples into somewhat abstract sonic components, which can then be recombined quite flexibly in the resynators. It seems clear that as DSP chips get faster, complex synthesis techniques of this sort will assume increasing importance in the synthesist's bag of tricks.

 ## Power Projects for Chapter 4

Project 4-1: **Listen to the Waveforms.** To do this project, you're going to need to create a default patch for your synth. Start by using the "initialize voice" command if the instrument has one, but be aware that the init voice may already have some types of processing (such as a tasteful amount of reverb) that you'll need to remove. The goal is to create a patch that has the following characteristics:

■ Only one oscillator should be heard. You may be able to do this by turning the others off, or by turning their output levels down to zero in the mixer.

■ The filter should be wide open. You may be able to shut it off entirely. If it's a lowpass filter, crank the cutoff frequency up to the max, and turn the resonance down to zero.

■ The amplitude envelope should be set to instant attack and full sustain level.

■ There should be little or no velocity-to-amplitude modulation: All the notes you play should sound equally loud.

■ The effects should be switched off or set to 100% dry.

■ The oscillator should have no modulation inputs. Either switch off the modulation, or turn the levels down to zero. Some synths hide their modulation routings in odd places, so you may have to hunt for them.

After creating this patch (and saving it as "MyInitPatch"), you're ready to proceed. Call up the relevant edit page of the active oscillator in the display and go through the synth's waveform selections one by one. Listen to the sound quality of each wave. Play them near the top and bottom of the keyboard, not just in the midrange. If your synth has velocity cross-switched multisamples, play at low, medium, and high velocities to hear the different samples.

This project has a dual purpose. First, you'll be getting acquainted with the full range of raw sounds available in your synth. Second, you may find that some of the waveforms don't sound very good in their raw state. Filtering, enveloping, keyboard scaling, and other techniques are needed to produce musically pleasing sounds. Once you know the raw materials, you'll be able to apply those techniques more intelligently.

Project 4-2: Combine Waveforms. Beginning with the default patch you created in Project 4-1, activate a second oscillator. Make sure the second oscillator's detune or fine tune control is set to 0 (no detuning). Try the following experiments:

■ Listen to two different waveforms mixed at the same loudness level. If your instrument has 100 waveforms, there will be 10,000 possible combinations with two oscillators, so you may not have time to listen to them all. Let your intuition be your guide.

■ Try some of the same combinations of waves with the second wave tuned an octave or two higher (or lower) than the first.

■ Try some combinations with the second wave mixed at a very low level, so that it adds a barely perceptible color, or filtered so that only its lowest or highest overtones contribute to the composite sound.

■ If your instrument allows each oscillator to have its own amplitude envelope, give the second oscillator a very short plucked envelope, so that it adds only an attack transient to the tone. Try tuning this attack transient up an octave or two, and try reducing its loudness.

■ Program the second oscillator so that its loudness responds more to velocity than the first oscillator's. The blend of the two tones should change, depending on how hard you strike the key.

■ When you've found a combination that seems interesting, refine other aspects of the patch to taste.

Project 4-3: Discover the Waveforms in the Factory Patches. Choose a factory patch that you like. Go into edit mode, and figure out how many oscillators it uses. Listen to each of the oscillators in isolation. (You may be able to mute and unmute oscillators, or you may need to turn their outputs down to zero to mute them.) Notice the contribution that each oscillator makes to the composite tone.

You may find that some oscillators seem to make no sound. This may be because they're active only at high (or low) velocities, or because they're only active in a restricted range of the keyboard.

Project 4-4: **Swap Waveforms.** Choose a factory preset in your synth. (Almost any preset will work for this experiment.) As in Project 4-3, go into edit mode and determine what contribution each oscillator is making to the tone. Then, without making any other edits, try changing the waveform of one oscillator to see how the character of the tone is altered.

Sometimes, changing the waveform is all you need to do in order to create a radically new and good-sounding patch. If you find something good, save it to one of the empty locations you created in Project 3-1. Other times, you may find a combination that seems promising, but that needs work. Experiment with the tuning of the oscillators, the envelopes, and the filter to help the new waveform blend in better with the other waves.

Chapter 5
Filters

Once you have an oscillator generating an audio signal, as described in Chapter Four, there are two things you can do with the signal to make it more interesting or more musically expressive: You can add new harmonic content, or you can take some of the existing harmonic content away. Adding new harmonic content is most often performed by effects processors, which are discussed in Chapter Nine, or by means of FM synthesis, which is discussed briefly in Chapter Four. In this chapter we'll cover the process of stripping away portions of the harmonic content from a signal. Modules that do this, or (to be a little more rigorous about it) that change the relative balance of the sound's partials without introducing any new partials, are called *filters*.

If you're not familiar with the nature of the harmonic spectrum, this would be a good time to review the material on that subject in Chapter Two. Filtering is a *frequency-based* process — that is, filters differentiate among the various frequencies in an incoming signal — so we'll be talking about the frequencies in the harmonic spectrum, and how filters treat them. In the discussion that follows, the words "harmonics" and "overtones" will sometimes be used to refer to the various frequency components of a signal, whether or not they're harmonically related to a fundamental. This usage is a little sloppy. The word "partials" is more correct, but is less commonly used.

Broadly speaking, a filter will reduce the amount of energy in certain parts of the spectrum, while perhaps increasing the amount of energy in other parts of the spectrum and leaving still other parts of the spectrum entirely untouched. With one exception, which we'll get to below in the discussion of resonance, filters don't generate any sound on their own. That is, if the signal being processed by the filter contains no harmonics within a given frequency band, the filter won't have any effect at all within that band. It won't create partials that don't exist in the raw sound. But if there's a harmonic component, which thanks to Fourier analysis we can visualize as a sine

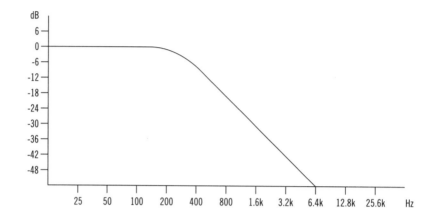

Figure 5-1.
The response curve of a
typical lowpass filter.

wave, within a band that the filter is operating on, the filter may decrease the amplitude of the sine wave, increase it, or simply pass it through without doing anything to it.

Actually, "without doing anything to it" is an oversimplification. In addition
to changing the amplitude of frequency components, filters can also change
their phase. This fact isn't usually of much significance to musicians who use synthesizers, because, as noted in Chapter Two, the human ear does a poor job
when it comes to distinguishing the phase relationships of harmonics within a tone.
If a synthesizer filter's phase response made an audible difference, you'd probably see lots of instruments with filters that included some form of phase control
as a feature. For some purposes in audio engineering, such as the design of filters
that are used in conjunction with analog-to-digital converters, phase coherence
(that is, keeping the overtones' phase relationships constant) is a real issue. These
filters are not discussed in this book.

The operation of filters is conventionally diagrammed in the manner shown
in **Figure 5-1**. If you don't understand this diagram, you're going to get lost pretty quickly, so let's dissect it in some detail. The frequency spectrum is plotted
on the graph on the X axis, with low frequencies at the left and high frequencies at the right. The amount of gain (boost) or attenuation (cut) introduced
by the filter is plotted on the Y axis. The response curve of the filter is drawn
on the graph.

The values on the X axis are plotted in an exponential rather than a linear manner. That is, each octave takes up an equal amount of horizontal space on the X

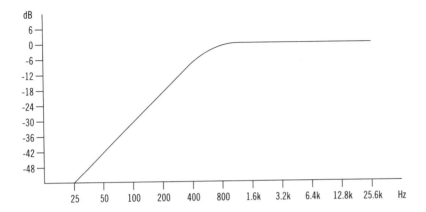

Figure 5-2.
The response curve of a
typical highpass filter.

axis. This is not the only way to do a frequency plot, but in the case of filters, it makes sense, as we'll see.

In the simplest case, the response curve would be a horizontal line stretching from left to right at the zero point on the Y axis. In this case, frequency components of the incoming signal would be processed with no gain and no cut, no matter what their frequency. (Believe it or not, this type of filter, which is called an allpass filter, is useful in some situations, such as building reverbs and phase shifters. This is because an allpass filter changes the phase of various harmonics.) At frequencies where the response curve dips below the zero point, the incoming signal will be attenuated, and at frequencies where the response curve rises above the zero line, the signal will be boosted.

How much boost or cut is introduced at any given frequency is shown by how far the response curve is above or below the zero line. If the response curve dips down to a low level, the corresponding frequency components of the signal being processed will be attenuated by quite a lot, rendering them nearly or entirely inaudible. If, on the other hand, the response curve is only a little below the zero line at a given spot, the frequency components of the signal in that part of the spectrum will be attenuated only slightly.

Explaining exactly how a filter can perform this type of magic on a signal is beyond the scope of this book — which is fortunate, because I'm not an engineer, so I have no idea how it works. All I know is, it works. Filters can cut some frequency bands while at the same time boosting others. A filter is a *frequency-dependent amplifier*.

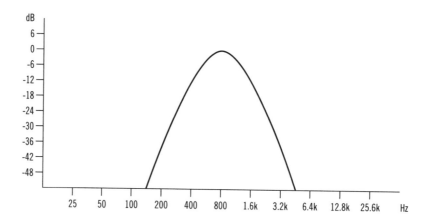

Figure 5-3.
The response curve of a
bandpass filter.

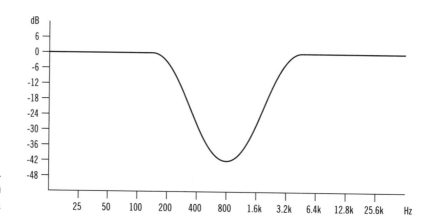

Figure 5-4.
The response curve of a
band-reject (notch) filter.

Types of Filters

The response curve shown in Figure 5-1 is characteristic of a *lowpass filter*, which is a very common type of filter. Lowpass filters are found on almost all synthesizers. A lowpass filter gets its name because it allows low frequencies to pass through unchanged, while attenuating higher frequencies. The opposite type of filter, as you might imagine, is called a *highpass filter*. A highpass filter (see **Figure 5-2**) allows high frequencies to pass through while attenuating lower frequencies.

A filter that attenuates both high and low frequencies, while allowing those in between to pass through, is called a *bandpass* filter (see **Figure 5-3**). Because bandpass filtering removes both the lows and the highs, it's a good choice for imitating the sound of an old-time recording. A bandpass-filtered string sound, for instance, will tend to have a distant and wistful but faintly menacing air.

The opposite of a bandpass filter is a *band-reject* filter, also commonly called a *notch* filter because the graph of its frequency response has a notch shape. As **Figure 5-4** shows, a notch filter allows both high and low frequencies to pass through, while attenuating the portion of the signal that falls between the highs and lows.

The range of frequencies that a filter passes through unaltered is sometimes called the *pass-band*. The range of frequencies that is significantly attenuated is called the *stop-band*. These terms are used more often in the literature on digital signal processing than in discussions of synthesizers, but they're sometimes useful.

These definitions are still a little vague. How high is high, and how low is low? How wide is a typical pass-band, if there is such a thing as a typical pass-band? To make the definitions more precise, we'll have to add a few more technical terms to the mix. Before we do that, however, we need to mention briefly a few other filter types.

In order to give musicians more options, synth manufacturers frequently build filters that can operate in more than one mode. For instance, a filter might be able to function as either a lowpass or a highpass filter. Or it might be able to operate in either lowpass, highpass, or bandpass mode. Such a filter is called a *multimode* filter. This is a catch-all term covering many different filter designs. One multimode filter might have three lowpass modes and one highpass mode, while another might have one lowpass mode plus bandpass, highpass, and notch modes. Also worth noting: Some multimode filters, especially those on modular analog synths, provide simultaneous outputs for their various modes. Other filters must be switched from one mode to another, and only one mode is active at any given time.

Less common, but musically useful, is the *state-variable* filter. Such a filter typically has a knob or control input (usually both) for changing the response curve in a smooth, continuous manner from lowpass to bandpass, or from lowpass through bandpass to highpass.

Some synthesizers offer EQ (equalization) in their filter modules. EQ is covered in Chapter Nine. A few instruments have exotic filter modes not covered in this book; the E-mu Proteus 2000's "BlissBatz" mode is as good an example as any. For information on these modes, consult the owner's manual.

A number of digital synthesizers have *comb* filters. As **Figure 5-5** shows, a comb filter has a number of notches, and a number of pass-bands between the notches. The number and spacing of notches will usually be user-programmable. You'll see only one parameter for this, which will control both the number and the spacing. As the number of notches increases, they'll get closer together. If you want individual control over the spacing of the notches and pass-bands, what you need is not a comb filter but a formant filter.

Formant Filters

A formant filter typically combines several bandpass/band-reject filters. For each band, you'll have control over the center frequency, the width of the band, and the boost/cut amount. A formant filter is similar in concept to a multiband parametric EQ, but you may find that the formant filter lets you attenuate unwanted frequencies more strenuously than an EQ does.

Typically, formant filters don't have inputs for envelopes or other forms of modulation. The response curve of a formant filter tends to remain static, both during each note and over the course of a phrase. This is not because of any limitations in engineering (the VirSyn Tera software synth, for instance, has a formant filter whose parameters can be controlled in real time) but because formants

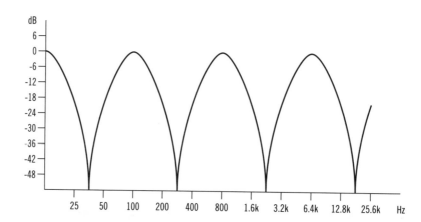

Figure 5-5.
The response curve of a comb filter.

are conceptually patterns of peaks and dips in frequency response that give sounds a unique and identifiable character. In some sense, moving a formant turns it into a different formant.

Vowel sounds offer the most important example of formants in action. Vowels are distinguishable from one another because the human vocal tract can impose various formant characteristics on the sound coming from the vocal cords. You do this mainly by moving your lips and tongue, which changes the shape of your mouth cavity. The vocal cords themselves don't give you a lot of waveform choices, but when formants are imposed on the sound of the vocal cords, the vowels take on a distinct character.

Some formant filters have presets named after vowels — "ee," "ah", "oo," and so on. You may also be able to morph (make a smooth transition) between one vowel sound and another. With a well-designed formant filter and a little clever programming on the part of the sound designer, it's possible to make a formant filter appear to be speaking almost-recognizable words.

Cutoff Frequency & Rolloff Slope

Referring back to Figure 5-1, you'll notice that there's a point on the lowpass filter response curve where the curve starts to dip downward. We can define this point in terms of where it falls on the X axis — that is, in terms of its frequency. This is the *cutoff frequency* of the filter. Scrutinize the panel of almost any modern synth and you'll see a knob labelled "cutoff" (or, if panel space is tight, simply "cut"). The cutoff frequency of a filter is perhaps its most important characteristic, and changing the cutoff frequency, as we'll see, is one of the most musically useful things you can do to alter the sound of the synth. Before delving deeper into this area, though, we need to talk about some other characteristics of the response curve.

The amount of boost or cut introduced by the filter at a given frequency is expressed in decibels (dB), a unit of measurement defined in Chapter Two. (For most listeners, a signal has to change amplitude by between 0.2dB and 0.4dB before the change can be perceived. These figures define the *just noticeable difference* for amplitude changes. A decrease of 6dB reduces the amplitude of a sound by 50%.)

You'll notice that the filter response curve shown in Figure 5-1 doesn't jump from zero down to infinite attenuation at one specific frequency. It looks more like a hillside than a cliff. The sloping part of the curve is called the *rolloff slope*, because it describes the part of the spectrum in which sound energy is rolled off (attenuated) by the filter.

The cutoff frequency is usually defined as the point on the rolloff slope where the signal is attenuated by 3dB. In the case of a bandpass filter, which has rolloff

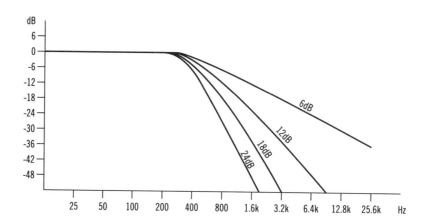

Figure 5-6.
Lowpass filter response
with rolloff slopes of 6dB,
12dB, 18dB, and 24dB
per octave.

slopes on both sides of the pass-band, the bandwidth of the filter is the distance between the –3dB points on both sides of the center frequency.

Depending on how the filter is designed and, in some cases, how its parameters are set, its rolloff slope can be steep or gradual. The steepness or gradualness — that is, the angle of the rolloff slope — is expressed in decibels per octave. A rolloff slope of 6dB per octave is fairly gentle, 12dB per octave is more pronounced, and 18dB or 24dB per octave qualifies as a steep rolloff slope. Lowpass filter response curves with these slopes are shown in **Figure 5-6**. Because the rolloff slope is defined in terms of octaves, when the X axis of the graph is marked in octave units, as mentioned above, we can draw the filter's response curve in the stop-band as a straight line. If the X axis used linear units, the response curve would indeed be displayed as a curve.

JARGON BUSTER: A filter's rolloff slope is sometimes described in terms of poles rather than in dB per octave. Each pole (a pole is simply one of the elements in the design of the filter) introduces 3dB per octave of rolloff. So a 2-pole filter has a rolloff of 6dB per octave, a 4-pole filter has a rolloff of 12dB per octave, and so on.

To explain cutoff frequency and rolloff slope in musical terms, let's assume you're sending a signal that's rich in high harmonics, such as a sawtooth wave or, better still, white noise, through a lowpass filter. If the cutoff frequency is extremely high (20kHz or so), the filter won't do much of anything. All of the harmonic components of the incoming signal will be passed through without attenuation. In this case, the filter's pass-band is the entire audible frequency spectrum.

As you begin to lower the cutoff frequency of the lowpass filter, perhaps by turning the cutoff knob on the front panel, the amount of energy in the high overtones will begin to diminish. The amount of attenuation at any given point in the frequency spectrum will depend on two factors: the cutoff frequency and the rolloff slope. As noted above, the energy of the signal at the cutoff frequency will be reduced by 3dB. Frequencies above the cutoff (assuming the filter is in lowpass mode) will be attenuated more sharply. For example, if the rolloff slope is 6dB per octave, fre-

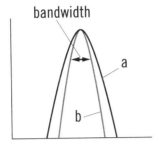

bandwidth

a

b

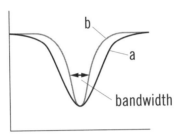

b

a

bandwidth

Figure 5-7.
The response curves of a
bandpass filter (top) and
a notch filter (bottom) with
a wide bandwidth (a) and a
narrower bandwidth (b).

quencies one octave above the cutoff will be attenuated by 9dB. Those two octaves above the cutoff will be attenuated by 15dB, and so on. If the rolloff slope is 24dB per octave, on the other hand, frequencies one octave above the cutoff will be attenuated by 27dB, those two octaves above the cutoff by 51dB, and so on — a much more significant attenuation.

As we continue to lower the cutoff frequency, the higher components of the signal will be more and more attenuated. Eventually the signal will become quite dull and muted in tone. Depending on the filter's characteristics and the nature of the input signal, it's even possible to lower the cutoff of a lowpass filter so far that the entire signal is filtered out, so that the filter's output will be silence.

TIP: If you're editing a synth patch and suddenly you don't hear anything when you play the keyboard, the first thing to check is the filter cutoff frequency. Quite likely, raising it (in the case of a lowpass filter) will allow you to hear the signal.

In the case of bandpass and notch filters, the term "cutoff" isn't quite applicable. Instead, you'll be dealing with the *center frequency* of the filter. In the case of a bandpass, the center frequency is the frequency at which incoming signals are not attenuated. In the case of a notch filter, the center frequency is the frequency at which incoming signals are *most* attenuated. While it's possible to talk about the rolloff slope of a bandpass or notch filter, you'll more often encounter the term *width* or *bandwidth*. A bandpass or notch filter with a high bandwidth has a shallow rolloff slope, and one with a low (narrow) bandwidth has a steep rolloff slope. This relationship is shown in **Figure 5-7**.

Resonance

If you've been around synthesizers for more than about two days, doubtless you've heard the term "resonant filter" or "filter resonance." Resonance has been used on synthesizers since the 1960s to make the sounds produced by filters more colorful and musically expressive. Resonance is referred to by some manufacturers as *emphasis* or *Q*. Technically, Q is a way of measuring the bandwidth of a bandpass filter, so it's a bit of a misnomer when applied to lowpass or highpass filter resonance. But the term is sometimes used as a synonym for resonance.

> **Q TIP**: The *Q* (which stands for "quality factor," though no one ever uses the term) of a bandpass filter is defined as the center frequency divided by the bandwidth. For instance, let's suppose the center frequency is 100Hz and the bandwidth is 50Hz. The Q of the filter it then 2. If the center frequency is 1kHz and the bandwidth is 500Hz, the Q is again 2. A narrower bandwidth results in a higher Q.

When you turn up the resonance amount on a highpass or lowpass filter, frequencies in the part of the spectrum nearest the cutoff frequency are boosted rather than being cut. As the amount of resonance is increased, the boost becomes more pronounced. Resonance introduces a peak into the filter's frequency response, as shown in **Figure 5-8**. Overtones that fall within the resonant peak will be amplified.

In many analog filters and some digital models, the resonance can be boosted to such an extent that the filter begins to *self-oscillate*. That is, it will emit a sine wave at the cutoff frequency even when no signal is present at the input stage. This is sometimes useful: If the filter is programmed to track the keyboard, for instance (see below), you may be able to use it as an extra oscillator. But it's also something to watch out for: Cranking the resonance up at the wrong moment could damage your speakers or even your eardrums. Even if the filter isn't self-oscillating, a prominent overtone in the signal at the filter's input can be boosted to a very high level by turning up the resonance.

When the filter's cutoff frequency remains static, adding resonance imposes a formant on the signal (see above). Modulating the cutoff when the resonance is high does a variety of interesting things to the tone, as discussed below under "Filter Modulation."

Depending on the distribution of energy in the signal being sent to the filter, cranking up the resonance can drastically increase the level of the signal emerging from the filter. Because of this, some filters provide *automatic gain compensation*: As the resonance increases, the overall output level is attenuated by a corresponding amount. As a result, gain compensation lowers the level of frequency components in the pass-band. Gain compensation is illustrated in **Figure 5-9**. Gain compensation can be good or bad, depending on the nature of the input signal and what you're trying to do musically. If you're using a lowpass filter to create a bass tone for pop music, gain compensation can work against you, because as you increase the resonance the bottom will tend to drop out of

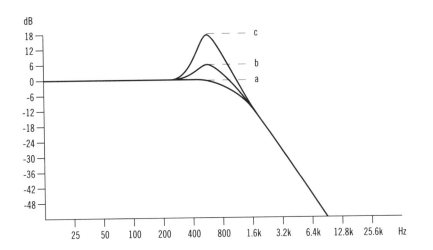

Figure 5-8.
The response curve of a lowpass filter with no resonance (a), some resonance (b), and a lot of resonance (c). Note that the resonant peaks rise above 0dB.

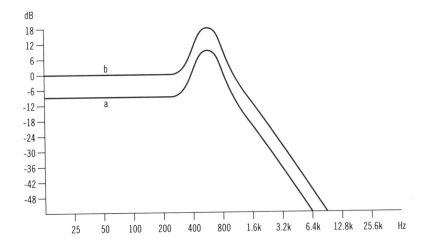

Figure 5-9.
Two response curves of a heavily resonant lowpass filter: with gain compensation (a) and without gain compensation (b).

the tone. Gain compensation is not a user-programmable feature on most resonant filters, but it's something you may run into from time to time.

Early digital filters, such as those on Korg's popular M1 synth (built in the late '80s), didn't have resonance. This was because the extra computation required to build a resonant filter would have required a faster processor, which would have made the instrument prohibitively expensive. Today, fast processors have become cheap enough that the bottleneck has disappeared. Very good simulations of resonant analog filters are found on most digital synths. Even so, purists maintain they can tell the difference between a real analog filter and a digital simulation.

In some synths, when a multimode filter is set to bandpass or notch mode, the resonance control usually turns into a bandwidth control. A few synths, however, have independent controls for filter resonance and filter bandwidth. If only one knob does double duty for resonance and bandwidth, increasing the "resonance" of a bandpass or notch filter will usually narrow the bandwidth (that is, it will increase the filter's Q). It's worth noting that narrowing the bandwidth of a notch filter will cause it to have *less* audible effect, because fewer partials will be filtered out. A notch filter produces the most striking effect when the bandwidth is at a maximum. In other words, adding more "resonance" with a notch filter (the knob being labelled with that word, although notch filters aren't usually resonant) will reduce the character of the filtering rather than increasing it. At high "resonance" settings, the notch filter may have no audible effect at all.

Overdrive

In order to make the sounds coming from their filters fatter and more satisfying, some manufacturers include an overdrive knob in the filter section. While this control adds new harmonics, which is not what filters do, filter overdrive is worth mentioning in this chapter simply because it's found in the filter section of the synth. The idea is that in real analog circuits, overloading the filter's input can produce a pleasing type of harmonic distortion. This effect can be simulated digitally. Unfortunately, manufacturers sometimes neglect to provide automatic gain compensation for the overdrive knob, so when you turn up the overdrive you have to turn down the volume parameter for the patch (or the instrument's volume knob). In some instruments, filter overdrive is achieved by turning up the inputs in the oscillator mixer past 8 or so. Between 8 and 10, increasing amounts of overdrive will be heard.

Filters & Polyphony

What I've neglected to mention up to now, because it wasn't germaine to the discussion, is that in most polyphonic synths each voice will have its own filter (or filters). When you play several notes on the keyboard, filtering will be applied separately to each note. When you start to apply filter modulation, this fact becomes vital.

In modern sample playback synths, you'll usually find each voice channel equipped with its own filter. If you program a sound that requires four oscillators, for example, you'll also have four separate filters, allowing the tone of each oscillator to be filtered in whatever way seems appropriate. In analog and modeled analog synths, it's more normal for the signals coming from the oscillators to be mixed and then sent to a single filter. Even in this situation, however, each note you play will still be filtered separately. Some synths provide more flexible ways of connecting oscillators to filters (see "Signal Routing," below).

Because each voice has its own filter, adding distortion in the filter by turning up the overdrive knob and then playing two or more notes doesn't give you the type of intermodulation distortion you'll hear when you run the same notes through a distortion effect. Distortion added within the filter will sound quite a bit cleaner, because each note is distorted by itself. As a result, you can play chord voicings without worrying about turning the sound into a crunchy mess.

Filter Modulation

Fixed filters, in which the cutoff frequency doesn't change during the course of a note or phrase, are useful for some musical tasks, such as adding formants (see "Formant Filtering," above). But the fun part of using filters comes when you start modulating the cutoff frequency. Just about all synth filters built today provide several modulation inputs with which to do this, and the time has come to discuss these in detail.

Modulation of the resonance amount is less crucial to the standard palette of synth sounds, so some filters have no facilities for real-time resonance modulation. Resonance modulation from an LFO tends to sound a bit artificial and gimmicky, in my opinion, but it can be useful with some types of sounds. When sweeping the filter cutoff with a mod wheel, however, you may find it very useful to shape the amount of resonance with the wheel at the same time.

When real-time resonance modulation is not provided in a particular instrument, there's a good chance the filter is set up in such a way that if you change the resonance amount parameter manually while holding a note on the keyboard, you won't hear the changes you're making. You may need to restrike the key in order to hear the new resonance amount. On modern instruments, however, restriking to hear changes in the cutoff frequency should never be necessary.

Six different control signal sources are commonly used for filter cutoff modulation: envelope generators, key number, note velocity, MIDI controllers, LFOs, and audio signals. Each has its own musical uses, so we'll look at them one by one. Before we start, however, it's important to understand that cutoff modulation is normally *additive*. That is, the control signals coming from all of the modulation inputs are added together and then added to the setting of the cutoff frequency parameter itself. The sum of all these values can easily drive the cutoff up so high that the pass-band of a lowpass filter contains the entire audible frequency spectrum, or for that matter down so low that the filter's output is effectively shut off. As you turn up the modulation amount from one or more sources, don't be surprised if you have to adjust the cutoff parameter to compensate. Jumping back and forth between, say, the envelope amount, the cutoff frequency, and the velocity amount knobs on a filter in order to get a playable sound out of a filter is very much the norm.

In acoustic instruments, the loudness and brightness of the tone are often closely related. Soft tones tend to be more muted, containing fewer overtones, while loud tones tend to be rich in overtones. In the case of plucked and percussive instruments such as acoustic guitar and piano, whose sound dies away gradually after being initiated, the sound of each note will become both quieter and more muted as it sustains. In order to simulate the response of acoustic instruments more realistically, filter modulation from both envelopes and velocity plays a key role.

Of course, there's no rule that says synthesizers can only be used to emulate acoustic instruments. Filter modulation is capable of many striking effects that have no counterpart in the acoustic instrument world. For instance, if your instrument has two or more filters available in a single preset, any of the modulation sources discussed below can be used for crossfading between two distinct sounds. This is accomplished by inverting the modulation amount applied to the cutoff frequency or output level of one of the filters. To take the simplest case, low-velocity notes might open filter A while closing filter B, while high-velocity notes open filter B and close filter A.

Keyboard Tracking. When filter cutoff is being modulated by the MIDI key number (or its analog equivalent, the keyboard control voltage), we say that the filter is *tracking* the keyboard. On most, though not all, filters, the amount of keyboard tracking is a user-programmable parameter. If the tracking amount is set to 100%, for example, the filter cutoff should rise by an octave each time you play an octave higher on the keyboard. When you play Middle C (MIDI key 60), the cutoff should be an octave higher than when you play the C an octave below Middle C (MIDI key 48).

Because each voice in a polyphonic synth has its own filter(s), when you play two or more notes at once, each filter will receive a different note number as a modulation input. If the filter is using any sort of keyboard tracking, it will use the note number to adjust the cutoff frequency.

Being able to adjust the keyboard tracking is especially helpful with oscillator tones that are rich in harmonics. To see why, let's assume for the moment that
there's no keyboard tracking, and that the filter cutoff frequency is fixed
at 500Hz (about one octave above Middle C). When you play the lowest C on a standard MIDI keyboard, the fundamental and the first six overtones
will all be in the pass-band, so the note will sound quite bright. But when you
play note 72 (an octave above Middle C), the fundamental itself will be attenuated by 3dB. Assuming the filter has a 12dB per octave rolloff slope, the first overtone of the higher note will be attenuated by 15dB, the third overtone by a
whopping 27dB, and so on. Thus the note will be perceived as much more
muted in tone than the note in the bass register.

    If the filter is programmed to track the keyboard with a 100% amount, on the
other hand, notes in the upper register will sound with the same number of
overtones as notes in the lower register (assuming the waveforms
coming from the oscillator are similar). Thus the synth's sound will
be much more uniform across the keyboard. But if the filter is tracking the keyboard at 100%, notes in the upper range may be
unpleasantly bright and harsh. Setting the keyboard tracking to
50% or 75% may make the patch musically pleasing across a
wider range.

    Many instruments allow keyboard tracking to be set to nega-
tive as well as positive amounts. This is useful in a few situations, such as programming keyboard crossfades. With a negative
keyboard tracking amount, the filter can be programmed so that
low notes sound quite bright while high notes are inaudible
because the fundamental and all of the overtones are in the stop-band. Most of
the time, though, keyboard tracking amounts between 0 and 100% will give you
what you need.

    Envelope Modulation. Changing the filter cutoff frequency in a controlled way
during the course of each note is a basic technique for giving shape to the notes
coming from your synth. This is accomplished by using an envelope to modulate
the cutoff. (For details on envelope generators, see Chapter Seven.) Because each
synth voice has its own envelope(s) and filter(s), each note will be shaped separately by the filter envelope.

    Some synths have dedicated filter envelopes. Others provide general-purpose
envelopes, whose output can be used to modulate the filter or other modules. Most
synths provide, as well, a way to *invert* the envelope being applied to the filter. This
may be accomplished with an invert button in the envelope, or with a bidirectional
modulation amount knob in the filter itself. When the envelope is inverted, the
filter cutoff will drop as the envelope rises, and vice-versa.

    The classic form of envelope modulation, beloved of electronic musicians

TIP: When programming the filter for a sound, don't just play one note over and over. Be sure to listen to notes across as wide a range of the keyboard as you plan to use. Adjust the filter's keyboard tracking so that the extreme upper and lower ends of the range have the sound quality you want.

everywhere, is to program the filter envelope with an instant attack, a short to medium decay, and zero sustain (see Project 5-2, at the end of this chapter). This patch can produce quick filter "blips" on the attack of a bass sound, a long sighing decay on a sustained chord, or anything in between.

Velocity Modulation. As noted above, acoustic instruments typically sound brighter as well as louder when they're struck, bowed, or blown harder. In synthesizers, this effect is duplicated by modulating the filter cutoff with MIDI velocity. Notes played with higher velocities will raise the cutoff of a lowpass filter higher, thus allowing more overtones to pass through the filter. To find the right balance between velocity control of the filter and velocity control of amplitude, you'll need to be sensitive to sound and knowledgeable about the capabilities of your synth.

As explained in Chapter Seven, in the section "Modulating the Envelope," velocity modulation applied directly to the filter cutoff has a somewhat different effect from velocity modulation applied to the filter envelope amount. Velocity modulation of the filter envelope time parameters, especially decay time, will also have a big effect on the character of your filtered sounds.

Modulation in Performance. Most MIDI synthesizers provide some way to control filter cutoff from MIDI. You may also be able to control filter cutoff from your synth's left-hand controller section. Recording a filter sweep into a MIDI sequencer as controller data is a classic technique for giving a shape to an entire phrase. The first notes in the phrase might be quite muted, notes in mid-phrase bright, and notes at the end muted once more. You may be able to record the filter sweep by transmitting controller data directly from the cutoff knob, or you may need to do it by assigning filter cutoff to a MIDI modulation wheel (CC1) and then recording the movement of the wheel or lever.

Other possibilities are worth investigating. Modulating cutoff from pitch-bend, for instance, can make your bends more expressive. This can be done subtly — an upward bend adding just a bit of extra brilliance — or aggressively. By inverting the filter modulation, you can program upward bends to drive the cutoff downward for a "choked" sound. Closing the filter in response to pitch-bends is helpful for simulating a harmonica performance.

LFO Modulation. Modulating cutoff from a sine or triangle wave LFO whose frequency is set to a medium rate (between 1Hz and 5Hz) produces the familiar "wah-wah-wah" effect. This isn't used a lot, because it tends to sound corny, but once in a while it's just what you need. The features available in your LFOs, such as start delay and mod wheel amount control (see Chapter Six), will go a long way toward making LFO modulation of the filter musically expressive rather than silly. With bright oscillator waveforms, an LFO square wave creating a timbral trill can be quite effective. A small to moderate amount of modulation from a slower LFO can add a bit of animation to sustained tones.

Because LFO signals can be either unidirectional or bidirectional, adding LFO modulation may alternately raise and lower the cutoff, or not. With a little experimentation, you should be able to figure out how the LFO signal is affecting the cutoff.

If your LFOs can be cranked up into the audio range (above 20Hz), you should be able to use them for audio rate modulation of the filter (see below). The full range of synthesis effects available from this type of modulation may not be available to you if you're using an LFO as the modulation source, however. For instance, a fast LFO may not have a frequency control input that will allow it to track the keyboard so as to play equal-tempered scales.

Audio-Rate Modulation. In real analog synths, it's usually possible to modulate the filter cutoff not from an LFO but rather from an ordinary audio-rate oscillator. This technique is not available on all digital synths, because it's processor-intensive. Updating the filter cutoff frequency thousands of times per second takes some extra computation time.

Audio-rate modulation, especially as the resonance amount is increased, generates *sidebands*. Sidebands are new overtones that are added to the sound; they get their name from the fact that on a frequency spectrum plot, the new overtones appear on both sides of both the fundamental and the original overtones.

Audio-rate modulation of the filter is similar in sound to FM and ring modulation (AM). Depending on the characteristics of the filter, however, it can sound brighter and thicker. If the modulating wave is at or near the frequency of the audio signal being processed by the filter, audio-rate modulation adds a buzzing, growling quality that can be very effective. If the frequencies of the modulating wave and the audio signal are different, the sidebands will be enharmonic (clangorous), and the original pitch will disappear in a thick wash of tone.

With an analog filter, sweeping the frequency of the modulating oscillator from an envelope is a lovely special effect. If the filter is heavily resonant, this technique produces a thick metallic swirl of sound as the sidebands move rapidly up and down through the frequency spectrum. On a digital synth, even if it allows audio rate modulation of the filter, the results may not sound as rich, because a digital filter is inherently band-limited. That is, none of the partials in its signal can ever be higher than the sampling rate. As a result, there are fewer high partials to produce difference tones. Setting a higher sampling rate (which may be possible on a computer-based synth) can add more and smoother sidebands.

Signal Routing

In most instruments with more than one filter per voice, you'll be able to choose the type of audio signal routing you'll use for a given patch. The most basic choice, when you have two filters, is between *series* and *parallel* signal routing. The difference between the two is shown in **Figure 5-10**.

In a few instruments, the filters are always in series. Typically in this case, the second filter will be capable of only highpass (or highpass and lowpass) operation, and will have only a few controls. It may not even have an input for envelope modulation.

When the two filters are connected in series, the second filter in the signal chain processes the output of the first filter. Only the frequency components in the pass-band of the first filter will arrive at the second filter. Depending on the modes and cutoff frequencies of the two filters, the output of the second filter may well be silence. In parallel routing, on the other hand, each filter processes the incoming signal in its original form, and the outputs of the two filters are mixed together again afterward.

Both series and parallel routing are useful. If one filter is set to lowpass operation and the other to highpass, connecting the two filters in series produces band-pass filtering, and connecting them in parallel produces notch filtering (see **Figure 5-11**). For this technique to work, the cutoff frequencies of the two filters have to be set appropriately. To produce a notch in the frequency response with a parallel routing, there have to be some frequencies in the middle of the spectrum that are filtered out by both filters. This will only happen when the cutoff frequency of the highpass filter is higher than the cutoff of the lowpass filter. If the pass-bands of the two filters overlap, nothing will be filtered out. Conversely, to produce a pass-band with a series routing, the cutoff of the highpass filter has

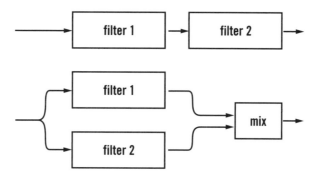

Figure 5-10.
The signal routing between two filters connected in series (top) and in parallel (bottom).

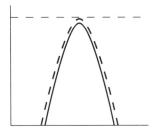

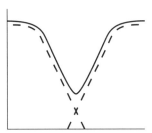

Figure 5-11.
Connecting a lowpass and highpass filter in series produces bandpass filtering (top), while connecting them in parallel produces notch filtering (bottom).

to be *lower* than the cutoff of the lowpass filter. Otherwise, the stop-bands of the two filters will cover the entire frequency spectrum, and you won't hear anything.

If this is still confusing, you might try thinking of it this way: In a parallel filter routing, the pass-bands of the two filters are added to one another, so any harmonic that is in *either* pass-band will be heard. In a series routing, the pass-band of one filter is subtracted from the pass-band of the other, so only harmonics that are in *both* pass-bands will be heard. (I'm using the words "add" and "subtract" conceptually rather than mathematically.)

Connecting two lowpass filters in series is a standard technique for increasing the rolloff slope of the output. If each filter has a 12dB per octave rolloff, and if their cutoff frequencies are set to the same value, the effective rolloff will be 24dB per octave. If the two cutoff frequencies can be offset from one another — again, a common feature on multi-filter instruments — you'll have other dimensions of control over the frequency response. If you can modulate each filter from its own envelope, things get even more interesting. One filter might produce a fast blip on the attack, while the other provides a long slow sweep.

A few synths, such as the Waldorf Q, provide quite flexible facilities for filter signal routing. For instance, you may be able to morph smoothly between series and parallel routing. You may be able to route one filter to the synth's left audio output, and the other to the right output, so that filter modulation from an LFO produces frequency-dependent stereo panning. The oscillator mixer may have two outputs, one for each filter, in which case you should be able to choose which filter each oscillator signal will be sent to.

 Power Projects for Chapter 5:

Project 5-1: Filter Modes & Cutoff Frequency. Create a patch in your synth with the following characteristics:

■ Use only a single oscillator.

■ Select a waveform rich in harmonics. If it's a sampled wave, choose one that sustains at a high level so you won't need to restrike the key. For this experiment, a simpler wave, such as a sawtooth, is better than one that has a lot of built-in animation.

■ Set the amplitude envelope for a fast attack and full sustain level.

■ Set all of the modulation inputs to the filter (from envelopes, LFOs, velocity, keyboard tracking, etc.) to zero. Depending on how your synth's operating system is designed, you may have to hunt around a bit. The modulation may be programmed in the source module, in the filter itself, or in a modulation matrix.

Begin with the filter in lowpass mode. If you have more than one lowpass mode, pick one at random. Play a note in the middle of the keyboard. While holding the note, move the filter cutoff frequency slowly from its lowest to its highest possible setting, and listen to the changes in the sound. If your instrument has a knob for the cutoff, pay attention as well to how smooth or grainy your knob movements are. Try faster knob movements, again listening for graininess. (Graininess can be cool, but unwanted graininess is less cool.)

Add some filter resonance, and repeat the manual cutoff sweep. Add still more resonance, and repeat it again.

Go through this process with each of the filter's modes (highpass, band-pass, etc.). This will give you a good feel for the range of tones you can get from your filter.

Project 5-2: Filter Envelope & Velocity. Starting with the patch you used for Project 5-1, do the following:

Program the filter envelope (or a general-purpose envelope that can be assigned to filter cutoff) for an instant attack, a reasonably quick decay, zero sustain, and a release that's about the same length as the decay. Make sure the envelope is not being modulated in any way by velocity.

Set the filter to lowpass mode (with a 24dB per octave rolloff slope, if possible). Turn the cutoff down to a medium-low value, and turn the resonance up about halfway.

While striking a key in some suitably interesting rhythm, gradually increase the amount of envelope modulation of the filter. You should hear the envelope adding a resonant sweep to the beginning of each note.

After setting the envelope amount to an intermediate level, neither too high nor too low, start adding velocity modulation to the envelope amount. Play the keyboard lightly and then harder, and observe the sonic differences. If your synth allows velocity to modulate decay time, add this type of modulation. You may need to shorten or lengthen the decay time to keep the decay segment in a usable time range.

Try inverting the envelope, so that the beginning of the sound rises from the floor rather than descending from the ceiling.

Chapter 6
LFOs

The humble low-frequency oscillator, better known as an LFO, is found in one form or another on virtually every synthesizer. Once in a while a manufacturer chooses a different term: For many years, Korg called their LFOs modulation generators (MGs). By any name, an LFO performs the same basic task: It's a source for control signals with which to add cyclic (repeating) modulation to the tone.

That's a bit abstract; let's see if we can make it more concrete. To begin the discussion, let's assume the LFO is producing a sine wave. When this sine wave is routed so as to modulate the pitch of an oscillator, the pitch will rise and fall in a smooth, regularly repeating manner. In other words, the LFO will produce vibrato. When the LFO's sine wave is modulating amplitude, the LFO produces a fluttering or stuttering sound called tremolo. This doesn't actually sound much like the tremolo (Italian for "trembling") that a string player produces by scrubbing the string rapidly with back-and-forth motions of the bow, but it's close enough conceptually that we can borrow the term.

When the LFO is modulating filter cutoff, the result can be anything from a subtle swell and fade in the high overtones, through a "wah-wah-wah" sound, to flat-out tremolo. (You'll recall that in Chapter Five we defined a filter as a frequency-dependent amplifier. If the LFO modulation of the filter cutoff is turned up high enough to sweep the cutoff through the entire frequency spectrum, it will affect the amplitude of all of the frequency components of the signal. Depending on the LFO waveform being used, filter-based tremolo will probably sound somewhat different from amplifier-based tremolo, but both types qualify as tremolo.)

LFOs can be used for many other types of modulation — for example, changing the pan position so as to sweep the sound from left to right and back again, changing some aspect of the timbre via pulse width modulation or FM amount modulation, changing the delay time in a chorus or flanger module, or even changing the rate of another LFO.

CD TRACK 11

In some instruments, an LFO will be "hard-wired" to the destination that its signal can modulate. You may see an LFO that's simply labelled "vibrato," for instance, because it's dedicated to modulating the pitch. In other instruments, one or more of the LFOs may be general-purpose modules, capable of modulating various aspects of the sound. Sound designers tend to prefer the latter approach, because it gives them more flexibility, but depending on the intended market for the synth, the manufacturer may feel that offering a dedicated vibrato LFO makes it easier for the user to understand what's going on. Most effects processors have dedicated LFOs, however, because the effect processor is usually monophonic — it's only instantiated once, and is operating on the summed signal coming from all of the synth voices. Because of this, using a voice LFO wouldn't make much sense (for more on monophonic vs. polyphonic LFO behavior, see "Trigger Modes," below).

Waveforms

LFOs typically offer the sound designer a choice of several waveforms (see **Figure 6-1**). The basic waveforms, found in most LFOs, are handed down from the early days of analog synthesis. Certain of these waveforms are ideal for producing familiar musical effects such as vibrato, trills, and tremolo. In recent years there has been a drift (calling it a trend would be too strong) toward adding more complex waves suitable for special effects. Because the waves are stored digitally, adding them costs the manufacturer almost nothing, but the jury is still out on how useful they'll prove to be musically. These odd waveshapes are not discussed below.

Waveform modulation, as described in Chapter Four, is available in some LFOs, but it's not too common.

Sine. As Figure 6-1 shows, a sine wave changes smoothly throughout its cycle. It's a good choice for vibrato and any other type of modulation in which you don't want to produce any abrupt discontinuities (jumps) in the sound.

Triangle. An LFO's triangle wave is similar in shape and function to its sine wave. In fact, the two are so similar that some synths offer only one type or the other, not both. The triangle wave has "corners" at the top and bottom of its travel, but I've never encountered a situation where these produced any audible glitching in the sound, because there's never a discontinuity in the level of the LFO signal. I tend to favor triangle waves over sine waves for common applications like vibrato and panning, because the sine wave spends more of its time at the outer ends of its travel — the upper and lower regions of the waveform — and less time transitioning through the middle of its range. This is audible: A sound being panned by a sine wave, for example, seems to slow down as it approaches the left and right speakers, "sticking" or "hovering" for a moment, and to whip rapidly through the

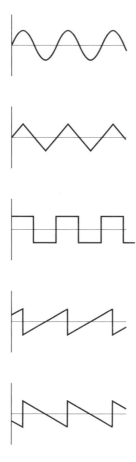

Figure 6-1.
The waveforms found most commonly in LFOs (top to bottom): sine, triangle, square, positive-going sawtooth, and negative-going sawtooth.

middle of the stereo field. When panned by a triangle wave, the same sound will be in constant motion.

Square/Pulse. When an LFO square wave is used to modulate an oscillator's pitch, the result is a trill: The pitch alternates between a higher and a lower value. Depending on how your synth is designed, tuning the trill to a musically mean-ingful interval may be easy or difficult, as we'll see in the section below on "LFO Amount." When a square wave is used to modulate amplitude or filter cutoff, the result is some type of tremolo. Depending on the depth of the LFO modulation, the tone could be chopped off entirely during the lower portion of the square wave's cycle, or the level could just drop a bit. Changing the amount of LFO modulation during the course of a note can pro-duce a striking effect.

In some LFOs, the square wave's pulse width (see Chapter Four) can be

CD *TRACK 12*

adjusted. Depending on what else is going on in the sound — for example, if you're creating a four-note pattern as described in Project 6-1 — a pulse width greater or less than 50% can be useful.

Square and sawtooth waves have abrupt discontinuities in their waveshapes. Unless your instrument smooths these transition in some manner, modulating amplitude or cutoff with either of these waves will quite likely produce clicks at the vertical edges of the waveform.

Sawtooth. Sawtooth wave modulation has no counterpart in acoustic instrument design or performance, but it has become part of the standard repertoire of synthesizer special effects. When pitch is being modulated by a sawtooth (or "saw") wave, it will rise (or fall) smoothly for some period of time, jump suddenly back to the other extreme, and then start to rise (or fall) smoothly again. If the LFO rate is between 0.5 and 3Hz, the pitch modulation is fairly extreme, and the oscillator is producing a continuous tone of some sort, sawtooth modulation sounds unnervingly like an electronic ambulance, an air-raid siren, or a spaceship weapon.

> **IDEA FILE**: If you're using a patchable analog-type synth, try processing an LFO square or sawtooth wave through a resonant lowpass filter whose cutoff is set extremely low (in the 5Hz range). Use the output of the filter as a modulation source for some other module, such as an oscillator. As you turn up the resonance, the vertical edge in the waveform will cause the filter to "ring" at its resonant frequency, which will produce a burbling effect in the module that's being modulated.

Some synths provide rising and falling sawtooth waves (see **Figure 6-1**) as separate waveforms. In other instruments, only one sawtooth wave is provided, but it can be used as a rising or falling wave by changing the modulation amount from positive to negative.

If a synth has some form of LFO waveform modulation, you may be able to morph a single waveform from negative-going sawtooth through a triangle wave to a positive-going sawtooth, as shown in **Figure 6-2**.

Stepped Random (Sample-and-Hold). In order to explain the last of the

Figure 6-2.
If an LFO is capable of waveform modulation, you may be able to morph the output from negative-going sawtooth through triangle to positive-going sawtooth.

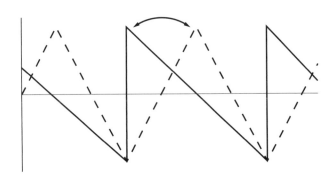

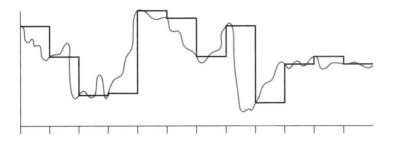

Figure 6-3.
The random input (curving line) and stepped output (horizontal lines) of a sample-and-hold circuit. Pulses from a clock source (shown along the bottom of the diagram) cause the sample-and-hold to change its output so that it matches the current level of the input.

common LFO waveform choices, we need to take a brief detour to explain what a sample-and-hold module is. The reason for the digression will become clear.

In an analog synth, a sample-and-hold module (often abbreviated *S&H* or *S/H*) is a type of control voltage processor. It usually has an input for the voltage to be processed; the input can come from any voltage source in the synth. Within the sample-and-hold is a clock source. A clock is similar to an LFO except that its output is a trigger rather than a waveform. (To learn more about trigger signals, see Chapter Seven.) Each time the clock sends out a trigger, the sample-and-hold measures (samples) the level of the incoming voltage. It then sends to its output a signal whose voltage level is the same as the level just measured. The crucial point is this: In between clock pulses, the output voltage doesn't change, *no matter what happens to the input voltage.* Even if the input fluctuates in a continuous manner, the output is always stepped. One possible result is shown in **Figure 6-3.**

Sample-and-holds are configured by manufacturers in various ways. Some have an external clock input, so that they can be triggered from some other module — even from a keyboard, so that each note played causes a new sample to be taken. Because white noise (a randomly varying signal) is the most commonly used input for a sample-and-hold, some S&H modules have built-in noise generators. Some have an input for the signal to be sampled, which is a very desirable feature, while others always sample their internal noise source.

When you select an LFO's sample-and-hold "waveform," the usual result is that you'll get a stepped random output. In other words, the LFO's sample-and-hold process will always sample a noise signal or the equivalent. Applying the S&H signal to pitch, filter cutoff, or both produces the somewhat hackneyed but still useful "electronic gizmo" effect heard in many science fiction films of the 1960s and '70s.

A few LFO-based sample-and-holds can be set up to sample other

IDEA FILE: If your sample-and-hold has an input for the signal to be sampled, send it a sawtooth wave from an LFO. For this to work, the S&H itself has to be getting its clock triggers from some other source, not the same LFO. While modulating the pitch of the oscillator(s) from the output of the S&H, change the frequency of the sawtooth wave. As the sawtooth speeds up, the rhythm of the steps will stay constant but the number of steps in each staircase will get smaller, while the individual steps get farther apart.

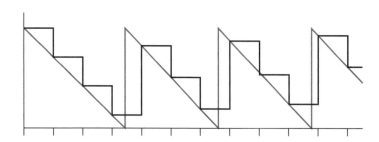

Figure 6-4.
When a sample-and-hold
is sampling a sawtooth
wave rather than noise,
the output is a stepped
control signal.

inputs, such as another LFO. If the other LFO is producing a sawtooth wave, the sample-and-hold will produce staircase effects, as shown in **Figure 6-4**.

For some reason, LFOs are sometimes designed so that when you choose the S&H "waveform," the clock source used by the sample-and-hold will be faster than the LFO rate you'll hear if you choose another waveform. I have no idea why this type of design is used, but I've seen it in more than one instrument.

Smooth Random. Related to the stepped random output of the sample-and-hold is the smoothed random "waveform." Found on only a few synths, this selection produces a smoothly varying but unpredictable signal. A very slight amount of smooth random modulation can add an attractive sense of "liveness" to the sound. Larger amounts are useful for special effects.

LFO Amount

As with most types of modulation, LFO amount (the amount of effect the LFO will have on the signal emerging from the modulation destination) is handled in some synths within the LFO module itself, in other synths within the destination module, and in still others in a general-purpose modulation matrix. No matter where it's handled, somewhere or other you'll find a parameter (and perhaps several of them) with which to control the LFO modulation amount.

In a simple synth, you may find one LFO amount knob within the LFO, and some switches, also within the LFO, which determine whether the LFO will modulate oscillator pitch, filter cutoff, amplitude, or other parameters. In an extremely simple synth, this switch may be a "radio button": You may be able to select only one destination.

You'll also find, somewhere or other, a parameter with which to control the amount of change the MIDI modulation wheel/lever produces in the LFO amount. By cranking this parameter up while keeping the basic LFO amount at zero, you should be able to apply LFO modulation to the selected destination(s) by pushing the mod wheel or lever, and have no LFO modulation the rest of the time. The mod wheel is a source of *secondary modulation*, a topic about which we'll have a bit more to say in Chapter Eight.

Most audio waveforms are inherently bidirectional. That is, some portion of the waveform represents an increase in air pressure above the background level while another portion represents a decrease in pressure below the background level. (For more on air pressure as it relates to waveforms, see Chapter Two.) So it's not surprising that standard LFO waves are much the same: The LFO's output signal varies both upward and downward from a zero level. If we're using an LFO to modulate pitch, for example, as the modulation amount increases the pitch will rise from its starting value — the pitch that the oscillator would produce if no modulation were applied — during part of the LFO's cycle, and drop below the starting value in another part of the LFO's cycle.

Quite often, this type of behavior is exactly what one wants musically. But not always. The most obvious problem occurs when an LFO square wave is applied to oscillator pitch so as to create a trill. When a trill is played on an acoustic instrument, the pitch varies in only one direction. The musician plays a note that supplies the base pitch and then rapidly alternates it with another note a half-step or whole-step above.

In order to recreate this effect on a synthesizer, we need an LFO that's capable of one-directional rather than bidirectional modulation. With a square wave, for instance, we want the lower portion of the wave to be the zero point. As the modulation amount is increased (with the aid of the mod wheel, for instance), the upper portion of the square wave should modulate the pitch upward, while the lower portion of the wave should return the pitch to its starting level.

In some synths, you'll find unidirectional waves among your waveform choices. These are most useful for pitch modulation, as just described, but they're also nice to have when you're modulating amplitude. It's usually very undesirable to have the maximum output level of your patch increase when you push the mod wheel to add tremolo. In the case of tremolo, the instrument may be designed to prevent this problem in a way that's invisible to the user. In the case of pitch modulation, though, you may be on your own.

Programming trills can also be tricky if your instrument won't let you tune the LFO's output in equal-tempered half-steps. This is one of the more subtle but infuriating lapses in synth design that you'll run into from time to time. Even if you're able to get in-tune trill intervals, you may find that the keyboard has been transposed to another key; you may need to use the coarse and fine tune parameters in the patch to get it back to concert pitch.

Another needless limitation is found most often in synths built by manufacturers whose background is in the home organ

TIP: Having trouble programming an in-tune trill with an LFO square wave? Your instrument may be set up so that trills will be in tune when one of the LFO amount controls (either in the oscillator section or in the LFO itself) is set to maximum. Try cranking one of the amounts up all the way and then listen to the pitches produced by changing the other amount.

market: Your instrument may be set up so that the maximum depth of pitch modulation from an LFO is only a half-step or so. This makes sense if you assume the LFO will always be used for vibrato and only vibrato, but it renders the modulation routing largely useless for other types of effects.

LFO Rate

The "low" in "low-frequency oscillator" means that an LFO typically cycles at a sub-audio rate — that is, below 20Hz (20 cycles per second). This makes it useful for types of modulation in which we're supposed to hear each shift in the sound as a more or less discrete entity. In vibrato, for example, we expect to be able to perceive the upper and lower bounds of the frequency, and to perceive the transitions between them. When the modulation rate exceeds 20Hz, the modulation is no longer perceived as discrete changes, but rather as a continuous change in timbre. (For more on this topic, see discussion of FM and AM in the "Audio Rate Modulation" section of Chapter Four.)

DANGER ZONE: In a well-designed synth, LFO rate should be constant, no matter how many or how few voices are being used. Depending on how the computer code for the operating system was written, however, this may not be the case. In poorly designed hardware instruments, playing thick chords can actually cause the LFOs to slow down, because the main processor is too busy producing audio (which has to be given top priority in order to prevent clicks and pops) to update the values of the LFOs in a timely fashion. If you encounter this problem, there are two solutions: Play fewer notes, or buy a better synth.

Some LFOs can be programmed to cycle very slowly indeed. A single cycle may last for many seconds. In fact, a zero setting for LFO rate may cause the LFO not to cycle at all. Believe it or not, this can be useful. If the LFO is doing random sample-and-hold and is set to retrigger from each keypress (see "Trigger Modes," below), a rate of 0Hz will cause the stepped output to remain stationary for each note, no matter how long the note lasts, while each new note you play will cause the LFO to output a new random value.

At the other extreme, some LFOs can be programmed to generate signals whose frequency is much higher than 20Hz, allowing them to be used for buzzy FM and AM effects. In some analog synths, such as the original Minimoog and its descendant, the Minimoog Voyager, a full-range oscillator can be used either as an audio signal or as an LFO.

An LFO is usually a poor choice for an FM modulator, however, for several reasons. First, an FM modulator needs to be able to track the keyboard so that its frequency will remain in a fixed relationship to the frequency of the carrier. While some LFOs can be programmed so that their frequency tracks the keyboard, most of them don't have enough precision to produce equal-tempered half-steps when doing this. (In the Minimoog, where the LFO is also a normal audio oscillator, this is not a problem.) Second, the amplitude of an FM modulator needs to be placed under the control of an envelope. Not all LFOs have this capability.

Third and perhaps most important, some digital synths (including most older models) are set up in such a way that they update their control signals at a fixed rate of between 100 and 200 times per second, if not less. When the LFO's frequency is sub-audio, this control rate is adequate to produce smooth modulation. But as the LFO rate moves up into the audio range, the modulation may acquire a pronounced chirpy or gritty character. At extremely high LFO rates, the modulation may acquire a pattern due to control-rate aliasing. At this point, small changes in the LFO rate (assuming the LFO can even change its rate by small amounts in this frequency range, which is not guaranteed) may cause changes in the pattern of chirps rather than the desired timbral shift. In sum, the fact that your LFO can generate signals of up to 150Hz is no guarantee that it will be useful for anything more than the most primitive form of FM or AM.

Being able to modulate LFO rate from an external source is quite useful. The vibrato produced by string and wind players doesn't have a constant rate, and speeding up or slowing down the vibrato is part of playing expressively. If your instrument allows you to modulate not only LFO amount but LFO rate from the mod wheel, you'll be able to simulate this effect: Pushing up on the mod wheel will both increase the amount of vibrato and speed it up. With a little judicious editing, the effect can be quite nice.

Ensoniq synths had a parameter with which you could randomize the LFO rate. In slight amounts, this may "humanize" the vibrato, but it always sounded a little artificial to me.

Some synths let you modulate the LFO rate from the MIDI key number or equivalent. In slight amounts, this type of modulation is useful: Acoustic instrument players often apply faster vibrato on high notes than on low notes.

Delay & Ramp-Up

As noted earlier, musicians who play acoustic instruments don't perform their vibrato at a constant rate. The rate changes to match the mood of the music. In the same way, the amount of vibrato often changes during the course of a note. In particular, players often increase the vibrato amount during long notes as a way of intensifying the emotion or sustaining the listener's interest. Quite often, short notes get no vibrato at all, both because it would be difficult technically to add vibrato when the fingers are already on their way to the next note and because vibrato would muddy the pitch of short notes.

One way to vary the vibrato amount on a synthesizer is by controlling it from the mod wheel. But what if both of your hands are busy playing the keyboard? This problem is solved in many synths by means of a parameter called *LFO start delay*. Don't confuse this with audio delay (see Chapter Nine) or oscillator start delay (see Chapter Four). When set to a non-zero value, LFO start delay causes the LFO's output to remain at zero for some period of time after the beginning of each note. (To learn more about how the LFO "senses" the start of a new note, see below.) If the LFO start delay is set to a time value approximately equal to an eighth-note at the current tempo, when you play eighth-notes you'll hear no vibrato or whatever other LFO modulation you've programmed, but when you play longer notes, the LFO modulation will kick in.

The hidden trap in the previous sentence is the word "kick." If the LFO's output goes suddenly from zero to some positive or negative value, the result will tend to sound unnatural. You may even hear a click. If the LFO is set up by the manufacturer so that at the end of the LFO start delay its waveform begins at zero and then starts moving up or down, you won't hear any clicks, but the result will still be a little artificial: No vibrato for a while, then suddenly, vibrato! To solve this problem, some LFOs include a ramp-up time parameter. The ramp-up time is the time the LFO takes, in each note, to move from its start level (usually zero) to its maximum level. With reasonable settings for start delay and ramp-up time, you can program the sound with a smooth, natural swell of vibrato on long notes.

On a few instruments, ramp-up time is included but not start delay. In this situation, the vibrato or other modulation always starts at the beginning of the note, but it may take some time to reach its full level. While this setup is not ideal, it's usually possible to work with it.

I've also seen two or three instruments in which the LFO amount could be ramped down instead of up. This is not too useful for emulating standard performance techniques; one seldom wants vibrato to start at the beginning of a note and then die away, leaving long notes to sustain with a static tone. If you crank the LFO rate up above 10Hz, however, and make the LFO amount fade-out fairly fast, you'll add a buzzy attack transient to the notes. It's not an effect you'll use every day, but it's a nice option to have.

In some instruments, you can control LFO amount (and perhaps also LFO rate) from an envelope generator. Assuming you have enough EGs to dedicate one to the task, this is an ideal setup for shaping the behavior of the LFO in a hands-free manner.

Trigger Modes

In the next couple of sections, we're going to look at how synthesizer designers address (or, on occasion, fail to address) a fundamental issue. Since LFO modulation causes the values of certain sound parameters to rise and fall during the course of each note, the issue that arises is, what will be happening to those parameters at the very beginning of a new note? Will they start at their base level and then rise? At their base level and then fall? At some higher level and then fall? At a level below the base level and then rise?

When described this way, the problem may seem like nitpicking or mere semantics, but it isn't. It has immediate practical consequences for the sound of the music. In order to explain the tools synthesizers give sound designers with which to control what happens, we're going to have to weave back and forth a little, so please read the whole discussion first and *then* get confused.

In a polyphonic synth, each voice will usually have its own LFO(s). By default, these LFOs are independent of one another: The LFOs for each voice produce their own signals, which modulate only the other modules within that voice.

In a true analog synth, be it monophonic or polyphonic, the LFO, because it's a piece of hardware, will always be cycling through its selected waveform, whether or not it's being used. Even when it's not modulating anything, or when you're not playing a note at all, the LFO is still cycling in the background. Polyphonic digital synths, however, are often designed so that, by default, the LFOs only cycle when the voice is actually producing a sound. Each time you play a note, the LFO(s) in the voice to which the note is assigned will start a new wave cycle.

You may be able to set an LFO to either *free-run* mode or *key trigger* mode. (Your instrument may use different names.) In free-run mode, the LFOs for each voice will operate independently, and should be cycling in the background even when the voice is not producing any sound. Even if the LFOs for all of the voices are running at the same speed, in free-run mode the relationships among their wave cycles will be undefined. In key trigger mode, when you play a block chord, all of the LFOs should begin at the same point in their cycle, producing a modulation pattern in which all of the voices are modulated in the same way at the same time. Unless some type of secondary modulation (such as velocity-to-LFO-rate) causes the various LFOs to get out of sync with one another as the note sustains, it should sound as if all of the voices are being modulated by the LFO(s) from a single voice. Another way to accomplish this, found on some synths, is a *global* LFO, a single LFO that can be used as a modulation source for all of the voices.

In free-run mode, even if the LFOs are all running at the same rate, when you play a block chord the modulation for the various notes won't necessarily be coherent. In the case of vibrato, one oscillator's pitch modulation may be at the top of its travel, another oscillator's may be at the bottom of its travel, and a third may be near the middle. With any appreciable amount of pitch modulation, the lack of coordination among the LFOs will tend to blur, if not entirely obliterate, the harmonic identity of the chord (see **Figure 6-5**). This may be what you want musically, but it may not be. Free-run mode can be useful because it makes the LFO's cycle less predictable, and therefore less monotonous from note to note.

IDEA FILE: Assuming your synth's LFOs can be set to key trigger mode, try setting up a patch in which a square wave does something interesting, such as changing the filter cutoff radically. Set the LFO to key trigger mode, program the LFO to a slow-to-medium rate, and then play some chords on the keyboard. But instead of playing block chords, start each note at a different time and observe the changes in the composite rhythm. For extra juice, add a digital delay whose delay time is synchronized with (or simply matches) the LFO rate. Now add a second oscillator and LFO, also synchronized but running at a different speed.

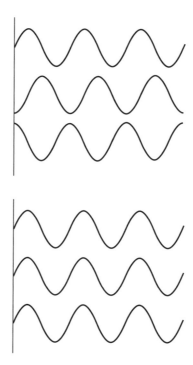

Figure 6-5.
Three LFO sine waves in free-run mode (top) and in key trigger mode when all of them have been triggered by notes that start at the same moment (bottom).

Phase

I f the LFOs in your instrument provide a key trigger mode, they may also have a start phase parameter. With this parameter, you can control the point at which the LFO waveform will start its cycle each time you play a new note. Phase is usually described in terms of degrees of arc: A full cycle of a wave encompasses 360 degrees of phase. (For reference, please refer back to Figure 2-3 on page 26.) If the sine wave in Figure 2-3 is coming from an LFO, setting the LFO's start phase parameter to 0 degrees will cause the sine wave to begin at the zero-point on the Y axis and then rise toward its maximum level. If the phase parameter is set to 180 degrees, the LFO will begin at the zero-point and then fall. If the phase is set to 90 degrees, the LFO will begin at its maximum output level and then fall.

In the case of other waveforms, the precise behavior of the output may be different, but the meaning of the start phase parameter will be the same. A setting of 180 degrees will cause the LFO to begin halfway through its waveform, and so on. A setting of 360 degrees is equivalent to a setting of 0 degrees.

In case it's not obvious, changing the LFO's rate (frequency) won't have any effect on a start phase setting. If the start phase is set to 45 degrees, for example, the wave will always begin ⅛ of the way through its full cycle, no matter how fast or slow the LFO happens to be cycling.

An LFO start phase parameter should have no effect when the LFO is in free-run mode, because the LFO should ignore key-down events.

CALCULATOR FORMULA: If you want the speed of an LFO or the delay time of a digital delay to match the tempo of your song, but the LFO or delay can't be synchronized, you can always set the parameter by ear. But if the parameter values are displayed in real-world form — as Hz or milliseconds — rather than in arbitrary units (0-127, for instance), you can use a calculator to find the correct setting.

Your sequencer will undoubtedly display the tempo in beats per minute (bpm). We're going to assume that "beats" is synonymous with "quarter-notes," which is usually a safe assumption. Here's how to do the conversion. If the parameter is shown in milliseconds (ms), the formula to use is:

60,000 / bpm = ms per beat

For example, if the tempo of the song is 100 bpm, you would divide 60,000 by 100, which gives a value of 600 milliseconds per beat.

But what if the LFO's speed is displayed in Hertz? Hertz, you'll recall from Chapter Two, is the same as cycles per second, so the first step is to replace milliseconds in the formula above with seconds:

60 / bpm = seconds per beat

The second step is to invert the fraction. We're looking for an LFO setting in cycles per second, not in seconds per cycle:

bpm / 60 = cycles per second

So if you want one LFO cycle per quarter-note beat at 100 bpm, the LFO needs to be set to 100 divided by 60, or 1.667Hz.

To arrive at the correct numbers for longer or shorter rhythm values, multiply or divide as needed. If an LFO at 1.667Hz produces one cycle per quarter-note, sixteenth-notes will be produced at 1.667 x 4 = 6.667Hz. If you want the delay line to produce triplet eighths rather than quarter-notes, you'd divide the millisecond value by 3. If you're using milliseconds, smaller rhythm values are found by dividing and larger ones by multiplying; if you're using Hertz, smaller rhythm values are found by multiplying and larger ones by dividing.

Synchronization

Because of the importance of rhythm in pop music, many synthesizers have LFOs that can be synchronized to outside clock sources. Typically, the clock source can be either the synth's own internal clock or an external MIDI clock signal. This type of synchronization is extremely useful if you're programming an effect that you want to coordinate with a song's tempo — for example, if you want an LFO to create a filter-based tremolo in an eighth-note rhythm, or if you want a triangle wave to sweep the filter up and down over the course of two bars. If you later decide to adjust the tempo of your song, or if you happen to write a song with tempo changes, a synced LFO will automatically adjust to the correct tempo.

To learn how (or whether) your instrument will sync its LFOs, consult the owner's manual. In some instruments, the LFO rate parameter can be scrolled up or down until you reach a group of synced settings. In others, switching on LFO sync will replace the normal rate parameter values with synced settings. Most often, these settings are indicated as fractions, with or without additional abbreviations. For instance, a setting of 1/8 should produce an eighth-note rhythm, 1/4 should produce quarter-notes, and so on. Settings followed by "t" produce triplets. Some instruments also have settings indicated by "d" or "." which produce dotted rhythms ("1/8." would produce a dotted-eighth value, for instance). More complex rhythm values, such as quintuplets, are not usually supported by synced LFOs. Nor are swing/shuffle rhythms usually provided.

LFOs that can be synchronized to MIDI clock don't usually respond to MIDI start commands. I can't help but feel this is a significant shortcoming in contemporary instrument design. The problem arises because MIDI clock is a "dumb" signal. A clock byte is transmitted by the sync master device 24 times for every quarter-note — but there's nothing in the clock signal to indicate which byte in any given series of 24 bytes falls on the quarter-note beat. As a result, if you're using a synced LFO but you happen to start sequence playback at some other point than the beginning of the song, the LFO may sound different than it did before. It will be running at the correct tempo, but it will have the wrong phase.

Here's the workaround: Set your synced LFOs to key trigger mode, and then always start the sequencer at or just before the beginning of a note that the LFO will be modulating.

Power Projects for Chapter 6:

Project 6-1: Trill Chords. If your instrument has two LFOs that can be set to a square or pulse wave and assigned to modulate the pitch of a single oscillator, you can create four-note trill/arpeggios. Begin by setting LFO 1 to a slow rate (0.5Hz or so) and selecting a square wave. Increase the pitch modulation amount while holding a key on the keyboard until you hear two alternating notes that are a perfect fifth apart. Next, set LFO 2 to a somewhat faster rate (between 0.75Hz and 3Hz) and increase its amount until it produces an interval of a minor third. At this point, holding one key on the keyboard should produce a minor 7th chord — C, E♭, G, B♭, for instance.

If you have two or more LFOs per voice but only one LFO can modulate a given oscillator, you should still be able to program one-finger rhythms by tuning each oscillator and its square wave modulation to different pitches.

If your LFOs can synchronize to an external or internal clock, try setting one to a quarter-note rate and the other to an eighth-note, triplet eighth, or sixteenth-note rate. To get a consistent pattern, set the LFOs to key trigger mode, so they'll retrigger at the beginning of each MIDI note. If your LFOs have a start phase parameter, setting the start phase of one of them to 90 or 180 degrees will change the rhythm of the trill.

Project 6-2: **Synced Timbre Grooves.** If your instrument has two syncable LFOs that can affect different aspects of the timbre (for example, filter cutoff and FM amount), you should be able to create some interesting rhythmic effects. With three or four LFOs, the results can be extremely colorful and exciting.

Start by syncing all of the LFOs to the same clock source, and set them to different rhythm values (such as half-notes, quarters, and eighths). Set them all to key trigger mode.

Add LFO modulation to taste, and then play and sustain two or three notes at a time in various rhythms. Try different LFO waveforms as well; unlike the trills in Project 6-1, which require square waves, the timbre effects in this exercise will be more interesting if you combine square, triangle, and perhaps sawtooth waves.

Chapter 7
Envelope Generators

Like a good story, a sound has a beginning, a middle, and an end. The devices with which synthesizer sounds are given coherent shapes—in other words, beginnings, middles, and ends—are called envelope generators.

An envelope generator (EG) makes no sound by itself. Rather, it's used as a source for control signals. These signals are routed to other modules, most likely (though not exclusively) modules responsible for generating and processing sounds. For details on how the signal routings can be handled, consult Chapter Eight.

The other modules change their behavior in some manner in response to the signal coming from the envelope generator. For instance, a lowpass filter might respond by increasing its cutoff frequency, thus making the sound brighter. But it doesn't matter to the envelope generator what type of response its signal is causing — if any. Its signal goes on its merry way, rising and falling in accordance with how the EG has been programmed, irrespective of what the receiving module is doing.

The signal coming from an envelope generator is called, naturally enough, an envelope. This term is a bit fuzzy: We can also refer to the *shape* of the signal coming from the envelope generator, rather than to the signal itself, as an envelope. The words "shape," "envelope," and "contour" (as in *contour generator*, an alternate name for the same device) are more or less synonymous.

Generally speaking, the signal coming from an envelope generator at any given moment is one-dimensional. That is, it can be higher (more signal) or lower (less signal). A few envelope generators operate in two dimensions (see "X/Y Envelopes," below), but this is a special case, and for the present we can safely ignore it. Because the one-dimensional envelope signal changes over time, we can diagram it conveniently in two dimensions, as shown in **Figure 7-1**. The passage of time provides the horizontal axis of the diagram. At this level of abstraction, we don't even need to know what sort of signal the EG is sending out: In a voltage-controlled analog synth, it would be a control voltage. In a digital synth, it would be a stream of numbers.

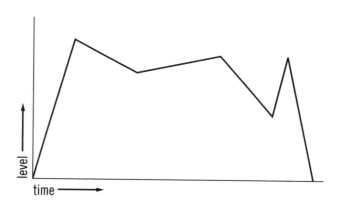

In the discussion above, I referred to envelope generators as giving shapes to sounds, not to notes. There's a reason for that. In most day-to-day usage, a given envelope will be applied to a single note. Each time a new note starts, one or more new envelopes will start at the same moment. Soon after the note stops, the envelopes will stop as well. But in some situations, as we'll see, there isn't a one-to-one correspondence between notes and envelopes. A single envelope may be used to shape a whole string of notes, or a single envelope might be triggered a number of times during one note.

Another common term for envelope generators, by the way, is "ADSR." If you've spent any time at all squinting at front panels or skimming synth manufacturers' websites, you will have run into this acronym. Because we're proceeding in a methodical fashion, however, I'm not going to explain quite yet what the letters stand for. Before we can talk about the shapes of particular types of envelopes (which is a clue: the letters "ADSR" refer to a type of shape, or rather to a family of shapes), we need to explore the kinds of command signals that will cause an EG to do its thing.

Gates, Triggers & MIDI

An envelope, as we said, has a beginning, a middle, and an end. The beginning is normally when the keyboard player presses down on a key. Everything that happens while the key is pressed down is the middle. The end comes when the player's finger lifts, releasing the key. Guitar controllers and other types of alternate MIDI controllers can also provide start/stop commands for envelope generators, but it's safe to consider them variations on the theme provided by the keyboard.

In order for the envelope generator to respond to the keyboard, the keyboard has to send it a message of some sort. In the days of analog gear, this message was

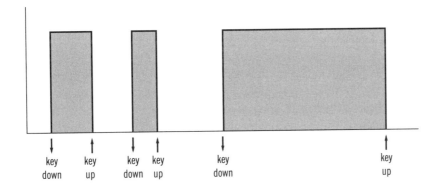

Figure 7-2.
An analog gate signal
coming from a keyboard.
The arrows along the
bottom show when a key
was pressed down
(down arrows) and
released (up arrows).

key
down

key
up

key
down

key
up

key
down

key
up

a form of control voltage called a *gate*. In the most common type of synth, the keyboard would transmit 0 volts when no key was pressed, and +5 or +10 volts during the period of time when a key was pressed. (Keyboards in those days were monophonic: They could play only one note at a time.) A gate signal is shown in **Figure 7-2**. It only takes a little stretch of the imagination to see why it was called a gate: The gate opened when the key was pressed, and it closed when the key was lifted.

With MIDI keyboards, the actual signals being sent don't look anything like Figure 7-2. One string of bits (a note-on message) is sent when the key is pressed, and a different string of bits (a note-off message) is sent when the key is released. But in a conceptual sense, we can still talk about a MIDI keyboard as sending gates to, or *gating*, envelope generators.

Another type of signal found in some analog synths was called a *trigger*. In an electrical sense, a trigger looked a lot like a gate, except that it might not last as long: The trigger was typically a rising-edge voltage transition, such as the transition from 0 volts to +5 volts shown in Figure 7-2. (Falling-edge triggers, called S-triggers, were used on some instruments.) The difference between a gate and a trigger was that as far as the receiving module was concerned, the trigger was essentially instantaneous. It didn't matter how briefly or how long the voltage stayed high. When responding to a trigger, the receiving module (often, though not necessarily, an envelope generator) would proceed to do whatever it was going to do, irrespective of when the incoming voltage fell back to zero. The equivalent in the MIDI world would be a module that responded in some manner to note-on messages but paid no attention to note-offs.

You may be wondering — what happens if the gate signal changes value between its start and end? The answer is, nothing happens. A gate is conceptually an on/off signal. If the actual voltage coming from an analog keyboard jumps from

0 to +5 volts and then wanders around between +4 and +7 volts before dropping back to 0, the envelope generator to which the gate is being sent should ignore the fluctuations. There are ways to send varying signals from a keyboard to an envelope generator or some other module during the course of a note, but those signals aren't gates.

The Shape of Things to Come

The first modern theorist to describe sound envelopes was Hermann von Helmholtz. In his classic book *On the Sensations of Tone* [Dover], written in 1870, Helmholtz described tones as having an amplitude contour consisting of three segments: an *attack*, during which the amplitude rises from zero to some peak value; the *steady state*, during which the tone sustains at the peak level; and the *decay*, during which the sound level falls again to zero.

While this is a fairly good description of the behavior of sounds produced by bowed and wind instruments, it's somewhat less accurate with reference to plucked and percussive instruments such as piano, guitar, and timpani. If you examine the sound of one of these instruments in a waveform editor, you'll see that it begins fairly suddenly and then falls back to zero at a more or less constant rate. There is no period of time in which the amplitude has a steady state.

When Bob Moog was building analog synthesizers in the mid-1960s, primarily for university music labs, he was approached by Vladimir Ussachevsky, who at the time was the head of the Columbia-Princeton Electronic Music Center. Ussachevsky suggested that Moog build a module that would provide a simple but practical and musically useful enhancement of Helmholtz's scheme, an enhancement that would allow both wind-instrument envelopes and percussive envelopes to be generated. Ussachevsky's control voltage generator had four knobs, which were labeled *attack*, *decay*, *sustain*, and *release*. Yes, this was the birth of the ADSR envelope generator.

In order to talk in a clear way about how an ADSR works, however, we need to pause for a moment to introduce a couple of new terms.

An envelope, as we noted earlier, is a signal that rises and falls in level over the course of time. The easiest way to describe such a signal is to consider that it consists of a series of *line segments*, as shown in Figure 7-1. Each line segment is defined by three data values: its starting and ending level, and the amount of time needed to move from the starting level to the ending level. Such line segments are often referred to as the envelope's *stages*.

Since the line segments will be joined end to end in a continuous contour, the ending level of each segment is also the beginning level of the following segment. This simplifies the description of the envelope: We really only need to define one level value and one time value for each segment. Also, we can build in some assump-

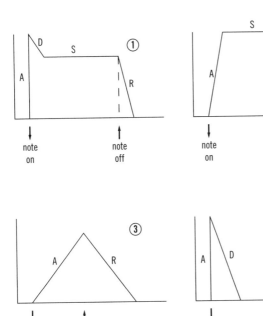

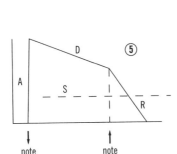

Figure 7-3.
A few examples of envelopes that can be produced by an ADSR (attack/decay/sustain/release) envelope generator. The gate begins at the point labeled "note on" and ends at the point labeled "note off." The full output level of the envelope generator is at the top of each graph. In diagram 1, attack is instantaneous, decay is rapid, sustain level is 75%, and release is also rapid. In diagram 2, attack and release are slow, and sustain level is 100%, so the decay setting has no effect. In diagram 3, the note-off occurs before the end of the slow attack phase, so both the decay and sustain settings are irrelevant and the envelope never reaches its full output level. In diagram 4, the sustain level is 0%, so the envelope falls to zero during the decay segment. As a result, the release setting is irrelevant. In diagram 5, the note-off occurs before the end of the decay, so the envelope goes immediately to the release stage, ignoring the sustain level.

tions, as Moog and Ussachevsky did: We can assume that the start and end levels will always be zero, and that the level reached at the end of the attack segment will always be the full level of the envelope (however that is defined in the synth).

The first knob (attack) in an ADSR envelope generator controls the amount of time that it takes the envelope to rise from zero to the maximum level of the envelope. This segment of the envelope works exactly as Helmholtz had described. The last knob, again as in Helmholtz, controls the amount of time the output will take to fall back to zero. Helmholtz called this the decay portion of the tone, but in Moog's instruments and most others since then, it's called the release.

In between the attack and the release, an ADSR envelope generator has two more knobs. One controls the level at which the output will sustain — Helmholtz's steady state — until the key is lifted. The other controls the amount of time needed for the signal to fall from its peak level to the sustain level. This is called the *decay time* parameter. Thus we've defined a complete envelope with three parameters (attack, decay, and release) that control amounts of time, and one (sustain) that controls a level.

Using these simple parameters, an ADSR envelope generator can create a variety of useful shapes, such as those shown in **Figure 7-3**.

In an ADSR, the sustain level is usually considered to vary between 0% and 100% of the peak level arrived at at the end of the attack segment. It can't be set any higher than the peak, but it can be set to zero. This fact has an important consequence: If the sustain level is set to 100%, when the envelope reaches its peak level at the end of the attack segment, it will simply stay there until the note-off message signals that it's time to begin the release segment. In this case the decay time parameter will be irrelevant, and changing its value will have no effect on the sound.

Conversely, if the sustain level is set to zero, once the decay segment has ended, it's the *release* parameter that becomes irrelevant. When the decay is finished, the output of the envelope is zero, so when the player lifts the key and the release segment begins, the envelope has nowhere to fall. It's at zero, and it stays there.

Let's walk through the ADSR's process step by step and watch what happens. Before the note begins, the output value is zero. When the gate signal arrives from the keyboard, the EG begins the attack segment of the envelope. The output rises from zero toward the maximum, increasing at a rate determined by the attack time parameter. This is the attack segment. At the end of the attack segment, the ADSR proceeds to the decay segment, during which the output falls from the peak level toward the sustain level. The rate at which it falls is controlled by the decay time parameter. Once the envelope reaches the sustain level, it stays there: The output remains constant until the gate signal ends. When the gate ends, the ADSR goes into its release segment, and the output falls from the sustain level back to zero at a rate determined by the release time parameter.

One question that immediately arises is, what happens if the player releases the key while the ADSR is still in the middle of the attack or decay segment — in other words, before the sustain level is reached? In most instruments, this common situation is handled by having the envelope fall immediately back toward zero, at the rate determined by the release parameter, starting at the moment when the gate ends. Figure 7-3 illustrates two of the envelope shapes that might result.

Another alternative is to design the envelope generator so that it will finish its attack and decay portions before going on to the release, whether or not the

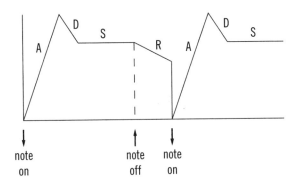

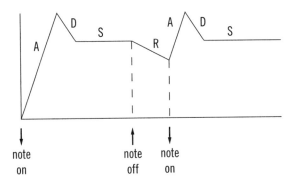

Figure 7-4.
When a new envelope begins before the release segment of a previous envelope has finished, the envelope generator will either restart from zero (top) or restart from its present position (bottom). On some instruments, you can choose either type of response.

note-off has been received. An envelope programmed to do this is said to be *free-running*. Once the sustain segment begins, if the gate is still open (if the note-off has not been received), the question of whether the envelope is free-running becomes moot. Unless it's not: Once in a while you might encounter an envelope generator that's designed in such a way that when it's in free-run mode, its sustain segment always takes zero time, so that it always proceeds from the decay segment directly to the release segment, whether or not a note-off has been received. (Such an envelope might better be described as an AR1BR2 envelope, since it has two release segments separated by a break point.)

A slightly more subtle question is what happens if the envelope is still in the middle of the release segment when the player starts a new envelope by pressing another key. This event can be handled in one of two ways, as shown in **Figure 7-4**. Either the envelope can jump from its current value back to zero in order to begin a fresh attack segment, or it can begin its attack segment from wherever it happens to be when the new gate signal arrives. On some instruments, you'll find

Figure 7-5.
The decay and sustain stages of a time-based envelope (top) and a rate-based envelope (bottom). In each case the decay parameter is identical, but the sustain setting is high (a) or low (b). When the decay parameter specifies an amount of time, the sustain level should be reached at the same moment whether it's high or low. But when the decay parameter specifies a rate, the slope of the decay segment should be the same, so the envelope will need longer to fall to a low sustain level.

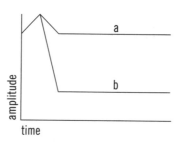

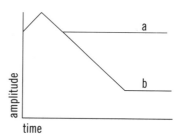

a switch that lets you choose which mode of operation you prefer for a given envelope in a particular patch. Restarting from zero gives all envelope attacks the same shape, which is often what one wants musically — but depending on what the envelope is being used for, the discontinuity that occurs when the output jumps back to zero can cause the sound to click, which may be undesirable.

Rates vs. Times

Up to now, we've been using the terms *rate* and *time* more or less interchangeably. They're not synonymous, however, and the distinction, while a bit fussy semantically, is not trivial.

If your synth's envelopes have time parameters, the parameters will (or should — it's not guaranteed that the manufacturer will use the term correctly) control the amount of time the envelope takes to proceed from one level to the next. For instance, if the decay time of an ADSR is set to 0.5 second, then the envelope should require 0.5 second to fall from the peak level to the sustain level, *no matter what the sustain level is.* If the sustain level is 95%, the envelope will fall from 100% to 95% over the course of 0.5 second. If the sustain level is 0%, the envelope will fall from 100% to 0% over the course of 0.5 second. During that 0.5 second, the sound will change much more rapidly if the sustain level is set low than if it's set high (see **Figure 7-5**).

If the synth's envelopes have rate parameters, however, they'll probably govern the *slope* of the segment, which should be constant irrespective of how far apart the starting and ending levels are. In this case, if an ADSR's decay is set to 50 (rate-based parameters are usually expressed in arbitrary units, not in degrees), the actual length of the decay segment will vary depending on where the sustain level is set. If the sustain is 95%, the decay will be relatively short. If the sustain is 0%, the decay will last much longer, because the envelope will have to move from 100% clear down to 0%.

In some EGs that use rates, if two adjacent envelope segments have the same level, the transition between them takes zero time. This shouldn't be the case if the EG has time parameters; if it uses times, you should be able to program a horizontal segment lasting some amount of time between two points whose levels are the same.

As noted in Chapter Three, instruments' parameters are often expressed in arbitrary values such as 0–99 or 0–127 rather than in real-world units. This is true of both rate and time settings. However, in the case of time parameters a setting of 0 usually means the segment will take a minimum of time, and 99 (or whatever value is the maximum) means the segment will last for several seconds. Rate parameters tend to work the other way around: A rate setting of 0 or 1 usually indicates a long, slow envelope segment, and a high rate setting usually indicates a high rate of change, resulting in a fast envelope segment.

More Stages

The fact that unadorned ADSR envelope generators are still being built testifies to the musical utility of the concept. Over the years, however, manufacturers have rung numerous changes on the original design. Most consist of added segments, but it seems someone is always coming up with a new wrinkle. For instance:

Delay. An ADSR with added delay segment is called a DADSR. The delay segment precedes the attack: After the gate begins, the envelope remains at zero for a certain length of time before the attack stage begins. By programming a short delay on one envelope while another begins immediately, you can create notes with double attacks. Delay is also useful if the envelope is being used to control LFO amount in order to add vibrato: Sometimes you don't want the vibrato to be heard at all with short notes.

Start Level. In some EGs, you can set the start level somewhere other than zero. In essence, the envelope is given a pre-attack segment which always has zero time. During this segment, the envelope

MINIMAL DELAY: Recently I found myself working on a patch that needed some filter resonance and lots of filter envelope. (The identity of the softsynth I was using will be concealed to protect the guilty.) I discovered that when I set the filter EG's attack time to a nominal value of zero, the filter still needed a couple of milliseconds to respond to the envelope. The result: A nasty click at the beginning of each note. Because the synth had DADSR envelope generators, I was able to solve the problem by adding a very slight amount of delay (less than 3ms) to the amplitude envelope. This amount didn't affect the responsiveness of the keyboard in any perceptible way. It simply inserted a little silence at the beginning of each note, so that by the time the sound started, the filter was ready.

Figure 7-6.
Many Korg synths have
used EGs in which a break
point and slope were
added between the decay
and sustain segments.
The break point can be
either above or below the
sustain level.

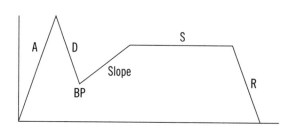

rises from zero to the start level. It then proceeds from the start level to the peak level at the rate determined by the attack parameter.

Hold. A hold segment can follow the attack. In this design, the envelope remains at its peak for a certain length of time before moving on to the decay segment. A hold segment has various musical uses. For example, if the sustain is set to zero and the attack and decay are quick, the hold parameter can be used to create fixed-length on/off envelopes for percussive effects. An ADSR with an added hold segment is called an AHDSR. (And that's entirely enough about acronyms. Feel free to make up your own.)

Break Point & Slope. Korg has long favored an EG design (see **Figure 7-6**) in which an extra time parameter and an extra level parameter were inserted between the decay and the sustain segments. The decay segment no longer falls to the sustain level; instead, it falls to the break point. The envelope then proceeds to the sustain level at a rate controlled by the slope parameter. Because the break point can be either higher or lower than the sustain level, the slope segment of the envelope can either rise or fall. This makes the design fairly versatile. Korg's envelopes can be used either for double-attack effects or to program a sort of two-stage decay, in which the decay rate speeds up or slows down part of the way through the envelope.

Sustain/Decay. In some Yamaha synths, the sustain segment has both level and time parameters. If the time is set to the maximum, the sustain level remains constant, as in a standard ADSR. If it's set to less than maximum, however, the sustain segment will sooner or later fall to zero. Again, this design is useful for programming two-stage decay envelopes, but unlike the Korg slope segment, the "sustain decay" always falls.

Multiple Release Segments. The envelopes in Kurzweil K2000 series synths have three time parameters and three level parameters for designing envelope releases. With this setup, you can program an extra click, thump, or swell and fade after the note-off arrives. The envelope will fall (or rise) from the sustain level to release level 1, then rise (or fall) to release level 2, and finally fall (or rise) to release level 3. The K2000 lets you program three attack segments in exactly the same way.

Below Zero. While the output of an ADSR always varies between zero and some positive value, many EGs are designed so that their level parameters can be set to either positive or negative values — to any value in a range of ±100%, for example. Depending on how the envelope is used, this setup can make a lot of sense. For instance, an envelope modulating pitch might start at 0% (the nominal pitch of the note), rise to 100%, then fall to –25%, and finally return to 0%. In some instruments, the start and end level of the amplitude envelope is always zero, but these levels can be varied in the other envelopes. This makes sense, because if the amplitude envelope ends at a non-zero level, the note will sustain indefinitely.

In some Yamaha FM synths, the start and end level of the envelopes was set with a single parameter, but it didn't have to be zero. Such a synth can play endless drones, even when no sustain pedal is hooked up.

Inverted Output

On many envelope generators, you'll see a switch that allows the output to be inverted. That is, instead of rising from its starting level, the envelope will fall. In other instruments, the inversion of the envelope signal is handled by the receiving module, whose modulation input will have a bidirectional amount parameter, or by providing two signal outputs for the EG, one of which is inverted. The latter designs are preferable, because they let you use a single envelope for both positive-going and negative-going modulation during the same note. If the envelope generator has a switch for inverting its output, you'll have to flip the modulation direction to positive or negative for *all* of the envelope's modulation destinations. With instruments that have a couple of extra EGs, however, this isn't usually a problem, because you can route various envelopes to their own destinations.

An EG whose output cannot be inverted in some manner, either in the EG itself or in the modulation routings, is a very undesirable feature. A few inexpensive instruments are designed this way.

Single & Multiple Triggering

The discussion up to this point has been based more or less explicitly on the assumption that each note played on the keyboard causes the envelope generators to start over. This is called *multiple triggering*, because when you play a line of notes, you'll trigger a succession of envelopes.

Many envelope generators have switches with which you can choose either multiple triggering or *single triggering*. Single triggering originated on first-generation synthesizers, which were mostly monophonic (capable of playing only one

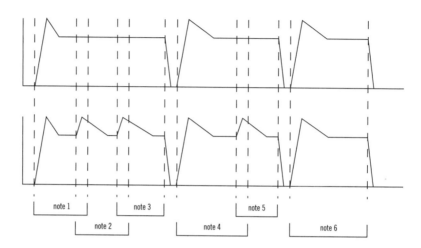

Figure 7-7.
Single-triggered
envelopes (top) and
multiple-triggered
envelopes (bottom). Single
triggering is an option in
many EGs; when it's
selected, lines that are
played in a legato
(overlapped) manner don't
trigger new envelopes.

note at a time). When you play a line on a monophonic synth whose EGs are set to single trigger mode, notes that overlap — what classical musicians call *legato* — don't trigger new envelopes. Instead, each EG generates only a single envelope for the entire legato phrase. The EG starts a new envelope only after a gap, however brief, during which no keys were pressed. The distinction between single and multiple triggering is illustrated in **Figure 7-7**.

TRACK 14

Single triggering doesn't make much sense when a synth is played polyphonically. Though the exact behavior of the synth depends on the number of voices available and the voice allocation scheme being used, it's fairly unlikely that two notes assigned to the same voice would ever overlap. Single triggering is used most often in a polyphonic synth when it's switched to mono or unison mode for lead playing. Once in a great while, however, you might find a synth with global EGs in addition to the voice EGs. Global EGs are inherently monophonic, so being able to set them to single-trigger mode makes sense.

Throwing a Few Curves

Up to now, I've been discussing envelope segments as if the envelope would rise or fall from one level to another at a constant rate. If diagrammed on paper, such an envelope would have segments that were straight lines. In some instruments, however, envelope segments can be curves.

The three types of segment curvature that are most often provided are shown

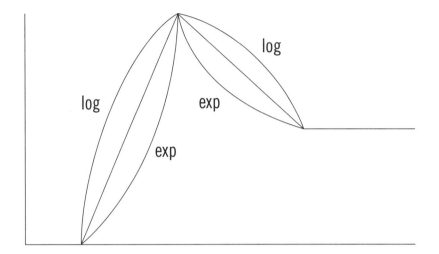

Figure 7-8.
Depending on the
features of your
instrument, you may be
able to program envelope
segments either as
straight lines or as
logarithmic or
exponential curves.

in **Figure 7-8**. In an *exponential* curve, the envelope changes more rapidly when its value is higher, and more slowly when its value is lower. A *logarithmic* curve is just the opposite. In a logarithmic curve, the envelope changes more rapidly when its value is lower, and more slowly when its value is higher. The meanings of these terms get a little fuzzy when the envelope's output drops below zero, so it may be safer to refer to them simply as concave and convex, respectively.

In some EGs, you have to choose exponential, logarithmic, or linear segments for the envelope as a whole, and you may be given only a three-position switch with which to do so. In other EGs (such as those in some Native Instruments soft-synths), segment curvature can be programmed differently for each segment, and can be varied from concave to convex in a continuous fashion by dragging a "handle" in the middle of the segment with the mouse.

It may not be intuitively obvious why changing the segment curvature should be useful. The primary reason is because the human ear perceives most audio phenomena in a logarithmic or exponential way. Consider pitch, for example: For every octave that the pitch of a note rises, the frequency doubles. This is an exponential relationship. To calculate the frequency of a note three octaves above a given note, we multiply the frequency of the lower note by 2 to the 3rd power. (In case your math is a little rusty, in this case the 3 is the exponent.) So what happens if we want a pitch envelope to drive the frequency of a note upward by three octaves over the course of a few seconds, and we use a linear envelope segment? The pitch will rise very rapidly at the start of the envelope, but will slow down as it approaches the destination, because the frequency is increasing by a fixed number of Hz per unit time. This may be exactly what the doctor ordered, musically speaking. But if we want the pitch to rise at a rate that the ear perceives as linear (that is, if we want it to rise the same number of half-steps per unit time), we need to use an exponential envelope segment.

In an actual instrument, this fact may have been built into the design of the oscillator. The oscillator's pitch modulation input may already be set up to respond to a linear change in the value of the modulating signal by changing the pitch in an exponential fashion. In this situation, sending the oscillator an envelope signal that rises in an exponential curve will cause the pitch to start changing at a relatively low rate and then leap up to the destination value at an ever-increasing rate. Which, again, might be what we want musically, or not. That's why it's good to have envelope generators that let you choose.

The ear also responds to amplitude in a nonlinear fashion. If you use a linear release segment in an amplitude envelope, the note will tend to be perceived as sustaining at a fairly high level for some period of time after the gate ends, and then falling rather suddenly to silence. To program a release segment that's perceived as smooth, an exponential curve is preferable. Again, the instrument's VCA (or digital equivalent) may handle this for you, translating a linear change at its modulation input into an exponential change in amplitude. The owner's manual may or may not explain this fact. As usual in synthesizer programming, your ears are your best guide to what's going on.

In an envelope generator that has lots of segments and can be set to loop, as in Native Instruments Absynth, for instance, adjustments in the curves of individual segments can be used to add articulations to notes within the loop.

Modulating the Envelope

String and wind players quite naturally play notes and phrases that have a variety of shapes — slow or fast attacks, notes that swell in the middle, and so on. Even on a plucked or percussive instrument, where the player has less control over the contour of individual notes, striking or plucking more aggressively will cause the sound to start at a higher level, and thus to take longer to decay to silence. So it shouldn't come as a surprise that one of the most important techniques we have for overcoming the inherent rigidity of the sound of a synthesizer is to modulate the envelopes in some way from note to note.

Depending on its design, your instrument may offer you one or several ways to do this. You may be able to modulate the overall output level of the EG, or (more rarely) the values of individual level parameters. You may also be able to modulate the time parameters — either the times of all of the segments together from a single modulation input, or the times of individual segments.

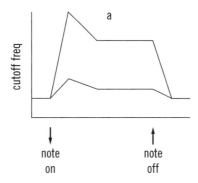

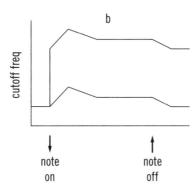

Figure 7-9.
Two types of filter cutoff response to velocity and envelope modulation. In (a), velocity is modulating the envelope amount, which in turn is modulating the filter cutoff. In (b), velocity and the envelope are modulating the cutoff independently of one another. Each diagram shows the result of playing a low-velocity note (lower line) and a high-velocity note (upper line).

The most usual modulation sources for envelopes are MIDI velocity and MIDI key number. Control of envelopes, and especially of individual segments, from LFOs and MIDI controller data is less common. I can't think of too many reasons (other than for wacky compositional experiments) where you'd want to use an LFO to control an envelope, but some instruments allow it. Being able to control the envelopes using MIDI controller data is useful primarily in situations where you want to crossfade between two sound colors with the mod wheel or a slider. In this situation, having a MIDI controller input to the EGs is vital. Even if you see such inputs, however, you need to be aware that some EGs are designed to read the value of the modulation input(s) only at the beginning of the envelope — which makes a certain amount of sense, since velocity data is defined only at the start of a new note. Changes in the position of a MIDI slider during the course of a note may or may not have an effect on envelope segments.

Let's look at the options one at a time:

EG Level Modulation. This type of modulation is fairly straightforward: When the modulation signal rises the EG output increases, and vice-versa. If you're using an envelope to modulate the pitch of an oscillator, for example, while modulating the envelope level from velocity, striking the key harder will cause the pitch to deviate more. This behavior is characteristic of many struck and plucked instruments.

If velocity is modulating EG output level while the envelope is being used to modulate the cutoff of a lowpass filter, striking the key harder will cause the envelope to open the filter further, resulting in a brighter tone — again, a characteristic of many acoustic instruments. (If the envelope is inverted, of course, higher velocities will close a lowpass filter further rather than opening it further.) You can achieve a similar result by modulating filter cutoff directly from velocity, and in fact some instruments give you one of these options, but not the other. It's important to note that while similar, they're not identical. As **Figure 7-9** shows, modulating the envelope amount from velocity causes the envelope to sweep the filter cutoff through a wider frequency range as velocity increases. Modulating the cutoff directly from velocity causes the start, peak, and end levels of the envelope to be higher or lower, but doesn't increase the range of the envelope sweep.

If the EG continues to read and respond to the value of a continuously varying controller during the course of the envelope, its output level can change even after the sustain segment is reached. This can be useful, especially on an instrument that has a limited number of modulation routings. For instance, it lets you apply both a pitch envelope and a vibrato LFO through a single oscillator modulation input, by modulating envelope amount from the LFO. Not all instruments respond this way, however.

Modulating the levels of individual envelope segments directly (as opposed to modulating the EG output level) gives you more flexibility. With an EG that has a break point/slope design, for instance, by modulating the break point level negatively from velocity, you can program the synth so that low velocities produce a smooth decay, while high velocities produce a double attack followed by a decay.

EG Time Modulation. As noted earlier, when a plucked or percussive instrument is played harder, the sound takes longer for the note to decay to silence. To produce a similar effect on a synth, we need to be able to modulate the EG's decay and/or release time with velocity. If the synth only provides one time modulation input to the envelope, however, and uses the incoming signal to change the rate of *all* of the envelope segments, there's a problem. When a plucked or percussive instrument is played harder, the attack transients in the sound will be more pronounced. So we'd like high velocities to produce a quicker attack (that is, a faster envelope rate) — but we'd like those same velocities to produce a longer decay (a lower rate). This is why a well-designed synth needs to be able to modulate the envelope times individually.

In some instruments, this challenge is met by having velocity-to-time modulation affect only the decay and release segments; attack time is not modulated. In others, notably synths from Korg, only one velocity amount parameter is provided for time modulation in each EG, but the modulation can be switched to positive, negative, or off for each time parameter. This is an effective compromise.

Another characteristic of plucked and percussive acoustic instruments is that high notes tend to die away more quickly than low notes. To accomplish this feat, a synth needs to be able to modulate envelope time from the MIDI key number or equivalent.

Looping Envelopes

In recent years, the trend has been to build envelope generators that are capable of looping. When the sustain level is reached, for instance, the envelope will start over with a new attack segment, cycling through its attack and decay segments over and over. With multi-segment envelopes, complex repeating shapes can be programmed.

In effect, a looping envelope functions like an LFO, providing repeating, cyclic modulation. A looping envelope offers a couple of advantages over an LFO, however. First, the segments of the modulation contour are individually programmable. Rather than being limited to a sawtooth or triangle shape, you may be able to program a shape that has a variety of rising and falling segments. Second, depending on how it's designed, the envelope generator may be able to loop through some of its segments rather than all of them. If it's programmed to loop segments 3 through 5, for example, segments 1 and 2 will only be activated once, at the beginning of a new note. Thus the "LFO" can begin with one contour that doesn't repeat and then settle into a different contour that repeats.

If your instrument provides multiple envelopes that can loop, you can program complex rhythms that will play when you strike and hold a single key. Striking and holding two or three keys, not at once but in a staggered rhythm, will produce polyrhythmic effects. Native Instruments FM7 is very capable in this regard. You may even be able to define the lengths of envelope segments in rhythmic terms (eighth-notes, sixteenths, and so on) and then sync the envelope to an external clock source, such as MIDI clock.

X/Y Envelopes

The Sequential Circuits Prophet-VS synth, which was produced in the early '80s, introduced the concept of two-dimensional *vector* envelopes (the "VS" stood

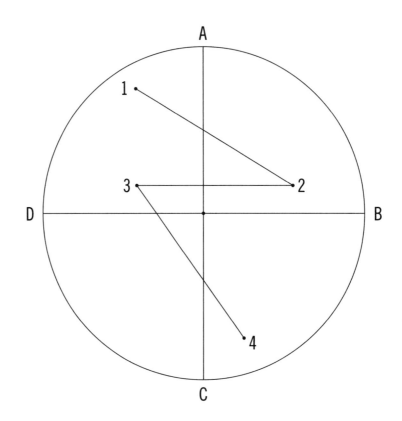

Figure 7-10.
A two-dimensional vector
envelope for controlling
amplitude. The levels of
sound sources
(oscillators) A through D
are determined by how far
the envelope is from a
given axis point at any
given moment: When it's
closer to A, sound source
A will be louder, while C
will be softer, and so on.
Note that the diagram
shows only the envelope's
output levels, not the time
required for the envelope
to move from one defined
point to another.

for "vector synthesis"). Shortly after Sequential was acquired by Korg, vector envelopes reappeared in the Korg Wavestation. Newer synths that have two-dimensional envelopes include VirSyn Cube and Steinberg Xphraze.

In place of level parameters, a vector envelope has X/Y coordinate points. It also has two simultaneous output signals, one for the current X value and the other for the current Y value (see **Figure 7-10**). At the beginning of a new note, the envelope begins at X/Y point 0 (which need not be the center of the X/Y modulation space). It then moves toward X/Y point 1 at a rate defined by time parameter 1. When it reaches point 1, it proceeds on toward point 2 at a rate determined by time parameter 2. This may sound sexy, but you can do the same thing and more with a pair of ordinary EGs. Essentially, an X/Y EG is like two separate EGs that share a single set of time parameters. One EG defines the X output levels and the other the Y output levels.

Most vector envelopes can loop, making them a good modulation source for various kinds of timbral animation.

Envelope Followers

An envelope follower is a device that senses the amplitude of a signal and outputs a control signal at a corresponding level. Envelope followers are found more often in effects processors than in synthesizers, but a synth that has an audio input (for processing external signals through its filter or other modules) may have an envelope follower, with which an envelope-type signal can be derived from the incoming signal. This envelope can then be used to control filter cutoff or other parameters.

An envelope follower usually has controls for attack and release. The attack control determines how quickly the envelope follower will respond to a rise in amplitude of the incoming signal. Typically this control is set to no more than a few milliseconds; if it's set too long, the envelope follower will fail to respond to short, percussive sounds. The release control determines how quickly the envelope follower's output will fall back toward zero when the amplitude of the incoming signal drops. The release time is usually set somewhat longer than the attack time; values in the 50–500ms range are likely to be useful. If the release time is set too short, the envelope follower's output will tend to become jittery. For instance, if attack and release are both set to less than 10ms and the input signal has a frequency of 100Hz, the envelope follower will rise and fall in response to individual wave cycles in the input.

A bank of envelope followers is one of the components of a vocoder, as explained in Chapter Nine.

Unusual Contour Generators

Any step sequencer, such as the Matrix module in Propellerhead Reason, can create multi-segment shapes that can be used as envelopes. Reason 2.5 lacks a lag processor, however, so Matrix envelopes will always be stepped, and it's not easy to start and stop Matrix in response to MIDI notes. In Native Instruments Reaktor, both of these necessities can be handled fairly easily, making Reaktor's step sequencer modules fully functional as contour generators.

In some modular synthesizers, you'll find modules that can serve as envelope generators, but that have features somewhat different from those discussed in this chapter. The Serge Modular, for instance, had a Dual Transient Generator module, which could function as an attack-decay envelope generator with the unusual property that it would only respond to a new trigger signal if the previous attack-decay cycle had finished. I'm not aware of any currently manufactured instrument that has this type of contour generator, but some modular software synths provide tools with which you could create one. With a program like Cycling '74 MaxMSP, you could even build a contour generator that would use or skip selected stages based on the value of some other signal, such as a MIDI controller.

Power Projects for Chapter 7:

Project 7-1: Snappy Segments. The attack of a sound — the first few milliseconds during which it's heard — has a big impact on how the sound is perceived. So it's useful to know just how crisp or flabby your synth's envelope attack segments are.

Create a single-oscillator patch. Choose a synth-type waveform such as a sawtooth wave, not a wave that has its own sampled-in attack transients. Open the lowpass filter all the way, or shut it off. Now program an amplitude envelope with an instantaneous attack, a medium-quick decay, and zero sustain. Get rid of any modulation of envelope times. While you're at it, get rid of any velocity-to-amplitude modulation, so that no matter how hard or softly you strike the key, the sound will be exactly the same. When you play the keyboard, you should hear a quick blip of sound, followed by silence.

While playing a single note repeatedly, gradually decrease the decay time until it reaches its minimum. If your instrument's EGs are fast enough, you may hear no more than a click. If they're slower, you'll hear a short burst of sound.

Reset the decay to medium-quick, and then increase the attack one increment at a time, again striking a key repeatedly as you do so. The notes' attacks should get gradually softer and smoother. Listen closely to how much control your synth gives you over the time of the attack segment: This is especially important to know when you're programming percussive sounds. Some synths will give you very precise control over how snappy the attack is; in others, an attack time of 0 may be instantaneous while an attack time of 1 is very perceptibly spread out. Knowing how your synth responds in this situation will help you design effective percussion.

You can repeat the experiment, if you like, with other envelope segments. You may find that an envelope release time of 0 creates a sharp click at the end of each note. Again, this is useful information. You may find that if you increase the release time to 5 or 6, the release will still sound instantaneous, but will be smooth enough that there's no click.

Project 7-2: Reverse Staccato. Program a synth brass type sound (two sawtooth waves with a little detuning) so that it has a quick attack, quick decay, zero sustain level, and a release time that's somewhat longer than the decay. When you play chords and hold the keys for a moment, the notes will die out, giving you a staccato sound. When you actually *play* staccato, however, releasing the notes before the end of the decay segment, the longer release time will be heard, so that the notes will "hang" for a while. The effect will be more audible if you don't use any reverb.

With a bit of practice, you can learn to control the length of the release segment from the keyboard.

Chapter 8
Modulation

f it weren't possible to shape the tone of synthesizers in a variety of ways, nobody would take the synthesizer very seriously as a musical instrument. The process of shaping the tone using control signals is called *modulation*. In the preceding chapters we've explored many of the features of synths that make modulation possible, and along the way we've touched on many specific modulation techniques and the musical issues that give rise to (or arise from) these techniques. The time has now come to look at modulation as a process in its own right. Inevitably, there will be some overlap between this chapter and the information on modulation in Chapters Four, Five, Six, and Seven. But modulation is important enough that you shouldn't have to search out a dozen scattered references in order to get a clear picture of how it works.

In this chapter, to an even greater extent than elsewhere in this book, I'm going to use the word "knob" to refer to any continuously variable control on the synth's front panel, be it a knob, a slider, a wheel, a two-dimensional joystick or touchplate (which are in essence two logical controls combined in one physical control), or on occasion a parameter in the operating system that has to be adjusted with a general-purpose data entry device.

Control Rate & Data Resolution

n analog electronics, as in the world of acoustic instruments and acoustical phenomena, processes are continuous, and the amount of any signal is infinitely divisible. When a control voltage rises from 1V to 2V, for instance, it passes through *all* of the intervening values — and there's an infinite number of values between 1 and 2. The signal may pass through the range between 1.53296V and 1.53297V very quickly, but if our instrumentation has enough precision, we can chart the signal's behavior in this range. Likewise, time itself is continuous in the analog world: If the signal takes one second to rise from 1V to 2V, beginning at 0 second and ending at 1 second, we can talk meaningfully about how it fluctuates during the time period between

0.53296 second and 0.53297 second. Up to the limits imposed by quantum mechanics and the uncertainty principle, we can discern ever finer gradations if we have the tools with which to do so.

This is not true of digital processes. In a digital synthesizer, no matter how powerful, there is only a finite number of discrete steps between 1 and 2. If the synth uses floating-point math for all of its calculations, the total range of values is large, but the number of steps within that range is still finite. In any case, few instruments use floating-point values for ordinary control signals; the cost in processor overhead would be significant, the musical benefits minuscule. In most synths, linear 8-bit, 16-bit, or 32-bit values represent everything except the audio signal itself, and in many instruments the audio is also a linear 24-bit or 32-bit signal.

What's more, everything that happens in a digital synthesizer happens at a discrete moment in time. In a computer that has a 500MHz processor, something (something extremely simple, such as copying a bit of data from one memory location to another) can happen 500 million times per second. But unless you're a chip designer, it's not meaningful to talk about what happens between event 239,153,296 and event 239,153,297, because *nothing* happens.

If a digital machine is working fast enough, it will appear to us that it's operating in a continuous fashion, because our senses are not very good at perceiving extremely fast changes. The ear is better than the eye in this regard, but it's still no match for a computer. Likewise, if the digital process creates percepts that are close enough to one another in value, our senses will perceive them as continuous rather than as separated into discrete steps. If you've ever used the blend tool in a paint program such as Adobe Photoshop, you'll be familiar with how a bunch of discrete screen pixels, each having a discrete numerical value for red, green, and blue, can appear, when viewed at a normal distance, to fuse into a smooth wash of color.

The speed with which a digital synth makes changes in its control values is sometimes referred to as the *update rate* or the *refresh rate*. It may be measured in Hertz or in milliseconds. The number of discrete data values available for a digital signal is referred to as the *resolution* of the signal. Typical resolutions are 8-bit, 16-bit, 24-bit, and 32-bit. In a more general sense, we can use the word "resolution" to refer to both the update rate and the bit resolution of the signal.

The question that naturally arises is how fast, and how high-resolution, digital audio processes need to be in order for us to perceive them as continuous. In Chapter Two, we discussed this question as it relates to the audio signal itself. In this chapter we'll be concerned primarily with control (modulation) processes. How often does the value of a modulation signal need to be updated so that we'll hear the result as a smooth, continuous change in the signal being modulated, and how close together do the steps of the modulation signal need to be?

For purposes of discussion, let's use a resonant lowpass filter as our modulation destination. While pumping a nice bright sawtooth wave through the filter, we're going to apply a modulation signal that will raise the cutoff frequency. To begin with, we'll send a signal that changes 10 times every second: The granularity (graininess) of the modulation signal with respect to time is 100ms. And we're going to change the value of the modulation signal in a way that will cause a minimum 100Hz change in the cutoff frequency.

During one second, then, the cutoff might rise from 500Hz to 1.5kHz. This modulation signal has an extremely low resolution, and the changes in the filter cutoff frequency will definitely be perceptible as discrete events. This phenomenon, in which discrete changes can be heard in the audio as a result of modulation, is called *stairstepping* or *zipper noise*. **Figure 8-1** shows what stairstepping would look like if we could see it. Zipper noise is generally undesirable from a musical standpoint, and manufacturers do their best to eliminate it.

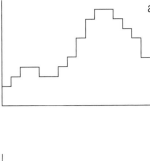

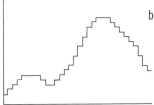

Figure 8-1.
A modulation signal with a very low resolution (a) will produce audible stair-stepping. As the resolution is increased (b and c) the stairstepping will become progressively harder to hear.

If we design our imaginary synth so that the control signal changes 100 times per second (a 10ms update rate), and so that it can make changes in the cutoff frequency of only 10Hz, we'll get a smoother filter sweep, but a little zipper noise may still be audible. If the control signal is updated at 1ms intervals and has a high enough data resolution that it can change the filter cutoff in 1Hz increments, the filter sweep should sound entirely smooth. Audio bliss will have been achieved.

So why aren't all synthesizers built to use extremely high-resolution control signals? From a manufacturer's point of view, the problem is financial. To have high-resolution control signals, the synth has to have a fast, powerful microprocessor. This increases the cost — or, in the case of a software-based synth, decreases the maximum polyphony available on a given computer. The manufacturer has an incentive to use as low-resolution control signals as possible, because a lower cost hardware instrument will probably sell better, and because lower manufacturing costs mean more profit (or, on occasion, the difference between a little profit and an outright loss). In the case of a computer-based instrument, musicians need as much polyphony as they can get, so again, the software developer has an incentive to economize when it comes to the resolution of control signals.

In general, you can expect, or at least hope, that expensive hardware synthesizers will have higher resolution controller response and a smoother sound. Inexpensive models may sound a little grainy.

The problem for the manufacturer is compounded by the fact that some types of controller graininess are more objectionable than others. The ear is fairly sensitive to changes in oscillator pitch, amplitude, and filter cutoff frequency, so these parameters need to be modulated in a fairly hi-res manner. But if the modulation destination is something like LFO rate, updating the modulation input 20 times per second is probably more than sufficient. Other parameters will fall between these two extremes.

As far as I'm aware, there aren't any hard scientific studies measuring just how high the resolution of a digital control signal needs to be before changes in various parameters are perceived as continuous — and even if there has been research on this topic, the manufacturer has to be concerned with other factors (such as cost and meeting a production schedule) in addition to the scientific ideal. As a result, it's quite normal to hear a little zipper noise when you push a modulation routing too hard. This can happen when the modulation signal changes rapidly, or when the amount of modulation is large, or both at once.

It's not guaranteed that all of the modulation signals in a synthesizer will have the same resolution. Nor is it easy to figure out what the resolution actually is. If you check in your synth's operating system, for instance, you may find that the filter cutoff frequency parameter has 8-bit resolution (a range from 0 to 255). You may also find that the filter envelope amount has 7-bit resolution (a range from 0 to 127). However, it's quite likely that internally, the envelope signal is applied to the filter cutoff with at least 16-bit resolution, so as to make envelope sweeps sound smooth.

Even if the envelope signal has a lower resolution, however, the filter sweep may still sound smooth, because the filter itself may *interpolate* between control signal values. In interpolation, a single change in value of the incoming control signal is replaced by several smaller changes that are closer together. Without interpolation, the filter cutoff might have to jump by 20Hz, that being the maximum resolution of the incoming modulation data, but with interpolation it might make four jumps of 5Hz each. Interpolation always imposes a slight time lag in controller response, but this is not usually perceptible, and if perceived it may actually sound good. If you grab the filter cutoff knob and whip it suddenly to its highest or lowest possible value, the filter may take a few extra milliseconds to reach the destination value — but this may make the filter feel more "organic" or "responsive," or at least less obviously digital.

Modulation Signal Routing

As mentioned in earlier chapters, three different schemes are commonly used for routing modulation signals to destinations and controlling the amount of modulation. You may be able to set up a particular modulation routing in the source module, in the destination module, or in a general-purpose modulation matrix that pairs sources with destinations. Just to make life a little more interesting, you may find two of these schemes (or even all three) used in a single instrument. The first two types are more likely to be found with commonly used routings, such as LFO to oscillator pitch, while a matrix may be available to handle more esoteric options, such as LFO to filter resonance.

Some modulation sources are permanently paired with specific destinations. This type of connection is referred to as "hard-wired." In an analog synth, there would actually be wires soldered between the source and the destination, but in a digital instrument the "wiring" is metaphorical.

The most common hard-wired routing, found in most instruments, is between an envelope generator and the amplifier module that controls the voice channel's output level. This routing is so integral to the functioning of the instrument that the amplifier itself will probably be invisible to the user. There won't even be an envelope amount control, because turning down the envelope amount would have exactly the same effect as turning down the instrument's output level. On the panel, you'll most likely see *only* the amplitude EG. Other common hard-wired routings are between a second envelope and the filter cutoff frequency, between an LFO and oscillator pitch, and between the MIDI modulation controller (CC1) and LFO output level.

In addition to the signal routing between modulation source and destination parameter, we need a way to control the *amount* of modulation. Again, the parameter that determines this amount may be found in the source module (an LFO's amount knob, for instance), in the destination module (a filter's envelope amount knob, for instance), or in the modulation matrix. In some instruments, you need to turn up *two* amount knobs, one in the source module and the other in the destination module, in order to hear the modulation. This can cause momentary confusion even for experienced sound programmers.

In general, the more powerful a synthesizer is, the more modulation routings it's likely to give you, both in absolute number and in the choices you have of source and destination for each routing. The more possible modulation routings there are, the more types of sounds you'll be able to create — but setting up complex modulations takes extra time and extra thought, and it can be confusing. Some manufacturers feel that a smaller set of useful routings is preferable to a larger set, because the added manufacturing cost (due to microprocessor speed requirements, design time, and the complexity of the front panel controls) and the difficulty musicians will have in learning to use the routings outweigh the musical advantages.

A modulation matrix is a general-purpose routing utility for modulation signals. Unless you're using a modular synth such as Native Instruments Reaktor or the Clavia Nord Modular, both of which allow signals to be split and summed with great freedom, the modulation matrix in your synth will most likely allow a fixed number of connections. In the E-mu Proteus 2000 series, for example, they're called Patchcords, and there are 24 for each voice channel. Typically, for each routing you'll be able to choose a source and a destination and set the amount of modulation. The sources and destinations available will depend on the design of your synth.

One advantage of a modulation matrix is that it's easy to program musical effects that the manufacturer might never have considered. Another advantage is that you'll probably be able to route a number of modulation sources to a single destination. This is often not possible in an instrument that has fixed routings: A filter may have only three hard-wired modulation inputs, for instance (one for the envelope, one for the LFO, and one for keyboard tracking). The disadvantage of a matrix is that the routings are usually found in a different part of the OS — in a separate menu, for instance — from both the source and destination modules. As a result, figuring out what's going on in a given patch can be a bit tricky. To shut off a particular type of modulation, you may have to hunt through a long list of routings.

Whether your instrument's modulation routings are hard-wired or buried in a matrix, it's very desirable that the modulation amount parameter be bidirectional. That is, you should be able to set it to an amount either greater or less than zero. A negative amount will invert the modulation signal: Increases in the signal will result in decreases in the value of the parameter being modulated, and vice-versa. In some synths, the modulation signal is inverted in the source module; an envelope generator may have an invert button, for instance, which will cause the EG's output to "flip over," descending rather than rising during the attack stage and so on. Inverting the signal in the source module is less desirable than a bidirectional amount control in the modulation matrix or destination module.

Even worse is a modulation setup in which the source module has the only amount control. In an inexpensive synth, for instance, an LFO may have both an output level (amount) control and a set of destination switches. If you switch on the LFO modulation for both the filter and the oscillator in such an instrument, you may find that you can't adjust the modulation amounts separately for the two destinations.

Secondary Modulation

Since the amount of modulation in any given routing is only another parameter, it's natural to expect to be able to modulate this parameter like any other. Modulating the modulation amount is called *secondary modulation*. (At least, that's what I call it.) The most common destination for secondary modulation is LFO amount: Just about all synths allow this to be controlled by MIDI CC1 messages. In most instruments, envelope amount can be controlled by MIDI velocity — another form of secondary modulation.

In an analog modular synth, secondary modulation will probably be set up using a VCA (voltage-controlled amplifier). The primary modulation signal is routed into the VCA's signal input, the secondary modulation signal is routed into the VCA's control voltage input, and the VCA's output is routed to the destination to be modulated. You can only set up this patch if your synth has two or more VCAs, because one will normally be needed to control the amplitude of the audio output. In a digital modular synth, a simple arithmetic module — a multiplier — takes the place of the VCA, making secondary modulation trivially easy. Hook the MIDI breath controller data to one input of the multiplier, the LFO signal to the other input, and the breath controller will modulate LFO amount. If you want the minimum amount of LFO (when the breath controller value drops to zero) to be greater than zero, a little extra arithmetic will be required: You'll have to add a constant value to the signal coming from the breath controller before it enters the multiplier.

A primary modulation routing can be set up with a non-zero *base amount*, which is the amount of modulation that will be applied when the secondary modulation amount (for instance, the MIDI mod wheel) is at zero. As the secondary modulation amount increases, the synth will either *add* to the base amount, or *multiply* it.

The difference is significant. In a synth that implements secondary modulation using multiplication, the primary modulation must have a non-zero base amount. If the base amount is zero, the secondary modulation controller will be multiplied by zero, so you'll never hear any modulation. If addition is used, the base amount can be zero. For that matter, the base amount can be negative (causing inverted modulation), so that as the secondary modulation increases, it will sweep the primary modulation amount *through* zero.

To give a concrete example, if your synth uses multiplication, and if you're applying secondary modulation to add vibrato from an LFO, you'll have to program some vibrato into the patch to start with. You won't be able to start a tone with no vibrato and then add vibrato as you move the mod wheel.

Modulation Signal Processing

Secondary modulation is a simple form of signal processing. In a few synths, more complex and interesting forms of signal processing can be applied to modulation signals. The Kurzweil K2000 series instruments (including the K2500 and K2600) have four *function generators* per voice channel. Each function generator — they're called FUNs in the display — takes two inputs, which can come from any modulation source, including other function generators. The two inputs are processed using any of a long list of equations, ranging from [a+b], which uses the FUN as a simple mixer, through exotic options like [min(a,b)], which outputs the lesser of the two signals, trigonometric functions like [sin(a+b)], and so on.

In the software world, the best modulation signal processing I've run into outside of modular instruments is in Image-Line's synth/sequencer Fruityloops (renamed FL Studio as of version 4.0). This program lets you write your own mathematical formula for any controller routing. For instance, you can enter the formula

(3 * Input) / 4

to scale the incoming MIDI controller data to ¾ of its original value. The Fruity Formula Controller goes even further: It accepts three streams of controller data as inputs, and lets you combine them by writing your own formula.

Even very simple synths usually have one hard-wired modulation signal processor. It's in the oscillator section, hidden under a knob labelled "glide" or "portamento." When the glide time is greater than zero, the pitch of the oscillator won't jump immediately to its new value when you play a new note. Instead, the oscillators

TROUBLE DOWN BELOW: If your synth allows you to enter or create mathematical formulas, you need to be careful not to inadvertently divide by zero. Dividing by zero is illegal, because the result would be infinite. If the variable in the denominator of a fraction ever reaches zero, the synth will, at the very least, shut down the voice in which this happens. It may crash.

You'll probably be able to do some form of error-trapping to prevent the value from reaching zero. For instance, if the possible range of a variable coming from a MIDI controller is 0–127, you could add 1 to it before using it. A formula like 56/(v+1) would work, as long as the variable v can't dip down to –1.

will take some amount of time to rise or fall to the new pitch. In first-generation analog synths, this effect was produced by a module called a *lag processor*. A lag processor is a lowpass filter for control signals: It limits the rapidity with which control signals can change, which has the effect of smoothing out abrupt jumps. Abrupt jumps in a signal are, by definition, high in frequency; that's what makes a lag processor a type of lowpass filter.

In some instruments, you may be able to use stepped rather than smooth glide: The oscillator may play a chromatic (half-step) scale each time it moves to a new pitch. This effect is created essentially by strapping another modulation processor — a *quantizer* — to the output of the lag processor. A few instruments, such as the Alesis QS series, provide quantizers with which you can process any control signal, turning a smooth sweep into stepped modulation.

A quantizer restricts its output to discrete values, but allows the output to change each time the input reaches an appropriate threshold. In a way, a quantizer is the opposite of a sample-and-hold (see Chapter Six). The latter allows the output to take on any value but changes the output at fixed time intervals.

Velocity Response Curves

Velocity response curves, also called simply "velocity curves," are a specialized type of modulation processing found in many synths. MIDI note-on velocity, you'll recall, can have any value between 1 and 127. A velocity response curve maps the incoming velocity data to some higher or lower value. Some typical velocity curves are shown in **Figure 8-2**.

The main point of using a velocity curve is to make the synth's keyboard feel more playable, both physically and in terms of the sound produced. If you tend to play hard, for instance, or if the keyboard has a light action, you may want to choose a concave velocity curve, in which intermediate velocities are mapped to somewhat lower values, so as to spend more time in the expressive middle velocity range of the sound you're playing. Conversely, if you tend to play lightly or are using a stiff keyboard, you may prefer a convex velocity curve, which will make it easier to produce midrange velocity data without having to pound the keyboard. A fixed velocity curve, in which the output velocity is always the same no matter how lightly or heavily you play, is useful once in a while, especially when you're triggering drum sounds that you don't want to get lost in the mix.

In some instruments, the velocity curve is selected at the global level, and processes velocity data before it's sent to the tone-generating circuitry. In other instruments, a velocity curve can be selected for each patch, or even for each envelope within a patch. The latter setup gives you more control, but it also requires more effort to program. Many players prefer to set the velocity curve at the global level and then never have to worry about it.

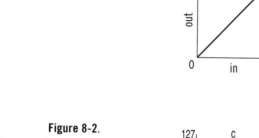
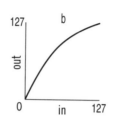

Figure 8-2.
Many synths provide a choice of velocity response curves, including linear (a), conyex (b), concave (c), S-shaped (d), inverted-S (e), and fixed (f). On some instruments, the fixed-velocity output can be adjusted up or down. In each diagram, the incoming note velocity is shown on the horizontal axis, and the output of the velocity processor is shown on the vertical axis.

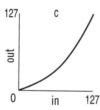
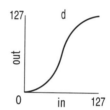

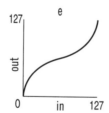
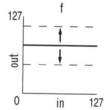

Some instruments offer only a few fixed velocity curves. Others have user-editable curves. However, the word "curve" is something of a misnomer. The output velocities, like the input velocities, will be able to take on only discrete values, usually the integers between 1 and 127. An input value (for example, 56) will always be mapped to some fixed output value (which might be 75 in a convex curve). When a nonlinear curve is selected, then, some of the possible output values won't be used. For instance, an input velocity of 1 might be mapped to an output velocity of 28. Since only 100 possible output values (28–127) are available while there are 127 possible input values, two or more inputs may produce the same output. For instance, input velocities of 100 and 101 might both produce an output of 112. Even so, a 127-node velocity map provides enough resolution for most musical purposes.

MIDI Control Sources

MIDI defines a number of types of signals that can be used for modulation. Most of them have been discussed at some point in this book, but a couple of them are used so seldom that I haven't mentioned them yet. For the record, here's a fairly complete list:

note-on velocity
note-off velocity
channel aftertouch (channel pressure)
polyphonic aftertouch (key pressure)
pitch-bend
note number
control change (also known as continuous controllers) 0 through 127
Registered Parameter Numbers (RPNs)
Non-Registered Parameter Numbers (NRPNs)
system-exclusive
clock

Velocity. Note-on velocity data is used by just about every synth built today. Its data range is from 1 to 127. A note-on message with a velocity of 0 is equivalent to a note-off: It stops a note from sounding. Velocity data is part of the note-on message, so it's defined only at the start of a new note. There's no way to change the velocity of a note while it's sounding. Velocity is used for just about every type of modulation in synth sound programming

Note-off velocity, which is included as part of the note-off message, is defined as a MIDI data type, but it's seldom used. It's one of the bright, or at least plausible, ideas that the people who wrote the original MIDI Specification had, which proved to be less useful in the real world than they had envisioned. The idea was that with a keyboard that sensed note-off velocity, you'd have separate control over the length of the envelope release stage for each note. Trouble is, a whole new kind of keyboard technique is required to transmit note-off velocities in a reliable, musically meaningful way, so the idea was quickly abandoned.

Some keyboards always send note-offs as note-ons with velocity 0 (which is allowed in the MIDI Spec for reasons having to do with efficiency). They never send true note-off messages at all. Most other keyboards send note-offs with a fixed note-off velocity of 64. Offhand I don't know of any keyboard currently being manufactured that senses and transmits variable note-off velocities, or any tone module that can respond to this data type, but I'm sure a few exist. Some sequencers let you edit the note-off velocities, but you'll probably have to use the event list rather than a convenient graphic interface.

Poly Aftertouch. Polyphonic aftertouch (also called key pressure) is a marginal technology, but it's a good deal more useful than note-off velocity. It was included in most Ensoniq keyboards, so if you can find one in good condition on the used market, you can play around with poly aftertouch. The idea was to allow the player to apply modulation separately to the individual notes within a chord. For instance, with poly aftertouch you can add vibrato to one note, open up the filter further, change the mix of two oscillators, and so on. This is actually a pretty slick capability, though it's not something you're likely to need every day. While keyboards that transmit poly aftertouch are no longer in production, a few synths, including the Kurzweil K2000 series, can respond to it. Many sequencers will allow you to create and edit poly aftertouch data graphically with a pencil tool.

A poly aftertouch message is a three-byte message. The first byte is the status byte (identifying the type of message and the MIDI channel), the second encodes the note number, and the third provides the actual amount of pressure (0–127).

Channel Aftertouch. Channel aftertouch (also called channel pressure) is implemented on many synths. Even instruments whose keyboards won't transmit aftertouch can often respond to it when it's received via MIDI. Aftertouch is used for most of the same musical tasks as the mod wheel (CC1). A few instruments will even let you map one of these MIDI messages onto the other, which is handy if you happen to be playing a keyboard that won't transmit aftertouch and don't want to go to the trouble of reprogramming the receiving module.

Channel aftertouch is a two-byte message, with a status byte followed by one data byte (value 0–127). This makes it marginally more efficient than control change data in situations where MIDI timing is critical. The downside of aftertouch is that your keyboard may be transmitting it even when you're not using it for anything. When recorded into a sequencer, it may clog up the playback data stream even when it's not producing any audible change in the synth sound. So it's a good idea to set up your sequencer to filter out aftertouch rather than recording it. (Some sequencers are set up this way by default.)

Pitch-Bend. MIDI pitch-bend is implemented on almost all synthesizers. While it's used by default to modulate oscillator pitch, on more capable instruments it can serve as a general-purpose modulation source. Modulating something else (oscillator detuning or filter cutoff, for example) along with pitch can make your bends more expressive.

Pitch-bend data is a bit different from other types of MIDI controllers in that zero is defined as being in the center of its range rather than at the bottom. This is so one data type can be used for both upward and downward bends. The actual depth of the pitch-bend — which could be anything from a half-step to several octaves — is programmed in the synth itself. It's not part of the pitch-bend message.

Pitch-bend is a three-byte message in which the status byte is followed by two data bytes. The first data byte is the Most Significant Byte (MSB) and the second is the Least Significant Byte (LSB). Together, the MSB and LSB give pitch-bend data 14-bit resolution. This is why you'll see it displayed in some sequencers with a range from −8192 to +8191 rather than from −64 to +63. However, many synths simply throw out the LSB data. Like note-off velocity and poly after-touch, the greater resolution of pitch-bend data was something that looked like a good idea to the people who created MIDI, but it has not proved to have a great deal of musical utility, at least for normal whole-step bends. Bends of an octave or more will definitely sound much smoother if you're using a bender that can transmit the LSB data and a synth that can respond to it.

Part of the art of synthesizer playing is learning to perform pitch-bends. It's a good idea to practice various types of bends, both so you can learn their expressive value and so you can get comfortable with the pitch-bend hardware provided on your MIDI keyboard. Most players seem to prefer to set the maximum pitch-bend range of their synths to ± 2 half-steps. This is a good compromise value: It's enough range for most of the types of bends played on guitar and other instruments, yet it's small enough that you'll have fairly precise control over the pitch. With a larger bend amount, bending a quarter-tone in a precise manner is difficult.

A few synths allow pedal-steel-type pitch-bending. (A pedal steel guitar has pedals and/or knee levers that can change the pitch of individual strings.) This is a nifty feature, but learning to use it requires practice. It's generally implemented as follows: The pitch-bend modulation is applied only to notes that are being held by fingers on the keyboard, *not* to notes that are being held with the sustain pedal. To bend the interval D–G up to E–G, you would play D and G, depress the sustain pedal, lift your finger from the G but not from the D, and then bend upward with the pitch-bend wheel or lever. The D, which is being held with a finger, will be bent, but the G, which is being held by the sustain pedal, will not.

Note Number. MIDI note number (0–127) is available in many synths as a general-purpose modulation source. It may be disguised with the term "keyboard tracking" or "key track." In some instruments, you can define keyboard tracking curves for the filter or other modules. This is a useful feature, because it allows the sound designer to make a synth patch playable across a wider keyboard range. Keyboard tracking curves generally allow for both positive and negative tracking amounts (see **Figure 8-3**). The keyboard tracking curve may include a "break point" parameter, which is the key (for instance, Middle C, which is MIDI note 60) at which the note number will be mapped to a modulation amount of zero.

Control Change Data. MIDI control change data (also known as continuous controller data, though it isn't actually continuous) is widely used for shaping synthesizer sounds. Control change (CC) data is a three-byte message, in which the

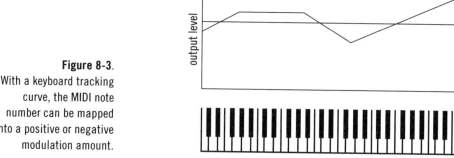

status byte is followed by a controller number (0–127) and a control change amount (also 0–127). Thus it's meaningful to talk about a controller 2 (CC2) message with a value of 13, for instance.

The meanings of some CC messages are defined, loosely or more precisely, in the MIDI 1.0 Specification. CC1, for instance, is the mod wheel (which might be a joystick, paddle, or touchplate on your synth), CC2 is the breath controller (which might be derived from an actual breath controller input on the synth's rear panel, or might come from a wheel or joystick), and so on. However, the musical effect of applying CC1 and CC2 data is not defined. CC7, on the other hand, is defined as Master Volume, which means that every synth ought to respond to a CC7 message with a value of 0 by turning its audio output down to zero. In this case, the MIDI Spec defines the result rather than the hardware input device.

Control change messages between CC64 and CC96 are defined in the MIDI Spec as switches (on/off controllers), which means that your synth should interpret CC64 messages (defined as the sustain pedal) with a value of 0 as meaning "the sustain pedal is up" and with a value of 127 as "the sustain pedal is depressed." CC64 values between 0 and 63 are usually interpreted as pedal-up messages, while values between 64 and 127 will cause the synth to sustain its notes.

Various items, such as the NRPN concept (see below), have been grafted onto the CC area of the MIDI Spec, with varying degrees of success. For instance, messages in the range CC32 through CC63 are supposed to be interpreted as the LSBs (Least Significant Bytes) of CC0 through CC31, respectively. This gives CC0 through CC31 a potential data resolution of 14 bits rather than 7 bits. However, your synth may or may not interpret CC32 through CC63 this way. And even if it does, there's no guarantee that your sequencer will be happy to display CC1 data with 14-bit resolution, using CC33 as the LSB. More often, in my experience, synths are designed so that their knobs can be assigned to any CC number between 1 and 63, if not between 1 and 97. (CC0 is reserved for the Bank Select message, a can of worms in its own right. CC98 and above are reserved for other purposes.) At this point, all of the CCs will have 7-bit resolution.

These days, many synths are set up so that each knob or slider on the front panel transmits a different control change message. These controller assignments may be hard-wired to the knobs, or you may be able to set up your own assignments. (Many software synths have a handy "MIDI Learn" feature: Right-click or option-click on the knob and then wiggle the hardware controller to send a few MIDI messages, and the knob will learn which CC you want it to respond to.) With this type of setup, you can record your knob moves into a sequencer and then edit the data as needed. This is an extremely effective way to make supple-sounding, expressive music with a synthesizer. A couple of limitations need to be noted, however.

First, your synth may allow only one knob at any given time to respond to a given CC message. If you assign this CC number to a new knob, the old assignment may be lost. This is fairly dumb, but quite common. If you want to move five knobs at once in an instrument that's set up this way, you may need to record five separate knob sweeps (or copy the data in your sequencer and change the CC number in the copies), which will eat up a fair amount of MIDI bandwidth, potentially causing timing problems.

Slightly less problematic, but still half-baked, are instruments in which the MIDI CC values always sweep the knob, slider, or other parameter through its full range. Ideally, one would like to be able to restrict both the input and output ranges. For one thing, your mod wheel or lever may be spring-loaded, and you may not want the parameter to slam down to zero when you let go of the lever. Also, it's nice to be able to create complex expressive sweeps with a single gesture on a hardware controller. For instance, you might want to have the filter cutoff rise from 1kHz to 2kHz as the mod

DON'T BANK ON IT: The MIDI program change message is a two-byte message, which means it can only specify 128 different patch memory locations. When MIDI was being developed, they figured that would be plenty — but these days it's not nearly enough. The Bank Select message allows any of up to 16,384 different memory banks (each with 128 locations) to be selected.

Bank Select is a three-byte message in which CC0 provides the MSB and CC32 provides the LSB. Some synths ignore the LSB, so CC0 messages with a value of 0, 1, 2, and so on are used for selecting the banks. Others expect that CC0 will always be 0, and use CC32 to select the banks. Some synths switch to a new sound program immediately when the Bank Select message is received, while others switch only when the next program change message is received. Some older synths don't recognize Bank Select, but use an alternate method to select banks. To make matters worse, many synths (especially those compatible with General MIDI) don't use consecutive banks. An alternative to the main electric piano sound, for instance, might be stored in bank 80, even though there's nothing in banks 1 through 79.

wheel moves up from 0 to 32, and then remain fixed at 2kHz as the mod wheel travels further. At the same time, you might want filter modulation from the LFO to remain at 0 until the mod wheel reaches 30, and then to increase from 0 to 15 as the mod wheel moves from 31 to 70. At the same time, you might want mod wheel values between 12 and 50 to *decrease* the level of oscillator 2 FM from 64 to 28. That may sound complicated and abstract when described in words, but the result, which is shown in **Figure 8-4**, could be a nice expressive sweep in which the filter cutoff opens and then begins to tremolo while the oscillator tone

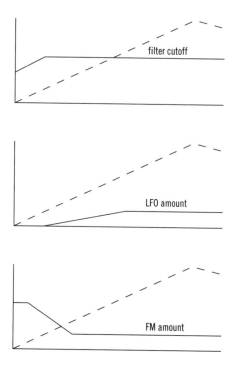

Figure 8-4.
Modulating three parameters (filter cutoff, top; filter LFO modulation amount, center; and oscillator 2 FM amount, bottom) from the same controller sweep.

becomes clearer and less raspy. To program this type of modulation, you need an instrument in which each knob's CC response can be range-limited.

Registered and Non-Registered Parameter Numbers. RPNs and NRPNs are a fairly obscure part of the MIDI Spec, but RPNs are used in a number of consumer-oriented synths, including the synths in some computer soundcards. These messages are sometimes embedded in Standard MIDI Files, as a way of controlling parameters that are not otherwise defined in the MIDI Spec.

RPNs and NRPNs are a clever way of using the existing set of 128 control change messages in a better defined and more consistent way. The RPN messages are by definition the same for each synth that implements them, but the NRPN messages can be different for each model of synth. It's up to the manufacturer to define a given synth's NRPN implementation, if it has one; there's nothing you can do about it as a user. Two CC messages are used to tell the receiving synth which parameter to get ready to edit, and then another CC message (CC6, data entry) is used to change the value of the chosen parameter. Since three separate CC messages are used, editing this stuff in a sequencer is best handled in an event list rather than graphically.

For a complete list of which RPNs and NRPN messages your synth can respond to and (one hopes) an explanation of how to program them in a sequencer, consult the instrument's manual. In case you're curious how it works, though, here's a real-world example. We're going to change the pitch-bend depth of a synthesizer that understands RPNs. First, we call up the pitch-bend parameter by sending a CC101 (the RPN MSB) with a value of 0, followed by a CC100 (the RPN LSB) also with a value of 0. Then we send a CC6 message with a value of 2. CC6 and, if needed, CC38 (the data entry LSB) set the value of the current RPN. In the case of pitch-bend depth, CC6 specifies the number of half-steps in the bend. Having set the new value for the RPN, it's good programming practice to conclude the data by sending CC101 and CC100 messages with values of 127. This chooses a null parameter, thereby insuring that stray CC6 messages later in the sequence won't unintentionally change the pitch-bend depth.

System-Exclusive. In many synths, parameters that can't be modulated with controller data can nevertheless be remote-controlled using MIDI system-exclusive data. (System-exclusive was explained briefly in Chapter One.) If you're lucky, you may be able to set up the knobs so that they'll transmit sys-ex. By recording this into a sequencer and then playing it back, you can gain fairly complete control over the sound of the synth. In other instruments, there is no way to transmit sys-ex for single parameters from the front panel, but you may be able to link editor/librarian software to your sequencer and record parameter changes from the editor/librarian into sequencer tracks.

The advantage of sys-ex modulation is that it often provides real-time control over parameters that can't be modulated any other way. In addition, it may (depending on how the manufacturer has implemented it for a given parameter) provide a higher data resolution than MIDI's standard seven bits (0–127). The disadvantages are, first, that sys-ex messages typically take up at least three times as much MIDI bandwidth as controller data, and second, that sys-ex control sweeps tend to be difficult, if not impossible, to edit in a sequencer. Sys-ex modulation is a last resort. If you can get where you want to go musically without it, you're better off.

MIDI Clock. The MIDI clock signal, a one-byte message, can in some sense be used as a modulation source. By syncing a delay line or LFO to MIDI clock, you can change the delay time or LFO rate by varying the tempo of the MIDI device that's sending the clock signals. Since all clock bytes are exactly alike, there's not much you can do with MIDI clock other than sync to it, but Kurzweil K2000 series instruments can divide the clock signal and derive a square wave from it, turning it into a general-purpose modulation source.

Audio Signals as Control Signals

I n many (but not all) analog modular synthesizers, control voltages (CVs) and audio signals use the same type of connector. In instruments of this type, an audio signal can be patched into a CV input — intentionally or by accident — and used for control purposes. Since audio signals typically change level rapidly, cycling up and down at a rate greater than 20Hz, using an audio signal for control purposes typically changes the timbre of the modulated signal by adding new partials, which are called sidebands. Modulating filter cutoff from an audio oscillator is a classic way to thicken the tone. Modulating amplitude from an audio oscillator is how you implement AM (amplitude modulation) synthesis, and modulating one oscillator's frequency from another oscillator produces FM (frequency modulation). For more on FM, see Chapter Four. Other types of audio-rate modulation are less useful: There's probably no reason to want to modulate envelope attack with an audio-rate signal, for instance.

 Power Projects for Chapter 8:

Project 8-1: Learn the Routings. Make a block diagram that shows all of the modules in one of your synth's voice channels. (This project may sound boring, but you might be surprised how useful it will turn out to be.) Include all of the modulation ins and outs for each module, and show the ways in which they can be interconnected. You may find that you need to draw the diagram in pencil, do a bunch of erasing, and then copy it onto a fresh sheet of paper to arrive at a clear layout.

Such a diagram makes visible in a two-dimensional way the connections that are hidden behind the synth's panel. The panel, especially in a digital synth with a big LCD, will probably show the connections only as cryptically abbreviated labels followed by numbers. This can make it hard for you to form a clear mental picture of what's going on in a patch. By drawing a map, you'll give your brain something more concrete to relate to.

Project 8-2: The Bends. If your synth allows pitch-bend data to be used for other types of modulation besides pitch-bend itself, try combining pitch-bend with filter cutoff modulation, LFO amount modulation, distortion amount modulation, reverb send or return modulation, and other effects. This should give you some new ideas about expressive performance techniques.

Chapter 9
Effects Processing

Since ancient times, musical instrument builders have used every means at their disposal to improve and enhance the sounds of the instruments they created. The grand piano, to give just one example, has not one but two groups of freely vibrating strings, which give the piano's tone a subtle "ambient" quality even in a small, acoustically dead room. So it's not surprising that synthesizer manufacturers routinely include digital effects processors in their instruments. The sound of most modern synths is heavily dependent on these effects, and would be much less enjoyable without them.

One of the very first popular analog synths, the ARP 2600, had a built-in effect — a spring reverb. Most first-generation instruments, though, lacked effects. At the time, the cost of including effects would have been prohibitive.

In the mid-'80s, however, falling prices for digital chips and the need to compete more effectively in the marketplace combined forces, and within a few years built-in effects were the norm. The success of the Roland D-50, which became the first synth to compete effectively with the Yamaha DX7, was due in no small part to the fact that the D-50 was the first synth to include included digital reverb and chorusing. Looking back on it, the D-50's reverb sounded pretty awful, but at the time it was a striking innovation. A couple of years later Korg upped the ante decisively with the M1, which included a surprisingly powerful multi-effects processor. Since then, instruments with effects have outnumbered their effectless counterparts by a wide margin. In recent years, the only major manufacturer who has bucked the trend has been Clavia, who scored a success with the effectless Nord Lead series. Many of the newer analog synths also lack effects — for two reasons, I suppose: The analog purists who buy these instruments may well turn up their noses at digital effects, even good ones, and the instruments are already expensive enough even without effects, so why add still more to the cost?

In this chapter we'll take a look at all the major types of effects. You won't find much technical discussion of how the effects are generated digitally, as that would take us far beyond the

SPRINGS WILL REALLY HANG YOU UP THE MOST. For those of you who are too young to remember, spring reverbs were considered essential in guitar amplifiers in the '60s and '70s. The device employed one or more actual metal springs, which were driven by a mechanical transducer mounted at one end of the spring. The sound waves bounced around within the metal coil of the spring and were captured at the other end by another transducer.

scope of this book. For the most part, I'll stick to explaining the effects parameters and what they're typically used for in creating synth sounds.

Before we get to all that, though, we need to take a look at signal routing and some other boring but essential topics.

Processors & Algorithms

One of the first questions neophytes learn to ask about synthesizers is, "How many effects does it have?" The answer gives a crude indication of the sonic prowess of the machine. Unfortunately, the answer can also be a bit misleading.

A digital device can do several things at once, even though it can't. The trick is, if it's cleverly programmed it can switch back and forth among two or more tasks, executing a bit of one task, then setting that task aside and moving to another. It's rather like a painter painting six paintings "at once" by running rapidly from easel to easel, adding a few daubs of paint to one painting and then dashing off to the next. To our slow-as-a-slug human senses, a digital device that's operating this way will seem to be doing all of the tasks at the same time.

In some cases, then, a synthesizer that boasts "three separate effects processors" may only have a single effects chip, which is giving you the impression that it's three separate chips by jumping from one audio processing task to another at a blindingly rapid speed. In a few cases, the synth may have no dedicated effects chip at all: The main chip that houses the oscillators and filters (all of which are digital processes) may also do the effects. In the case of software synthesizers, this is absolutely the case, because all of the processes are running "simultaneously" on the computer's CPU.

Each effect requires a certain amount of computation time, however, and better-sounding effects require more computation time. In many synths, the total number of effects processes that can be carried out at once is fixed: The manufacturer makes the decision that there will be three effects, and you get to figure out how to make the best musical use of them. In other instruments, the user is given some limited control over the number of effects. Bearing in mind that higher-quality effects take more computation time, you may be allowed to choose, let's say, a higher-quality reverb that uses up the whole effects chip or a lower-quality reverb that can run at the same time as a couple of other less computationally intensive effects.

By the way, the word "expensive" is sometimes used as a synonym for "requiring lots of computation time." Within a given effects system, the statement, "This is an expensive reverb," means that the reverb sounds good but also takes up a lot of the system's resources. Another term you'll hear from time to time is

DSP. This is an acronym for "digital signal processing." A synth with three effects processors will sometimes be referred to as having "three DSPs" or "three effect DSPs."

Even in an instrument that has, in theory, a fixed number of effects, tradeoffs between effect quality and total number of effects will quite likely be allowed. In such an instrument, the list of effects might include the following items:

> chorus
> overdrive
> chorus + overdrive

If you choose the "chorus + overdrive" effect, you're not magically increasing the speed of the effects chip so as to be able to run both the chorus and the overdrive effects at once. What's happening is that you're getting a lower-quality chorus, which is running in tandem with a lower-quality overdrive. The two together take up the same amount of computation time as the higher-quality chorus or overdrive by itself.

As a result, a synth that will do "three simultaneous effects" may in fact allow you to do five or six lower-quality effects at once. A reputable manufacturer will still call this a three-effect synth, but a salesperson might try to inflate the number to impress you. Trying to be smart, you might ask, "Yeah, but how many separate separate effects processors does it have?" The real answer to this might be, "one," if all the effects are being computed on one chip — and yet the correct answer may be three, if you can always use three different higher-quality effects at once and send a separate audio signal to each of them (a topic we'll look at more closely below).

In the list above, the items "chorus," "overdrive," and "chorus + overdrive" are usually called effects *algorithms*. For each effects processor (or what appears to the user as a separate processor), you can choose a separate algorithm — reverb, chorus, flanger, or whatever. If an instrument has 43 different algorithms in its list of effects, another correct way of answering the question, "How many effects does it have?" is to say, "Forty-three." Only two or three effects may be available at the same time, but for each of these, you may be able to choose any of the 43 items in the list.

Or not. Some synth effects are set up in such a way that each effect processor has its own list of algorithms. You may find, for instance, a dedicated reverb/delay with 17 algorithms, a dedicated chorus/flanger/phaser with another nine algorithms, and a third, more versatile processor with 43 algorithms, some or all of which are

JARGON BUSTER: An *algorithm* is a mathematical procedure. In math, it's simply a way of solving a problem. In computers, it's a procedure or method designed to produce some type of output. In a technical sense, digital oscillators and digital filters are produced by algorithms. For that matter, in a technical sense a patch in an analog modular synth is an algorithm. In digital music circles, however, the word is usually used in a narrower sense, to refer to two types of processes: effects, and the configurations of oscillators and envelope generators that produce frequency modulation. (The latter is discussed in Chapter Four.)

the same as the 17 reverbs and nine choruses. So does the synth have three effects, or 69, or some number in between?

In most instruments, you'll find several algorithms for a single type of effect — several different reverbs and so on. Even when you adjust the user-programmable parameters so that they appear identical, two reverb algorithms will probably sound somewhat different from one another. This is because each algorithm includes some settings that are not user-programmable. In a few instruments, however, what are displayed in a list as separate "algorithms" may in fact all be based on a single underlying algorithm. When you choose a different item from the effects list (for instance, the "dark room" reverb as opposed to the "Grand Canyon" reverb), the difference in sound might be due simply to the fact that the reverb is initialized with different values for the user-programmable parameters. In other words, you may be loading a reverb *preset* rather than a new reverb algorithm. The owner's manual probably won't tell you this; the only way to find it out, if it's important to you, is to adjust the user parameters of the two separate reverb selections so that they're identical, and then use your ears.

Signal Routing

Generally speaking, effects are the last part of the audio signal chain. Sounds are created in the synthesizer voice section, the sounds of the separate voices are combined, and then the combined signal is sent through the effects section. The output of the effects section is fed straight to the instrument's audio output jacks. Within that broad outline, however, you may encounter many different options.

The signal paths through which the synth voices are sent to the effects are usually called either *buses* or *sends*. "Bus" is a general term for any path through which an audio signal flows; the word can also be a verb, as in, "We're busing this signal to this input over here." "Send" is more specific; it's a shorthand term for "effects send," which is a bus that's used as an input for an effects processor. Each effect will also have an output bus. The signal coming from the effect will appear on its output bus, and your synth may give you further options for what to connect that output bus to.

Buses can be either mono or stereo. A mono bus carries a single audio signal. A stereo bus is actually just two mono buses side by side, a left bus and a right bus, which have the same source and destination. In a hardware mixer, it's usually a simple matter to send the left and right sides of a stereo signal to different destinations, in the unlikely event that you need to. I've never seen a synth that allowed stereo buses to be split in this way, but I'm sure somebody has built one. In most modular synths, however, especially digital modulars, "stereo" buses are often separate mono buses running side by side, so splitting them is a simple matter.

In effects signal routing, the signal that is being sent to the effect — that is, the signal to which the effect process has not yet been applied — is called the *dry* signal. The output of the effect is called the *wet* signal. Most effects processors include some method of controlling the relative levels of the wet and dry signals. Often, but not always, this is in the form of a wet/dry balance parameter. The wet/dry balance is conventionally considered to be in the range 0–100%. When the balance is 100% wet, the output contains only the output of the effect, with none of the input signal. At 0%, the output contains only the signal that was input to the effect, and the effect itself has, if you will, no effect. When the wet/dry balance is 50%, the output contains equal amounts of the dry (uneffected) and wet (effected) signals. In some instruments, 0% is referred to as 100% dry, and 50% is referred to as 50/50.

If your synth seems not to have a wet/dry balance control *per se*, it will probably allow you to set the wet/dry balance in some other manner. For instance, you may have separate level controls for the dry and wet output buses. With this type of setup, a little care is needed. A few instruments provide *both* a level control for the dry bus and a wet/dry control within the effect processor. In this situation, if you turn up the dry bus (which is routed *around* the effects rather than through them) and also set the wet/dry control within the effect to less than 100% wet, the dry signal will appear at the output through two signal paths — via the dry bus and also after passing through the effect. You might not expect this to be a bad thing, but it is. The problem is that the effects processor will most likely delay the signal passing through it by some small amount. Even the dry signal will be delayed as it passes through the effect. As a result, when the two dry signals are recombined, there will be some phase cancellation, which will alter the sound, usually in an undesirable way. (Phase cancellation is explained in Chapter Two.)

Even if your synth doesn't allow you to set up signal routings that cause phase cancellation, setting the correct wet/dry balance is important. A sound with too much effect can sound good when you're checking out the synth in the store, because the sound programmers at the factory wanted the instrument to sound big and impressive. But if you use that sound in a recorded track without lowering the wet/dry balance ("lowering" means lowering the wet part of the signal and increasing the dry part proportionally), or especially if you use several factory sounds without doing so, you're quite likely to end up with a mix that's a muddy mess. When evaluating effects settings of any kind, always consider how the patch sounds in conjunction with the other musical parts that will be heard at the same time.

A few synths, mostly consumer models, are set up in such a way that the dry output is always at full level, while the wet output (the effects output level) is programmable. In this situation, the wet/dry balance can be no wetter than 50/50. For most musical purposes, this is not a huge problem, but once in a while it can hang you up. For instance, you might want the cavernous sound of a snare drum passing through a reverb 100% wet, without the dry signal.

Many synths have effects *bypass* buttons on the front panel. A bypass button sets the output of the effect temporarily to 100% dry. This is a handy shortcut when you want to listen to a sound both with and without the effect, in order to judge whether certain parameters need a little more massaging: Not only does the bypass button save you the trouble of digging through the menu to find the wet/dry control, pressing the bypass actually leaves the wet/dry parameter set where it was before, so that you don't have to remember the setting in order to restore it when you're done listening to the dry sound. And if you're playing in an auditorium where there's a lot of natural reverberation, being able to bypass the synth's reverb for the entire gig with one button-press may be very useful.

In some instruments, an effect on/off button is provided instead of a bypass button. The result is usually the same. Pressing bypass will give you the dry signal by itself.

Many synths sum the output of their voices to mono before sending them to the effects. In a few instruments, you can not only pan individual oscillators left or right within the dry bus but also choose the effect send bus that each oscillator will use. Another common option is to allow each of the sounds in a drumkit multisample to have its own effect send level and/or bus assignment.

When a synth has more than one effects processor, the question of how signals are routed through the effects section becomes more interesting. In Chapter Five, in discussing instruments with more than one filter, we introduced the concept of *series* vs. *parallel* routing (see Figure 5-10, page 96). Like filters, two effects can be connected in series or in parallel. If they're routed in series, the output bus of the first effect becomes the input bus of the second effect. If they're routed in parallel, each effect receives its own input signal, and the two outputs are sent to whatever physical output you've chosen. (Output busing is discussed below.)

In some synths, the effects routing is fixed. You may find, for instance, a distortion effect, a chorus effect, and a delay effect connected in series, so that the output of the distortion feeds the input of the chorus and so on. In other instruments, the effects configuration is partially or entirely user-programmable. The effects might always be connected in series, for instance, but you might be able to choose the order of effects in the series. In a more flexible instrument, such as a Roland JV series synth, you'll have separate control over the dry output level, the output level for the chorus (the amount of chorus signal being passed directly to the instrument's physical outputs), the send level for the bus that goes from the chorus to the reverb, and also the output level for the reverb.

If there are three effects, still more possibilities present themselves. You may be able to patch two of them in series and run the third parallel to those two, or run two in parallel and then mix their outputs before sending it to the third.

For many standard types of sounds, this amount of programming power is overkill. When you're laying down an electric piano track, a little chorus and reverb are most likely all you'll need. But if you're working in a genre — pop music, to name one — where fresh sounds are important, being familiar with all of the tools in the tool kit can pay big dividends. Running a flanger in parallel with the reverb or EQing the heck out of a signal before sending it to the distortion effect may be exactly what you need to put your recording over the top. So don't neglect effects.

Multitimbral Setups & Physical Outputs

As noted in Chapter Three, individual synth programs on most instruments contain parameter settings for the effects. When you recall a program in single mode, you'll hear whatever effects were chosen for that program. In multitimbral mode, however, the single programs that are part of the multi are usually heard without their effects. Instead, all of the programs will use whatever effects settings are active in the multi. Since the instrument has only a limited number of effects, this is more or less inevitable. However, we're starting to see instruments, including some computer-based synths and some modeled analog hardware synths from Europe, in which the single-mode programs retain some or all of their own effects in multi mode. Such an instrument might legitimately boast 40 simultaneous effects. Typically, the effects will be a lot less computationally expensive than their counterparts in an instrument with only three effects. I'm not going to say they're lower-quality, because musical quality is partly subjective, but you can tell what I'm thinking.

If your synth has more than two outputs (one stereo pair), the multi will let you assign different single programs to different outputs. At this point, the effects busing situation gets a little more complex. In some instruments, the effects are always tied to the signal going to the main stereo outputs, and all of the other outputs will receive a dry signal. Other instruments let you bus various effects outputs to various physical outputs. Dry outputs are useful, however, because they allow you to patch some of your sounds, such as drum tracks, into additional mixer channels in order to process them with outboard effects.

External Audio Inputs

Given the amount of audio processing power found in synthesizers, it's very natural to want to process other types of signals through the instruments. Some instruments are set up to do this, but many aren't; if you're not sure whether yours allows it, check the owner's manual. Most audio input jacks on hardware synths are clearly labelled, but some instruments allow these to be used as external inputs for the filter and/or effects, while others use them strictly for sampling.

The external signal will generally come from one of two sources — either a microphone or a previously recorded audio track. If your synth is a sampler, it may have a microphone input. If its inputs require a line-level signal, you'll have to use a mic preamp to boost the mic signal before sending it to the synth. Some computer-based synths have external audio inputs, but when trying to process a live mic signal through the computer you may encounter an audible amount of latency (time delay between audio input and audio output), which can be disorienting if the person using the mic is listening to the computer's audio output at the same time. If you run into this problem, ask the softsynth manufacturer for recommendations on how to reduce the latency of your audio system.

When an external audio input is being used, the synth is basically operating as an effects processor rather than as a musical instrument. A full discussion of how to use effects processors is beyond the scope of this book, but there is one special factor that you need to be aware of when using your synth in this way:

In order to produce an audio output, you may need to send the synth a MIDI note to trigger its envelope generators and open its amplifier. This is often the case when the signal is being processed through the filter, but not when it's being processed through the effects. If the effect in question is part of the voice signal chain, however (this is often true of ring modulators), rather than being in the effects section, this type of MIDI gating is often needed.

If you're using a vocoder effect (see below), your synth may be set up so that its own voices will always provide the carrier signal. In this situation, you won't hear anything when you patch in the external audio signal, until you play at least one MIDI note so that a carrier signal is generated.

If your synth is also a sampler, you can process external audio through its effects even if it isn't set up to do this in real time. Simply sample the sound you want to process, assign the new sample to a preset, and then assign effects to the preset in the usual way.

Reverb & Delay

Reverberation (better known as reverb) and delay (also known as a delay line) are different but related effects. Both are sometimes referred to, imprecisely, as "echo." Reverb simulates what happens when a sound bounces around in a real acoustic space, such as a concert hall, gymnasium, or tiled bathroom. Without getting fancy about it — and some digital reverbs let you get very fancy indeed — we can say that a reverb effect produces a smooth, blurred wash of echoing sound. A delay line, on the other hand, produces a series of one or more discrete, non-blurry echoes of the input signal after some period of time has elapsed.

Reverb. Because reverbs are designed first and foremost (though not exclusively) to simulate acoustic spaces, many of their parameters have familiar-sounding names or use familiar metaphors. For instance, you may be able to select the "room size" in "meters." In the discussion below, please bear in mind that all of the acoustical behavior of the physical space in question is being simulated digitally by the reverb effect. Digital simulations are, at best, approximations — and in inexpensive synthesizers the approximations are likely to be relatively crude.

Consider what happens when a sound is generated in an auditorium: It travels outward from the source (perhaps a revolver being fired) in straight lines in all directions at once. You can visualize the sound wave as a rapidly expanding sphere with the sound source at the center. Before very long, the leading edge of the sound wave strikes the nearest wall. As it hits the wall, it rebounds. To be slightly more technical, we can say that it's reflected. Unless the auditorium happens to be perfectly spherical, however, and the sound source situated in the center of the sphere, the sound wave won't strike all of the walls at the same time. As it's reflecting from the nearest wall, it will still be traveling toward walls that are farther away. By the time the sound wave reaches the wall farthest from the source, it will quite likely have rebounded twice from walls that are closer together. Within a fraction of a second, the rebounding waves will be bouncing around the auditorium in very complex ways. As a result, the energy of the original sound is rapidly dispersed into a diffuse, overlapping, blurred cluster of echoes, which together constitute reverberation.

The precise sound color of the reverberation depends on a number of factors, principally the size and shape of the auditorium; the relative positions of the listener, the sound source, and the walls; and the hardness of the wall surfaces. Harder surfaces reflect sound more efficiently, while softer surfaces absorb more.

Eventually, the energy of the original sound will be absorbed by the walls, the bodies of the audience, or whatever else is in the room, and the reverberation will die out. The parameter with which this phenomenon is duplicated in a reverb is called *decay time*. The units with which the decay time parameter is programmed are usually seconds, but the number of seconds you see in the LCD may correspond imperfectly to what you hear. In some digital reverbs, decay time is defined as the amount of time required for the signal level to drop by 60dB; as a result, the decay time you're actually hearing may seem to be half of what the parameter indicates. As in most aspects of synthesizer programming, let your ears be the guide.

In an acoustic space, high frequencies are absorbed more read-

CLAP YOUR HANDS: An easy way to hear how sounds are reflected from the walls in an acoustic environment is to clap your hands. If you're standing between two walls that are parallel to one another and have hard surfaces, you'll hear a distinct buzz as the sound waves bounce back and forth between the walls.

ily than low frequencies. To simulate this, many reverbs provide a high damping parameter. When *high damping* is active, the high-frequency components of the reverberant sound die away more quickly than the low-frequency components. Other reverbs allow you to set the decay time separately for low and high frequencies. If the high decay time is shorter than the low decay time, the result is similar to high damping, but an artificial-sounding "space" can be created by reversing the settings.

Some digital reverbs let you choose the "material" that the walls are made of — tile, cloth, and so on. These options put a human face on high damping. In some cases, the wall material parameter may provide a more complex type of frequency filtering than simple discrimination between highs and lows.

If you're sitting close to the sound source in an auditorium and the walls are far away, you may hear the direct (dry) sound first and then, after a short delay, the reverberant sound. This is simulated in a reverb with the *predelay* parameter. Predelay provides some important control over the perceived nearness of a sound in a mix: By increasing the predelay to 50ms, you give the listener the impression that he or she is close to the sound source and the nearest walls are 50 feet away. Conversely, if the intent is to make a sound appear to be far away from the listener, when turning up the wet/dry mix you should probably reduce or eliminate the predelay.

For a brief period of time after a sound is generated in an auditorium, the listener will be able to perceive the reflected sound waves not as a continuous wash, but as discrete echoes bouncing from the nearest walls. This phenomenon is simulated in a digital reverb with the *early reflections* parameters. You may be able to program the amplitude of the early reflections, the number of reflections, and even their separation in time.

Many digital reverbs include a *diffusion* or *dispersion* parameter, or both. These give you a way of controlling the thickness of the wash of sound. Low diffusion and dispersion settings give the reverb a hard, brittle character. At an extremely low diffusion setting, the reverb may sound a bit like beebees rattling around in a tin skillet.

Specialized reverb algorithms are found on many instruments. The most common is probably gated reverb, which is a combination of a reverb with a noise gate (see below). Gated reverb was used by Phil Collins for processing drums in some hit songs in the '80s. For a while the sound was so identified with Collins that anyone else who used it sounded derivative, but in recent years the stigma has fallen away. It's a useful effect, especially for percussive sounds, because it allows you to create a big-sounding reverb and yet shut down the reverb decay quickly so that it doesn't smother everything else in the mix. It's also an exciting sound, because it plays with our psycho-acoustic perceptions: Each drum hit seems to be in a cavernous space one moment, and in a small, dead room the next moment.

"Reverse" reverb is also widely found. True reverse reverb can only be accomplished by recording a sound to analog tape or a hard drive, playing the sound backwards, sending the playback through a reverb, recording the output of the reverb, and then reversing this recording in turn. This trick was used in some well-known recordings in the 1960s, by Jimi Hendrix and others. A reverse reverb algorithm attempts to simulate the effect by applying an envelope with a rising slope to the output of the reverb. The envelope is triggered by loud transients in the incoming signal, with the result that the reverberant sound of the peaks gets louder rather than dying away. Early reflections may also increase in loudness, and be output near the end of the envelope rather than at the beginning. Given how much work the reverb is doing, the results tend not to be musically inspiring.

Delay. Reverb and delay are often lumped together because they both extend the input sound in time. In a delay line, each sample word in the input signal is stored in a memory buffer; after some period of time, it's read from the memory buffer and passed on to the output. (For you technical types, this is a FIFO — first-in, first-out — buffer. Generally speaking, the delay line reads the contents of the buffer in the order in which they were written. If it reads the buffer in a non-linear order, the result is a form of real-time granular synthesis.)

To take a simple case, let's assume the wet/dry mix is 50/50, and that the delay time parameter is set to 500ms. First we hear the dry sound; then, half a second later, we hear it again. If the wet/dry mix is set to greater than 50% dry, the echo will be softer than the original, which sounds more natural.

The most important parameter of a delay line is the *delay time*. This can usually be set in milliseconds. Because a delay line requires a certain amount of memory to operate, the maximum delay time is always fixed. In many synths, the delay time can be synchronized to a clock signal, which can come either from the synth's own internal clock or from an external MIDI clock. When the delay is synchronized, the delay time may be programmable in beat units (eighth-notes, quarter-notes, and so on). Because the total amount of memory is fixed, however, the actual delay you'll hear when you choose a larger rhythmic unit, such as a whole-note, may depend on the tempo. At a fast tempo, the delay may have enough memory to delay the signal by a whole-note, but at a slow tempo it may only be able to give you a half-note, or three quarters. For information on how to calculate the correct delay time for a given tempo if your delay can't be synchronized, see the "Calculator Formula" sidebar in Chapter Six, page 113.

A single short delay (under 50ms) is called *slapback echo*. Slapback echo is often used in conjunction with reverb in processing vocals; it provides a distinct early reflection. Panning the slapback delay's output to a different point in the stereo field than the dry signal is a useful technique. Slapback echo tends to spread out the attack transients of percussion sounds, so you may want to avoid using it on drum tracks.

Many delay lines have a *feedback* parameter. When the feedback is greater (or less) than zero, some portion of the delay line's output is fed back into its input. This produces a string of echoes from a single input. If the feedback amount is less than 100%, each succeeding echo will be quieter than the one before it, and the echoes will gradually die away. If the feedback is set to 100%, the echoes will keep cycling through the delay line until you reduce the feedback amount, switch to a new preset, turn off the synth, or die of boredom.

Feedback parameters can generally be set to negative as well as positive values. When the feedback is negative, the polarity of the signal is reversed before it's fed back into the delay line's input. Reversing the polarity of the feedback signal changes the nature of any phase cancellation that may be occurring as a sustaining sound is mixed with its own echoes, causing different overtones to cancel or be reinforced. The difference between positive and negative feedback may or may not be audible with any given input; let your ears be your guide.

A nonresonant lowpass filter with a gentle rolloff slope is often included in the delay line's feedback loop. This causes successive echoes of a given input sound to lose progressively more of their high-frequency content. The cutoff frequency of the filter can usually be programmed. The result is rather like high damping in a reverb. In fact, a delay line with a short to moderate decay time (between 100ms and 500ms), a moderate amount of feedback (between 20% and 50%), and a bit of high damping can be used to provide pseudo-reverb in an instrument that lacks a true reverb. Especially when the input signal is sustained rather than percussive, the separate echoes in the delayed signal will tend to blend together into a wash of ambience.

Many synths provide stereo delay algorithms. The input to a stereo delay is usually mono, but you'll be able to set separate delay times for the left and right delay channels. Each channel may also have its own feedback amount parameter. In addition, a stereo delay will usually provide some type of *cross-feedback*. In cross-feedback, some amount of the output of the left channel is sent to the input of the right channel, or vice-versa. This allows the delayed signal to bounce back and forth between the left and right speakers, which can be an interesting effect. Some synths provide delay algorithms or presets that are set up to do this; they're sometimes called *ping-pong delay*, by analogy with the sound of a game of table tennis.

With a stereo delay that includes both feedback within each channel and cross-feedback from one channel to the other, you may be able to program runaway feedback. If the sum of the cross-feedback amount and one of the channels' feedback amounts is greater than 100%, the sound coming from the delay will get louder and louder rather than fading away. This is not usually desirable, but it's possible to create an endlessly sustaining wash of somewhat distorted sound with this type of patch. If you're into sonic experiments, you might want to try it.

A multitap delay provides two or more separate outputs for the delay, each of which can be given its own time, level, and pan settings. A multitap delay is a good tool when you need a more complex rhythm-based echo than can be provided by a simple ping-pong delay algorithm. With short delay times, a multitap delay is also good for customizing the early reflections in a reverb (or adding early reflections to a reverb algorithm that doesn't have any). To do this, patch the delay in series before the reverb, so that the outputs of the taps will be reverberated.

Some delay lines allow the delay time to be modulated. The modulation source is usually an LFO within the effects section itself (not a voice LFO). When the delay time is increasing, the output will be pitch-shifted downward; when the delay time is decreasing, the output will be pitch-shifted upward. If the delay output is set to 100% wet, this type of modulation will add vibrato to the sound. If the wet/dry mix is 50/50, the pitch-shifted signal, whose frequency is constantly changing, will combine with the dry signal to produce phase cancellation. As the amount of pitch shift changes, the frequencies that will be reinforced and cancelled will move up and down. Small amounts of modulation will impart a pleasing richness to a sound.

The effect is so useful, in fact, that even if your synth offers nothing called a time-modulated delay, it will probably provide a number of algorithms that produce the effect. The technique I've just described is called *chorusing*.

Chorus, Flanger & Phaser

Chorusing, flanging, and phasing (more correctly called phase-shifting) are all ways of adding motion to the overtones of signals being processed. All three modulate the signal with one or more LFOs, so you'll generally see LFO rate and depth parameters. The differences among the three effects are fairly easy to hear, though, once you know what to listen for.

Chorusing gets its name from the fact that it's impossible for a large group of singers to sing perfectly in tune with one another. There will always be small pitch variations from voice to voice; the result is a thick, blended sound. Electronic chorusing adds a rich, swirling coloration to the sound. It's created with one or more time-modulated delay lines, as discussed above at the end of the "Reverb & Delay" section. A computationally inexpensive chorus may use only one delay line, but many choruses use two or more delays, which will be modulated by LFOs with different rates. In some synths, some of the chorus algorithms will have special but probably meaningless names like "ensemble" and "symphonic."

In a good chorus effect, all of the overtones will be changing in amplitude at once, some increasing and others decreasing. Flanging is similar, but has a more "pointed" sound. With a flanger, you'll usually be able to hear a prominent peak in the harmonic structure, which moves up and down. This peak is created by adding a feedback loop to the delay line, whose delay time is typically somewhat shorter than for a chorus. As the flanger's feedback amount increases, the peak will become more prominent. The delay time will govern the placement of the peak in the frequency spectrum: Longer delay times result in lower-frequency peaks. The LFO amount parameter controls how far the peak sweeps up and down through the frequency spectrum. By setting the LFO amount to zero, you can create a fixed peak, which will be quite pronounced if the feedback amount is large.

Phase-shifting produces a similar peak, but it tends to be higher-pitched and more metallic-sounding. As with a flanger, you'll probably find a feedback parameter that can make the peak more or less prominent, and an LFO for sweeping the peak up and down. Phase-shifting is not in fact produced by a delay line, but the results are pretty much the same as what you'll get from a flanger with a very short delay time.

Rotary Speaker

A rotary speaker effect is a specialized algorithm that attempts to mimic the sound of a rotating Leslie speaker. Leslies were commonly used with Hammond organs, and this effect is most often used in synths in conjunction with organ presets. It can be a good choice for other types of sounds, however, such as acoustic and electric guitars or even vocals.

A real Leslie has two components, a high-frequency horn and a low-frequency woofer, which rotate independently of one another. They add animation in two ways. First, as the speaker moves toward and away from the listener, the perceived frequency moves up and down due to the Doppler effect. Second, as the speaker points in different directions in the room during its travel, it causes different amounts of reflected delay depending on the relative positions of the speaker, walls, and listener. The sound reaching the listener after bouncing off a nearby wall may be moving upward in frequency (again due to the Doppler effect) at the same time that the sound reaching the listener directly from the Leslie is moving downward in frequency. Thus the result is a form of chorusing. In a lower-cost synth, in fact, the organ presets may use an ordinary chorus effect rather than a true Leslie simulation.

In a true Leslie, the acoustic chorusing will be applied independently to the high frequencies and the low ones, because the horn and woofer are rotating independently of one another. A true

COMIN' ATCHA: If you stand near the train tracks and listen to the sound of a train's whistle as the train approaches you, passes you, and recedes, you'll notice that the whistle seems to be higher in pitch as the train approaches and lower in pitch after it passes you and is headed away. That's the Doppler effect in action. The sound produced by the whistle doesn't actually change pitch. The illusion is caused by the fact that the train's speed is a significant fraction of the speed of sound. As the train approaches, the peaks of the whistle's waveform are "bunched up" in the air because the whistle itself is chasing its own sound waves. As the train recedes, the peaks of the waveform are stretched apart.

The Doppler effect is caused by the relative motion of the sound source and listener. If you're on the train, the whistle's pitch will be constant, but you'll hear the Doppler effect as you approach and then recede from the clanging bells at a crossing gate.

Leslie can also be switched between slow and fast rotation speeds, and the rotation can also be switched off entirely. When the speed is switched to fast or slow, the woofer and horn speed up or slow down at different rates. In a good Leslie simulation, you may be able to program the ramp time of the speed change independently — the parameters may be called *braking* and *acceleration*. You may even be able to control the crossover frequency (the point in the spectrum at which the horn will take over and the woofer will drop out).

In some sample playback synths that lack a Leslie simulation effect, the manufacturer tries to simulate the slow-to-fast Leslie transition by crossfading between samples. Two samples are recorded from a Hammond/Leslie combination, one with the Leslie rotating slowly and the other with it rotating fast. In the preset, pushing the mod wheel up causes the slow-rotation sample to fade out and the fast-rotation sample to fade in. This is utterly unconvincing to anyone who knows what a Hammond sounds like, and is in my opinion one of the more repellant uses of sampling technology. Still, I suppose it's better than nothing.

A real Leslie can be overdriven — that is, it can be sent a signal that's too hot for it to handle. This will result in a type of distortion. Some rotary speaker effects include this type of distortion, and even add a bit of the whooshing noise created by the horn spinning around.

Distortion

Rumor has it that distortion was first applied intentionally for a musical effect in the late '50s, when guitar players started slicing up the cones of the speakers in their amps with razor blades in order to add a buzz to the sound. Before long, manufacturers were selling stomp boxes called fuzztones, which gave the same kind of buzzing effect but allowed it to be switched on and off at will, something that was hard to do with a sliced-up speaker.

Other forms of distortion that have been used intermittently since those days involve sending to a circuit a signal that exceeds the intended electronic tolerances of that circuit — overdriving the circuit, in other words. Both analog tape recordings and the vacuum tubes in amplifiers can be overdriven, which usually results in a warmer, more subtle form of distortion than slicing up the speakers.

Today, these and other types of distortion are produced by overdrive effects algorithms. The purpose of overdrive is to add new frequency components to a signal. The new overtones will usually (but not necessarily) be harmonically related to the overtones already present in the signal, which will cause the sound to get thicker and perhaps brighter without changing in a way that would alter its perceived fundamental pitch.

Unlike most of the effects discussed in this chapter, overdrive distortion is an *amplitude-dependent* effect. That is, the number and loudness of the new overtones that will be generated, and thus the amount and depth of coloration imparted by the effect, depend directly on how loud the incoming signal is. If the overdrive doesn't seem to be doing much, it may be because you're not sending it a hot enough signal. Many overdrive algorithms include an input boost parameter (called "drive" or something similar) that can add gain to a signal whose level is too low to provide a satisfying amount of distortion. However, cranking up the drive is likely to increase the effect's output level drastically, which may not be what you want. You'll probably find an output attenuation parameter, with which you can scale back the output so that it doesn't destroy your speakers, but in some synths the output has to be turned down with the master volume knob after the overdrive has finished boosting it.

The amplitude-dependent nature of overdrive distortion means that the synth's envelope generators will quite likely have an effect on the distortion. A sound that starts loud and quickly drops to a low sustain level, for instance, will probably have a "crunch" on the attack but less distortion on the sustain. Cranking up the effect's input gain (and backing off on the output gain) will make the distortion more consistent throughout the note, but may also obliterate this envelope shape.

Conversely, when you play several notes at once on the keyboard, the amplitude of the signal reaching the distortion effect will be higher, so you'll hear more distortion. In addition, you'll hear harmonically related *intermodulation* distortion caused by the relative frequencies of the notes in a simultaneous interval, triad, or other chord. Unless the frequency ratio between two notes can be expressed by a relatively simple whole-number fraction (such as 3/2 for a perfect fifth), the distortion effect will add a considerable amount of beating and roughness to the sound.

This, incidentally, is one reason why rock guitar players tend to play open fifths in the bass register rather than full triads or other intervals. An equal-tempered fifth is a relatively consonant interval, so there isn't much beating when it's distorted by an overdriven amp or fuzz device. An equal-tempered major third, however, is badly out of tune compared to the ideal 5/4 ratio of a major third in just intonation, so the major third will produce rapid, unpleasant beating when distorted.

As noted in Chapter Five, many synth filters allow their inputs to be overdriven to add distortion. The essential difference between this and a distortion effect is that the filter's distortion is usually applied separately to each voice, while the distortion in an effects device processes the outputs of all active voices at once. By adding distortion at the filter stage, you can play thirds or other chord voicings without fear of intermodulation. If two oscillators within the voice are tuned to anything other than a unison, however, intermodulation between the oscillators will take place as filter distortion is added.

Other types of distortion found in some synth effects sections include *exciters* and *lo-fi* (low-fidelity) effects.

An exciter (also called an enhancer) adds new overtones to the sound, but only in the high frequency range. A little bit of this effect can bring out sounds (such as acoustic guitar) that would otherwise be lost in the mix, but using an exciter too liberally can give you a mix that's harsh and strident.

Lo-fi effects come in several flavors. Some add noise (such as simulated vinyl crackling and rumble) to the signal. Others simulate a lower sampling rate or bit resolution. This can add both noise and harmonic artifacts to the sound.

Pitch-Shifting

As its name suggests, a pitch-shifting algorithm raises or lowers the pitch of an incoming signal. Some pitch-shifters have two separate pitch-shift channels. The usual parameters are coarse- and fine-tune amounts for each channel. With a 50/50 wet/dry mix, small amounts of pitch-shifting sound rather like chorusing. Large amounts can produce intervals or three-note chords.

Unlike a modulated delay line, which alternately raises and lowers the pitch of the delayed signal, a pitch-shifter produces an unchanging pitch offset. This might seem like an unarguable advantage; the downside is that pitch-shifters seldom sound very good. They tend to introduce a gargling quality into the shifted sound, which will be more noticeable as the amount of shift gets larger.

Recent technological advances have made possible a technique called *formant-based pitch-shifting*, in which the fundamental pitch of a note is moved up or down while the formants (the peaks in the frequency spectrum of the incoming signal) remain fixed, or vice-versa. With formant-based pitch-shifting, you can do tricks like transposing a vocal up a fifth without having it sound as if it was sung by chipmunks. Formant-based pitch-shifting can also do exotic things to sound sources such as drums and acoustic guitar.

Filter & Envelope Follower

Some synths include a resonant lowpass filter among their effects algorithms. Because all of the synth voices are summed to a mono or stereo signal before being passed through this filter, and because the synth voices may start and end their notes at different times, it doesn't make much sense to modulate filter cutoff from any of the voice envelopes. Instead, the filter effect usually incorporates a device called an *envelope follower*. An envelope follower senses the amplitude of an audio signal (in this case, the signal entering the effects processor) and outputs a control signal with a corresponding amplitude. The control signal, in turn, modulates filter cutoff. As a result, when you play the keyboard harder or play more notes, the envelope follower will open the filter cutoff further. As the sound coming from the voice section dies away, the filter cutoff will fall. In many effects processors, this is called an *auto-wah* effect.

Like other lowpass filters, a filter effect will probably have parameters for cutoff frequency, resonance, and envelope amount. The envelope follower will probably have two parameters: attack and decay or release. In this case, "decay" and "release" mean essentially the same thing. The attack parameter controls how quickly the envelope can rise as the amplitude of the incoming signal increases: With a fast attack time, the envelope will respond more quickly. The decay parameter, in turn, controls how quickly the envelope can fall back toward zero when the amplitude of the signal decreases.

You might expect that it would be a good idea to set both attack and decay to short time values (fast attack, fast decay). But if you do this, the output of the envelope follower will tend to be a little jumpy. Most often, a fast attack should be combined with a medium-to-slow decay. In some instruments, these are the defaults, and you can't change them.

Equalization

Equalization (better known as EQ) has been used in recording studios for decades. An equalizer can boost or cut the frequencies in selected parts of the frequency spectrum while leaving other parts of the spectrum untouched. Unlike many of the effects discussed in this chapter, which can alter sounds in spectacular ways, an equalizer is more or less intended to improve the sound without being noticed.

Equalization is used most often not for enhancing or controlling the timbre of individual sounds by themselves, but for shaping their frequency content so they'll "sit better" in a mix with other sounds, either onstage or in a recording situation. Because of this, some synths put their EQ not in the effects section, where it would be programmable separately for each patch, but in the global output section, so that the EQ settings won't change when you select new patches.

With an equalizer, you'll be able to define the frequency range to be affected and the amount of cut or boost to be applied to partials that fall within that range. The amount of cut or boost is usually specified in dB — a range from −18dB to +18dB may be about average. Other than that, there's not much to say about cut and boost. There's more variety in the way the frequency range is defined.

For each range of frequencies to be affected, we can talk about the *bandwidth* and the *center frequency* (see **Figure 9-1**). The bandwidth is measured in Hertz. For instance, if we want to boost frequencies between 800Hz and 1,200Hz, the bandwidth would be 400Hz. The center frequency of this band is 1,000Hz (1kHz).

A *graphic EQ* (see **Figure 9-2**) provides a number of frequency bands (10, 15,

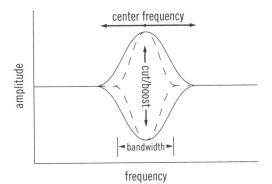

Figure 9-1.
The frequency response of one band of a parametric equalizer is governed by three controls. The cut/boost parameter changes the height of the "bump" in the response curve, the center frequency parameter moves the bump from left to right, and the bandwidth parameter changes the width of the bump.

Figure 9-2.
A hardware graphic equalizer. The term "graphic" comes from the fact that the front-panel sliders provide a visual representation of the frequency response.

or more) of boost/cut. The bandwidth and center frequency of each band is fixed, in such a way that all of the bands together cover the entire audible frequency range. Each band might cover one octave, for instance. In that case, the center frequencies might be 24Hz, 48Hz, 96Hz, 192Hz, 384Hz, and so on. If there are more bands, each band can have a narrower bandwidth, thus giving you more control over the frequency spectrum.

Graphic EQs are seldom found in synthesizers. More often, you'll see a *parametric* or *semi-parametric* design (or some combination of parametric and semi-parametric). A parametric EQ provides fewer bands, but gives you more control over each band, the assumption being that for the most part you'll want to leave the signal untouched. A single parametric band may be all you need to dial in the required boost or cut for a troublesome sound.

A parametric EQ band contains three controls: boost/cut amount, center frequency, and bandwidth. A three-band parametric EQ (not an uncommon design) provides three independent bands, each with these three controls.

A semi-parametric EQ band has only two controls: boost/cut amount and center frequency. The bandwidth is not directly controllable. Some synths, for example, provide EQ effects with two fully parametric bands for processing midrange frequencies, plus semi-parametric high and low *shelving* bands. A shelving band (so called because the EQ curve looks rather like a shelf, as **Figure 9-3** indicates) can cut or boost the lows or highs, but it will cut or boost *all* of the partials that fall above or below the frequency set by the frequency parameter. This parameter is sometimes called the *corner frequency*, because the frequency response curve has an angled shape. With a low shelf EQ whose corner frequency is set to 150Hz, for instance, all of the partials below 150Hz will be cut or boosted. In effect, the frequency parameter of a shelving EQ band controls both the bandwidth (which in this case goes from 0Hz to 150Hz) and the center frequency (75Hz), which is halfway between the corner frequency and the outer end of the frequency range.

Many EQ algorithms in synthesizers limit the parameter settings in various ways. For instance, you might find two fully parametric mid-bands, one whose center frequency can be set between 100Hz and 1,000Hz and the other with center frequency settings between 800Hz and 8kHz. The low and high shelving might have no frequency parameters at all, only cut/boost parameters.

When using EQ, it's important to understand that an equalizer can neither cut nor boost overtones that don't exist in a given signal. If a sound has no high-frequency content to begin with, cranking up a high shelving EQ will only add a bit of background noise. To use EQ effectively, you need to develop a sensitivity to what's going on in various parts of the frequency spectrum.

Removing DC Offset. In some programs, such as Csound and Max, that will do experimental digital synthesis, certain types of DSP, such as digital reverbs, may

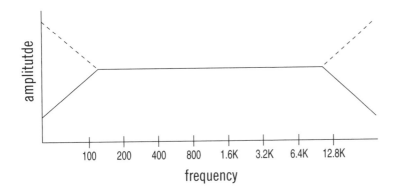

Figure 9-3.
A low shelving band in an equalizer (left) affects all of the frequencies below the corner frequency. A high shelving band (right) affects all of the frequencies above its corner frequency.

introduce a *DC offset* into the signal. A DC (direct current) offset is a nasty form of distortion: While inaudible for the most part, it causes clicks and pops at the ends of sounds. DC offset can be spotted in a waveform display. As a sound decays toward silence, the waveform won't converge on the center line but will instead taper to a line above or below the center line.

Since DC is by definition a partial with a frequency of 0Hz, a low shelving EQ or highpass filter set to an extremely low frequency (such as 5Hz) will remove DC offset without affecting the sound of the music.

Compressor, Limiter & Gate

Compressors, limiters, and noise gates provide various ways of controlling the amplitude of a signal. To do their job, these algorithms have some method of sensing the amplitude of the incoming signal — either an envelope follower (see the section on filters, above) or the equivalent. The information coming from the envelope follower is used to adjust, in one way or another, the gain of the signal being passed through the effect.

To explain how the devices work, we'll start by talking about compressor/limiters (sometimes called comp/limiters), because noise gates turn the process on its head. Trying to explain them both at once would make for confusing reading.

A comp/limiter has a threshold level parameter, which is usually defined in dB. Signals that fall below the threshold level — that is, signals whose highest dynamic peaks are quieter than the level defined by the threshold parameter — pass through the effect without any change. For instance, if the hottest peaks in the signal are at –17dB and the threshold is set to –15dB, the comp/limiter has no effect on the signal passing through it.

When the incoming signal rises above the threshold, the comp/limiter reduces (attenuates) the level of its output. The amount of attenuation is controlled by the *compression ratio* parameter. Typical compression ratios range from 2:1 to 20:1.

I'm not even sure how to explain what this ratio means in a single concise sentence, so I'm going to give you an example. Let's say the threshold is at −15dB, as before, and the incoming signal rises to −7dB. That's 8dB above the threshold. If the compression ratio is 2:1, the compressor will turn that 8dB increase into a 4dB increase (compressing the added gain by a 2:1 ratio). Thus the output signal will rise to a level of −11dB (−15 plus 4), as shown in **Figure 9-4**. The amount of attenuation is half of the amount by which the incoming signal exceeds the threshold, because the ratio is 2:1. If the ratio is increased to 8:1, the same 8dB rise above the threshold would be compressed to 1dB above the threshold, resulting in an attenuation of 7dB and an output of −14dB.

If that still seems a little abstract, don't worry about it. The point is, a higher compression ratio will cause the comp/limiter to "squash" loud peaks more forcibly, and a lower threshold will increase the effect by causing the comp/limiter to look at lower-level signals as "loud."

If the compression ratio is infinite, the comp/limiter will prevent the signal from ever rising past the threshold. This is called limiting.

Many comp/limiters have attack and release parameters. The attack parameter controls how quickly the dynamic level is reduced — how quickly the compressor starts to do its job — when the incoming signal rises above the threshold, and the release parameter controls how quickly the uncompressed dynamic level is restored after the signal drops below the threshold. A relatively slow attack setting (more

Figure 9-4.
A compressor reduces the amplitude of signals that are higher than its threshold value, while letting lower-level signals pass through intact.

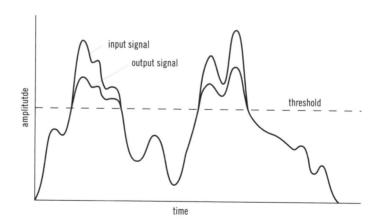

than a few milliseconds) will allow the percussive attack transients of sounds to pass through without being compressed. This can add "snap" to compressed drum sounds.

Compression is often used to give pop music recordings a uniformly high dynamic level, which is felt to make the recordings sound better on the radio. Too much compression, especially when it's applied to an entire mix, can squash the life out of a performance. Applied to individual drum samples, however, large amounts of compression can produce a startling and colorful effect. The compressor raises the low-level room ambience at the end of the sample to a point where it's clearly audible.

In a noise gate, which is a type of *downward expander*, the amplitude of the signal is unchanged as long as it *exceeds* the threshold. The gate reduces the amplitude of its output (or shuts off the signal entirely) when the signal falls below the threshold, as shown in **Figure 9-5**. If the threshold is set to a low value, the gate can clean up a recording by removing background noise without audibly affecting the timbre of the music. When the threshold is set high, a noise gate can chop a signal apart and produce unusual stuttering effects.

Vocoder

Vocoders have been around (in analog form) since the '60s. They're used most often to make a novelty "singing synthesizer" effect, but they're capable of other musical effects as well. They're a potent resource for processing drum loops, for

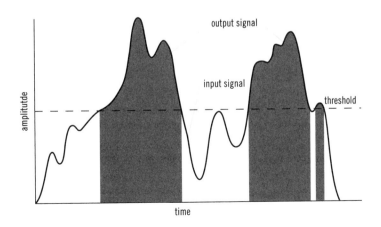

Figure 9-5.
A noise gate reduces the output level when the signal being processed falls below the threshold.

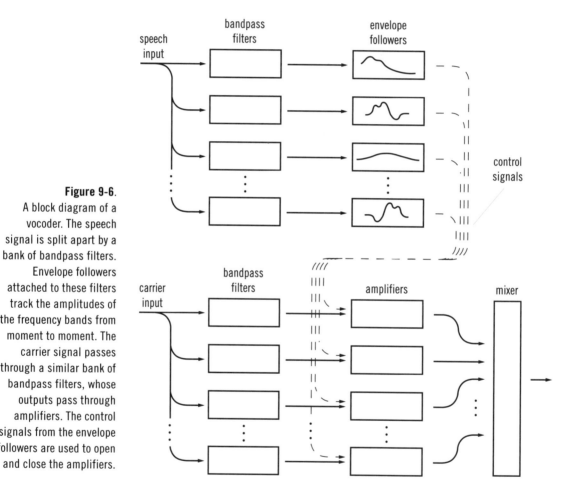

Figure 9-6.
A block diagram of a vocoder. The speech signal is split apart by a bank of bandpass filters. Envelope followers attached to these filters track the amplitudes of the frequency bands from moment to moment. The carrier signal passes through a similar bank of bandpass filters, whose outputs pass through amplifiers. The control signals from the envelope followers are used to open and close the amplifiers.

example. A vocoder requires two inputs to function: a *speech* signal and a *carrier* signal. What it does is impose the moment-to-moment frequency spectrum (the overtone structure) of the speech signal onto the carrier signal.

A vocoder consists of two banks of bandpass filters, a bank of envelope followers, and a bank of amplifiers. A block diagram of how it operates is shown in **Figure 9-6**. The two signals are split into narrow frequency bands by banks of bandpass filters. In ordinary operation, these filters will be set to matching frequencies, but this is not a requirement, and in fact some synth vocoders allow the bandpass frequencies to be offset or reassigned in various ways.

The outputs of the bands coming from the speech signal are tracked by a bank of envelope followers, which register the amplitude of the overtones in a given band at a given moment. The control signals from the envelope followers are then used to raise and lower the levels of the signals coming from the carrier's bandpass bank. The carrier signals are then mixed and sent to the output.

In order for a vocoder to work effectively, the carrier must have a rich overtone structure. Sawtooth waves and wind (white noise) are good carriers. If the carrier lacks overtones in a given band, the vocoder won't create them; all it does is raise and lower the levels of the carrier's existing overtones. In many synths, the vocoder effect uses the synth's own voices to produce a carrier signal. Generally, the speech signal will come from an external audio source.

Human speech contains some prominent high-frequency components, which are created by consonants such as f and s. If these are missing from the vocoder's output, the speech will be more difficult to understand. Since the carrier may not have enough energy in the high-frequency range to reproduce these consonants effectively, some vocoders have a pass-through for the highs: They mix the top end of the speech signal with the carrier before sending it to the output.

Vocoders shouldn't be confused with speech synthesis. Speech synthesis (robotic-sounding computer-generated speech) is an emerging field that may have some interesting musical applications in the future.

Ring Modulator

Like a vocoder, a ring modulator needs to receive two input signals. It's much simpler, however: It multiplies one signal by the other, a process that produces the sum and *difference* frequencies at the output, but not the original signals themselves. To give a simple example, if we feed two sine waves into a ring modulator, one with a frequency of 250Hz and one with a frequency of 350Hz, the output will consist of sine waves with frequencies of 100Hz (the difference between the two) and 600Hz (the sum). If, instead of sine waves, we use signals that have overtones, the output will contain the sum and difference frequencies for each pair of overtones.

Some ring modulators contain their own sine wave generator, which will produce one of the two signals. If there's a sine wave generator, you'll be able to adjust its frequency, and it may also be able to change frequency in response to MIDI note messages.

In many synths, the ring modulator is in the oscillator section, and has inputs from two oscillators. If the two oscillators are tuned to a harmonically consonant interval such as a fifth, mixing the output of the ring modulator with the oscillator waveforms will produce a sound that's richer in overtones. If the oscillators are tuned to some other ratio, the ring modulator will add non-harmonic components to the sound, altering or destroying the sense of a pitch center.

A close relative of the ring modulator, found in a few analog modular systems, is the *linear frequency shifter*. This device outputs only one side of the ring modulation process — either the sum frequencies without the difference frequencies, or vice-versa. When a signal is processed by a linear frequency shifter, all of its partials are shifted up or down in a linear manner. This warps the harmonic ratios among them, resulting in clangorous tones.

Real-Time Control of Effects

Many synthesizers provide some form of real-time control of their effects, either from front-panel controls, via MIDI, or both. Your owner's manual will provide specifics. It's worth noting, however, that real-time control of effects is often more limited in scope than real-time control of other synthesis processes. There's a reason for this. With effects that use digital delay lines in some way (including reverb, delay, and chorus), any change in a delay time parameter is likely to add ugly clicks and pops to the sound. To avoid customer dissatisfaction, manufacturers simply don't allow those types of modulation.

At the very least, a modern synth will probably let you modulate the send level or wet/dry mix of your effects in real time. You'll be able to add more reverb to selected notes, for instance. The levels of non-delay-based parameters, such as chorus LFO depth and rate, may also be available as modulation destinations. If your synth allows an effect's output level to be modulated, and if you have two effects processors that can be run in parallel, you'll be able to crossfade between two entirely different effects during the course of a single note or phrase.

Power Projects for Chapter 9:

Project 9-1: Dry vs. Wet. Choose a few of your favorite synth presets and disable or bypass all of the effects so as to hear only the dry sound. You may be surprised at how dull and lifeless the sound suddenly becomes. Without adjusting any of the voice parameters, choose different effects for a preset to hear what your effects are capable of. Move the wet/dry level control up high enough that you're hearing too much effect and not enough dry signal, and then back it off until you hear just the right mix (this is a matter of taste — what's too much for you might be just right for someone else, or vice-versa).

Project 9-2: Effects Chaining. If your synth has two (or more) separate effects processors that can be linked in series, try reversing the order of two effects: Put effect A before effect B and listen to the sound, and then put B before A and listen again. Some combinations are more effective than others; in a few cases, the second effect will mostly obliterate the sound coloration imposed by the first effect. Try these combinations:

- Distortion and reverb.
- Chorus and reverb.
- Flanging and distortion.
- Phasing and delay.

Appendix:
CD Track Listing

Track 1, 1:11 (**Chapter 2**). These five tones show what partials sound like. The first three are similar, but with different groups of harmonic overtones. The fourth illustrates detuning of partials, and the fifth shows the inherent bias in our ability to perceive amplitude.

Tone 1: This tone begins with a sine wave. Shortly, the first overtone (the second harmonic) enters, followed by the second overtone and the third.

Tone 2: Here, the initial sine wave is followed by a band-limited square wave containing the first six odd-numbered harmonics. After a moment, the even harmonics are filled in, producing a band-limited sawtooth wave. At the end of the tone, more high harmonics are added.

Tone 3: After the initial sine wave, a cluster of very high harmonics is added to the sound. These then fade out, being replaced by some midrange harmonics. The same thing happens again, the midrange harmonics being replaced by lower harmonics. The tone ends with a type of loop that can be created only with additive synthesis, in which the three sets of harmonics alternate.

Tone 4: At the beginning of this tone, the partials are harmonically related, producing a reasonable approximation of a sawtooth wave. As the tone continues, higher partials become progressively sharper. The stairstepped effect is due to the limited resolution of VirSyn Cube's Spread parameter, which controls the detuning of the partials.

Tone 5: The beginning of the tone is a sine wave. As overtones are added using FM synthesis, the sound seems to get a lot louder, but in fact its amplitude isn't changing.

Synthesizers Used: Tones 1–4 were created with VirSyn Cube, an additive software synthesizer. Tone 5 was created in Native Instruments FM7, an FM-based software synth.

Track 2, 0:46 (**Chapter 2**). Problems with digital audio caused by clipping distortion and aliasing. In all of the clipping examples, the clipped tones sound louder than the unclipped tones, even though their actual peak amplitudes are lower. This is caused by a combination of three factors. First, the initial input level of the sound source was raised in order to produce the clipping, so that clipping the output produced a form of compression. Second, clipped tones have more high-frequency content. Third, the distortion makes clipped tones sound more aggressive in a subjective, emotional sense.

Tones 1–3: The first of these three stereo arpeggios (with delay) has no clipping. The second has a bit of clipping, and the third has quite a lot.

Tones 4–9: A conga drum (unclipped and then slightly clipped), an acoustic kick drum (unclipped and slightly clipped), and an electronic kick tone (unclipped and then very clipped). The clipping in the first two drum tones is so brief that it isn't perceived as clipping, but rather adds slightly to the percussive character of the tone.

Tone 10: A diatonic scale is played from the bottom of the keyboard up four octaves. On the last note the pitch-bender is used to change the base frequency of the tone. The synth patch itself doesn't change from the first tone to the last, but because the patch produces so many high harmonics, prominent aliasing occurs in the top two octaves: High harmonics "fold over," producing lower-frequency partials that are not harmonically related to the fundamental. The pitch-bend changes the relative frequencies of these partials, producing something that doesn't sound much like a bend.

Synthesizers Used: The clipping tones were produced by a Korg 01/W. The clipping in tones 1–9 was created in Steinberg WaveLab software using the gain change command to boost the recorded tone past the maximum level possible in a 16-bit file. Clipped tones were then scaled back, again using the gain change command, so that they would have about the same subjective loudness as the unclipped tones. The aliasing example was created in Native Instruments FM7.

Track 3, 0:46 (**Chapter 2**). Beating and difference tones caused by phase cancellation.

Tone 1: Two sine waves are heard simultaneously, one at 439Hz and one at 441Hz. Beats occur at a rate of 2Hz. If you look at this tone in an audio editing program, you'll see that at the points where the two waves are 180 degrees out of phase, the waveform is momentarily silent.

Tone 2: Phase cancellation between complex waveforms can produce a rich, musically interesting effect. Here, two sawtooth waves are heard at the same time, one slightly detuned from the other. In the second half of the tone a third sawtooth wave enters the mix, resulting in much more complex phase cancellation and thus a richer tone. While the effect is similar to chorusing, this example was produced without a chorus effect.

Tone 3: Two sine waves whose difference tone rises into the audio range. One wave remains at 3kHz while the other falls from 3kHz to 2.1kHz. If you listen closely, you'll hear a third tone rising from the sub-audio range to 900Hz. This is the difference tone: It's not being generated directly by an oscillator, but is caused by phase cancellation between the two sine waves.

Synthesizers Used: Tones 1 and 3 were generated in Csound, a non-realtime (rendering) software synth programmed by typing lines of computer code. Tone 2 was produced in VirSyn Tera, an analog-type software synth.

Track 4, 1:07 (**Chapter 4**). The raw building blocks of synthesizer sound: A four-bar lead line played first by a sawtooth wave, then by a square wave, then by a thin pulse, then by a triangle, and finally by a sine. In the lowest register, the fundamental pitch of the square and pulse waves tends to be obscured.

Synthesizer Used: VirSyn Tera.

Track 5, 1:01 (**Chapter 4**). Using a noise source or envelope for pitch modulation.

Phrases 1–3: The frequency of a sine wave is modulated first by white noise, then by pink noise, and finally by low-frequency noise. I'm a little suspicious of the white noise, which doesn't seem to have quite as much high-frequency energy as I'm used to hearing, but the pink noise modulation is audibly lower in frequency. The low-frequency noise causes the frequency of the sine wave to vary only slightly, in a random way.

Phrases 4–5: A simple bell-like FM tone (processed by a moderately resonant lowpass filter) plays a short phrase, first with no noise modulation and then with a brief burst of frequency modulation from a noise source on the note attacks. The noise creates the "knocking" sound.

Phrase 6: This phrase, played by a sawtooth wave, is heard twice, first with no pitch envelope and then with a quick pitch envelope driving the frequency upward during the note attacks.

Synthesizers Used: I created my own instrument using Native Instruments Reaktor 4.0, which is a completely modular software synth, in order to demonstrate noise modulation. The pitch envelope patch is from VirSyn Tera.

Track 6, 2:43 (**Chapter 4**). Detuning, oscillator sync, and fractional scaling of oscillator pitch.

Tone 1: A two-oscillator patch in which one oscillator is detuned from the other. In the lowest octave the beating is very slow (though faster beating can be heard among the higher overtones). For each octave that I play up the keyboard, you'll hear the speed of the beating double. This happens because the detuning is a constant fraction of a half-step, and the distance in Hz between adjacent half-steps doubles for each octave the base frequency rises.

Tones 2 & 3: In these tones, we're listening to an oscillator whose frequency is synced to a master oscillator (the latter not being heard). In tone 2, the frequency of the slave oscillator is modulated by a slow envelope decay, causing it to descend slowly. In tone 3, the frequency of the slave is being modulated by an LFO, and the tone is being processed by a resonant lowpass filter to make it a little more pleasing.

Phrases 5–9: This two-oscillator patch uses a choir-type sample for the main body of the tone and a bandpass-filtered bongo drum sample for an attack transient. The key follow parameter of the attack transient is set to 20% (100% being normal tuning). The phrase is heard four times: first with the complete patch, then with the choir-type comp sound but no attack transient, then with *just* the attack transient, and finally with the two elements combined again (repeating the first phrase). The third phrase has not been gain-normalized, so you'll hear it with the same amplitude it has in the composite sound. Notice how much less colorful the second phrase sounds.

Synthesizers Used: VirSyn Tera (tones 1–3) and a Roland JV-2080 rackmount synth (phrases 5–9).

Track 7, 1:42 (**Chapter 4**). Sample start point modulation and wave sequencing.

Phrase 1: In this short example, sample start point is being modulated by velocity. The only thing being modulated is the sample start point; the sound gets louder between note 1 and note 13 because as note velocity increases, more of the short, unlooped, and rather rude percussive waveform has a chance to be heard before the end of the wave data is reached.

Phrases 2 & 3: Sustained tones that use factory wave sequences in the Korg Wavestation. In each phrase, the tone begins with a single note, to which a fifth and then an octave are added. In the first phrase, the waveforms in the wavesequence crossfade with one another, producing a blend of harmonics, while in the second they're rhythmically distinct.

Phrases 4 & 5: Sequencing of single-cycle waves in a software emulation of the PPG Wave 2.2. The wavetable in each case is being swept by an envelope, which causes the oscillator to switch from one wave to another at regular time intervals. Each phrase includes four single notes (root, fifth, root, then fifth again) followed by a chord (root, fifth, octave).

Synthesizers Used: For sample start point modulation, an E-mu Proteus 2000 rackmount synth. For phrases 2 and 3, a Korg Wavestation SR rackmount synth. For phrases 4 and 5, the Steinberg/Waldorf PPG Wave 2.V.

Track 8, 1:55 (**Chapter 4**). Brief examples highlighting several types of synthesis: frequency modulation (FM), additive, and granular.

Tone Group 1: The point of this example is to show the effect of various carrier/modulator frequency ratios on tone color. Ratios included are (in order) 1:1, 2:1, 3:1, 4:1, 5:1, 1:2, 1:3, 1:4, 1:5, 1:6, 8:5, 5:8, 8:7, and 7:8 (the modulator frequency is given first). In each case, the FM amount (modulation index) is the same. The modulator envelope has a slightly slower attack and faster release than the carrier envelope, to allow you to hear a bit of the unmodulated carrier sine wave at the beginning and end of the tone.

Tone Group 2: Modulator enveloping in an FM tone. Two modulators were used for this tone, one with a quick decay to provide attack transients and the other with a long, smooth decay. The amount of FM is greater in each note than in the note before, and the last note sustains to illustrate the similarity of an FM amount envelope to a lowpass filter envelope. If you listen closely, you may be able to hear that the amount of fundamental in the tone decreases as the FM amount increases; this is because each note has the same total amount of energy. As more overtones are added and their amplitude increases, the available energy has to be distributed among them.

Tone Group 3: This chord illustrates both additive synthesis and envelope looping (a topic explored in Chapter 6). The two-dimensional looping envelope changes both the relative amplitudes and pan positions of various individual overtones.

Tone Group 4: This example begins with the source audio (my voice), which is unprocessed except for a bit of compression to give the granular process a more uniform signal level with which to work. This audio is then manipulated by automating the playback controls of a granular synthesis algorithm.

Synthesizers Used: Tone groups 1 and 2 use Native Instruments FM7. Tone group 3 uses VirSyn Cube. Tone group 4 uses Grainstates SP, one of the software synths provided with Native Instruments Reaktor 4.0.

Track 9, 2:03 (**Chapter 5**). Various types of filtering.

Tones 1–4: Slowly sweeping the cutoff/center frequencies of a lowpass, highpass, bandpass, and notch filter with an envelope generator. In each case the source signal is a raw sawtooth wave.

Tone 5: Gradually increasing the amount of resonance of a lowpass filter. The cutoff frequency is set to a moderately low value. There is no resonance at the beginning of the tone, and the amount gradually increases to just short of self-oscillation. Although the cutoff frequency seems to rise slightly as the resonance increases, no modulation of the cutoff frequency was employed; this frequency shift is a result of the design of the filter.

Tone 6: A simplified illustration of a synthesis technique that can be useful in an instrument that provides two or more filters per voice. This tone crossfades between a lowpass filter and a highpass filter under the control of a slow LFO.

Synthesizer Used: VirSyn Tera.

Track 10, 1:09 (**Chapter 5**). Modulating the cutoff frequency of a lowpass filter in various ways.

Phrases 1 & 2: The notes in these two phrases are identical, rising seven octaves. In the first phrase, the filter's cutoff frequency tracks the keyboard, which results in a fairly uniform tone across the full range. In the second phrase, the cutoff frequency remains unchanged. As a result, the lowest notes are far brighter than in the first phrase, while the highest notes almost entirely fade out.

Phrase 3: A three-note broken chord in which a multi-stage envelope modulates a moderately resonant lowpass filter. During the release stage, the filter envelope rises rather than falling toward zero.

Phrases 4 & 5: A short lead lick in which both oscillator frequency and filter cutoff are being modulated by MIDI pitch-bend data. In the first phrase, the two types of modulation are in the same direction: Bending downward closes the filter, while bending upward opens it. In the second phrase, the filter modulation is reversed.

Tone 6: The cutoff frequency of a moderately resonant lowpass filter being modulated by an LFO. The amount of modulation gradually increases: At the beginning of the tone there's none, but by the end of the tone the cutoff is sweeping down to 0Hz, completely shutting off the sound.

Phrase 7: Modulating the cutoff frequency (again, of a moderately resonant lowpass filter) from an envelope generator. The envelope generator is set to zero attack, a quick decay, and zero sustain level. The amount of modulation increases from note to note; there's none in the first note and a great deal in the last note. A sawtooth wave is being used as the source signal.

Synthesizers Used: LinPlug Delta III (phrases 1–5) softsynth, Native Instruments Reaktor 4.0 (phrase 6), VirSyn Tera (phrase 7).

Track 11, 0:59 (**Chapter 6**). Various types of LFO modulation. Tones 1–5, all of which use a triangle waveform in the LFO, begin with no modulation, and the modulation depth gradually increases under control of a MIDI mod wheel.

Tone 1: Oscillator frequency.

Tone 2: Cutoff frequency of a lowpass filter.

Tone 3: Amplitude.

Tone 4: Panning.

Tone 5: FM amount.

Tone 6: Secondary modulation of one LFO's rate by another LFO. The LFO whose rate is being modulated is modulating, in its turn, three primary sound characteristics: FM amount, panning, and filter resonance.

Synthesizer Used: VirSyn Tera.

Track 12, 1:35 (**Chapter 6**). More examples of LFO modulation.

Tone 1: Oscillator frequency modulated by a square wave.

Tone 2: Oscillator frequency modulated by a rising sawtooth wave.

Tone 3: Oscillator frequency modulated by a falling sawtooth wave.

Tones 4 & 5: Bidirectional (tone 4) vs. unidirectional (tone 5) modulation from a square wave. The amount of modulation increases during the course of each tone under control of a MIDI mod wheel. Unidirectional modulation produces a more musically usable trill.

Tone 6: The LFO is producing a stepped random (sample-and-hold) output, which is being applied to oscillator frequency and also slightly to filter cutoff.

Tone 7: Again, a stepped random LFO output, this time applied to the frequency of a synced oscillator and also to panning.

Tones 8 & 9: Polyphonic vibrato. In tone 8, the LFOs in the four voices are in phase with one another, while in tone 9 they're out of phase. The major 6 chord retains its harmonic identity in the first example, while the harmony is somewhat obscured in the second example.

Synthesizers Used: VirSyn Tera and (for tones 4 and 5 only) Native Instruments Reaktor 4.0.

Track 13, 1:29 (**Chapter 7**). Some basic envelope shapes.

Tone 1: An ADSR envelope with a slow attack and slow release.

Tones 2–6: The envelope generator settings on these five chords are exactly the same: slow attack and fast release. The longer notes get louder because the envelope generator has time to open up further before the note-off message starts the release stage.

Phrase 7: With fast attack and release settings, playing clearly articulated lines is easy.

Tones 8–12: Fast attack and fast decay with varying amounts of sustain level. The first chord has a sustain level of 0, and in succeeding tones it's raised progressively higher.

Tones 13–14: An academic demonstration of linearly and exponentially decaying amplitude envelopes. Both notes are the same length, but after three seconds the note with linear decay still has about 20% of its initial amplitude, while the note with exponential decay has less than 1% of its initial amplitude. The note with linear decay sounds almost as if it's "hanging" at a relatively high amplitude level as it starts to decay and then decays more rapidly as it fades out, when in fact the amplitude is falling at a uniform rate from the very beginning of the note.

Synthesizers Used: VirSyn Tera and (for tones 13 and 14 only) Csound.

Track 14, 0:37 (**Chapter 7**). More types of envelopes.

Phrases 1a & 1b: Phrase 1a uses a single-triggered filter and amplitude envelopes. Phrase 1b is identical, except that the envelopes are multiple-triggered.

Phrase 2: A looping envelope (16 sixteenth-notes in length) animates a sustaining tone. The notes of the chord were triggered on different beats of the bar in order to give the envelope a polyrhythmic aspect.

Tones 3–5: The performance technique known as reverse staccato. As performed on the keyboard, the first chord is long and the last one short, while the middle chord is of intermediate length. Holding notes longer on the keyboard produces shorter notes, because envelope sustain is set to 0, envelope decay is fast, and envelope release is slower.

Synthesizers Used: VirSyn Tera (phrases 1a and 1b) and Native Instruments FM7.

Track 15, 0:56 (Chapter 8). Examples of modulation.

Tones 1 & 2: Control signal granularity in a rising FM amount envelope. In the first tone, the FM amount is being updated 14 times per second, while in the second tone it's being updated 3,150 times per second. The first tone contains audible stairstepping artifacts, while the second is entirely smooth.

Phrase 3: Fingered portamento. When notes are connected by playing legato, the pitch glides between them, but when there's a moment of separation, the new note begins at its normal pitch.

Phrase 4: Keyboard tracking of envelope generator decay time. The envelope generator's keyboard tracking shortens the decay time as the MIDI note number increases.

Synthesizers Used: Csound, Roland JV-2080, VirSyn Tera.

Track 16, 1:39 (Chapter 9). Reverberation.

Phrases 1–3: Long and short reverb decay times. A phrase on an organ patch is heard three times: first with a relatively long reverb decay, then with a short reverb decay, and finally dry (no reverb). The dry phrase is included to make it easier to hear the short reverb; only a portion of the dry phrase is heard.

Tones 4–9: A "hall" reverb algorithm set to no high damping, moderate high damping, and lots of high damping. Two chords are played with each setting to make it easier to listen to the differences. If you listen closely, you'll hear that the reverb's output is in stereo: The left-channel sound is independent of the right-channel sound, which adds to the sense of space.

Phrases 10–12: Predelay and early reflections. A kalimba phrase is heard three times, first with essentially no predelay, then with a long predelay, and finally with the same long predelay but no early reflections. The second and third phrases are very similar in sound, but if you listen closely you'll hear that the beginning of the reverberant sound is softer in the final phrase.

Synthesizers Used: Roland JV-2080 (organ phrases) and Korg 01/W.

Track 17, 0:33 (Chapter 9). Two examples of rhythm-based delays.

Phrase 1: Each arpeggio is played (by a MIDI sequencer) only once. The repeating pattern, which causes the notes to blend into chords, is created by a delay line.

Phrases 2 & 3: The delay line here is set to 50/50 wet/dry. In phrase 2, there is no delay feedback; the second note in each pair is created by the delay. In phrase 3, the feedback is turned up. In addition, I waited an extra two beats before playing the arpeggio so you could hear the first note being delayed repeatedly.

Synthesizer Used: Korg 01/W.

Track 18, 0:52 (Chapter 9). Chorus, flanging, and phase shifting. The same phrase, played by a one-

oscillator sawtooth patch, is heard four times — first dry (no effect), then with chorusing, then with stereo flanging (the left and right LFOs are 90 degrees out of phase), and finally with phase shifting. The animation heard in the dry recording is due to the beating inherent in equal-tempered intervals.

Synthesizer Used: Roland JV-2080.

Track 19, 2:07 (Chapter 9). Assorted effects.

Phrase 1: A Hammond organ patch, first with no rotary speaker emulation (in bar 1), then with a slow rotary speaker. During the first long chord the rotation speeds up, and during the second long chord it slows down again.

Tones 2–7: Distortion as it affects intervals. The first interval, a perfect fifth, sounds smooth when distorted, while the second and third intervals (a major third and a minor second, respectively) produce harsh beating. The same intervals are heard again without the distortion effect, for comparison. This patch also illustrates a useful programming technique: The second oscillator has a very slow attack, and is tuned a fifth above the primary oscillator. As it increases in level, it mimics the sound of a guitar feeding back through an amplifier. Acoustic feedback often causes higher partials to become more prominent than the fundamental, due to the resonant characteristics of the speaker cabinet and the room.

Phrase 8: A vocoder. I played a synth sound using a basic two-oscillator sawtooth-wave synth in Reaktor, while letting a Reaktor sample player play the vocal loop (which is heard dry at the end). The vocoder is one of Reaktor's factory effects.

Phrases 9 & 10: Ring modulation. In both phrases, a square wave is ring-modulated with a sine wave. In the second phrase, the pitch of the sine wave is modulated by an envelope with a 2-second delay time, so that short notes have a stable pitch, while long ones are swept. A stereo delay effect is also used in the second exmple.

Synthesizers Used: CreamWare Noah (rotary speaker), Korg 01/W (distortion), Native Instruments Reaktor 4.0 (vocoder), and VirSyn Tera (ring modulation).

Index

A

ADC, 20–21
ADSRs, 2, 118, 120–24
Aftertouch, 150
AHDSRs, 126
Alesis QS, 147
Algorithms, 159–60
Aliasing, 25, 56–57
Allpass filters, 81
Amplitude
  definition of, 15
  effects dependent on, 171–72
  loudness vs., 18
  measuring, 18–19
  modulation, 72, 73
Analog-to-digital converter (ADC, A/D),
    20–21
Applied Acoustic Systems Tassman, 75
ARP 2600, 157
Attack. *See* ADSRs
Attack transients, 69
Audio rate modulation, 71–73, 95
Audio signals, 155–56, 163–64
Auto-wah effect, 174

B

Bandpass filters, 82, 83, 87, 88
Band-reject (notch) filters, 82, 83, 87, 90
Bandwidth, 87, 174, 175
Bank Select messages, 153
Bass recording, 14
Beating, 27, 28, 58
Binary numbers, 23
Bit resolution, 22–25
Bits, definition of, 23
Break points, 126
Buchla, Don, 1
Buses, 160
Bytes, definition of, 40

C

Cahill, Thaddeus, 1
Center frequency, 87, 174, 175
Cents, 59
Channel aftertouch, 150
Channel messages, 7
Channel pressure, 150
Chorusing, 169
Circuits, analog vs. digital, 32–33, 139–40
Clangorous sounds, 17
Clavia
  Nord Lead, 157
  Nord Modular, 144
Clipping, 25
Clock signal, 155
Collins, Phil, 166
Comb filters, 84
Compare feature, 38
Compressor/limiters (comp/limiters),
    177–79
Contour generators. *See* Envelope
    generators
Contours. *See* Envelopes
Control change data, 151–54
Corner frequency, 176
CreamWare Noah, 33
Cross-feedback, 168
Csound, 73, 74
Cursor, 42
Cutoff frequency, 85–87, 98, 101
Cycling '74 MaxMSP, 33, 74, 136

D

DAC, 21
DADSRs, 125
Data bytes, 6
Data entry, 42–43
Data resolution, 140–43
DC offset, 176–77

Decay. *See* ADSRs
Decay time, 165
Decibels, 18–19
Delay
  as envelope stage, 125
  LFO start, 109–10
Delay line, 164–65, 167–69
Detuning, 58–60
Difference tones, 27, 28
Diffusion, 166
Digital audio, 20–21
Digital-to-analog converter (D/A,
    DAC), 21
Disk mode, 45
Dispersion, 166
Distortion, 171–73
Doppler effect, 170
Dropouts, 24
Drum kit multisamples, 69–70
DSP (digital signal processing), 159
Duty cycle, 55

E
Echo. *See* Delay line; Reverb
Edit buffer, 37–39
Edit mode, 44–45, 49
Editor/librarian software, 4–6
Effects
  algorithms, 159–60
  bypassing, 162
  chaining, 183
  chorusing, 169
  compressor/limiters, 177–79
  delay, 164–65, 167–69
  distortion, 171–73
  equalization (EQ), 84, 174–77
  external audio inputs for, 163–64
  filter and envelope follower, 173–74
  flanging, 169–70
  history of, 157, 158
  linear frequency shifters, 182
  in multitimbral mode, 48, 163
  noise gates, 179
  number of, 158–60
  phase-shifting, 170
  pitch-shifting, 173

  processors, 158–59
  real-time control of, 182
  reverb, 160, 164–67
  ring modulators, 181–82
  rotary speaker, 170–71
  signal routing and, 160–63
  timbre, 115
  vocoders, 179–81
  wet/dry balance, 161–62, 182–83
Emagic SoundDiver, 4, 5
Emphasis, 88
E-mu Proteus 2000, 42, 64, 69, 84, 144
Ensoniq, 36, 109
  ESQ-1, 70
  Mirage, 33, 66
Envelope followers, 135, 173–74
Envelope generators (EGs)
  with additional stages, 125–27
  ADSR, 2, 118, 120–24
  definition of, 117
  inverted output from, 127
  keyboards and, 118–20
  unusual, 135–36
Envelopes
  definition of, 117, 118
  diagrams of, 118
  examples of, 121
  free-running, 123
  looping, 133
  modulating, 62–63, 93–94, 130–33
  one-dimensional, 117
  rates vs. times for, 124–25
  segment curvature of, 128–30
  single- vs. multiple-triggered,
    127–28
  stages of, 120–24, 125–27, 136
  X/Y (vector), 133–35
Equalization (EQ), 84, 174–77
Exciters, 173

F
Feedback parameters, 168
Filter effects, 173–74
Filters
  allpass, 81
  bandpass, 82, 83, 87, 88

band-reject (notch), 82, 83, 87, 90
center frequency of, 87
comb, 84
cutoff frequency of, 85–87, 98, 101
definition of, 79–80
formant, 84–85
highpass, 81, 83
lowpass, 80, 83, 86, 89
modulating, 91–95, 98–99
multimode, 83, 90
overdrive of, 90
polyphony and, 90–91
resonance of, 88–90
response curves of, 80–82, 84, 86,
    87, 89
rolloff slope of, 85–87
signal routing between, 95–98
state-variable, 83–84
Flanging, 169–70
Foldover, 25
Formant filters, 84–85
Fourier analysis, 16–17
Fractional scaling, 63
Free-run mode, 111–12
Frequency
center, 87, 174, 175
corner, 176
cutoff, 85–87, 98, 101
definition of, 16–18, 54
equalization and, 84, 174–77
modulation, 72–73
Nyquist, 22
Function generators, 146
Fundamental, 17

G
Gain compensation, 88–90
Gated reverb, 166
Gates, 119, 179
Global mode, 44
Granularity, 141
Graphic equalizers, 174–76

H
Hardware synths, 8–10
Harmonics, 17

Hartmann Neuron, 42, 75
Helmholtz, Hermann von, 120, 121,
    122
Hendrix, Jimi, 167
Hertz, 16
Hexadecimal numbers, 6
Highpass filters, 81, 83
Hi-hat groups, 70
Hohner Clavinet, 56
Hold segments, 126

I
Image-Line Fruityloops (FL Studio),
    146
Initialization, 38
Intermodulation distortion, 172
Internet resources, 10
Interpolation, 66, 143

J
Just intonation, 63

K
Kawai
    K5, 73
    K5000, 73
Keyboards
    envelope generators and, 118–20
    MIDI, 119
    tracking, 92–93, 151, 152
    velocity response curves and, 147
Key pressure, 150
Key trigger mode, 111–12
Kick drum samples, 26
Knobs, 31–32, 139
Korg, 41, 101, 126
    M1, 65, 90, 157
    Poly-61, 31–32
    Wavestation, 42, 71, 134
Kurzweil K2000 series, 37, 60, 126,
    146, 150

L
Lag processors, 147
Legato, 128
Leslie speakers, 170–71

LFOs (low-frequency oscillators)
   amount, 106–8, 145
   modulating filter cutoff with,
      94–95, 101
   ramp-up, 110
   rate, 108–9
   start delay, 109–10
   start phase, 112–13
   synchronization of, 114
   trigger modes, 110–12
   uses for, 101–2
   waveforms found in, 102–6
Limiters, 177–79
Linear frequency shifters, 182
Local off mode, 44
Lo-fi effects, 173
Loudness, 15, 18
Loudspeakers, 19–20, 170–71
Lowpass filters, 80, 83, 86, 89

M

Mark of the Unicorn Unisyn, 4
Memory, 35–40
Menus, 41–42
Microphones, 19–20
MIDI
   Bank Select messages, 153
   bulk dump, 6
   clock signal, 155
   control change data messages,
      151–54
   control sources, 149–55
   data bytes, 6
   implementations, 6, 10–11
   keyboards, 119
   local off mode, 44
   messages, 6–7
   note number, 151
   pitch-bend messages, 61–62,
      150–51, 156
   program change messages, 49–50,
      153
   RPNs and NRPNs, 154–55
   status bytes, 6
   system-exclusive data, 4, 155
Minimoog, 63

Modeling, physical, 74–75
Modes, 43–48
Modulation. *See also* Signals
   amplitude, 72, 73
   audio rate, 71–73, 95
   definition of, 139
   envelope, 62–63, 93–94, 130–33
   filter, 91–95, 98–99
   frequency, 72–73
   importance of, 139
   LFO, 94–95, 101
   matrix, 144
   pitch, 61, 62–63
   ring, 73
   secondary, 107, 145–46
   velocity, 94
Monitoring
   evaluating setup for, 29
   tips for, 7–8
Monophonic synths, 45
Moog, Bob, 1–2, 120
Multimode filters, 83, 90
Multisampling
   definition of, 66–67
   drum kit, 69–70
   problems with, 67–68
   velocity cross-switching and, 68–69
Multitap delay, 169
Multitimbral mode, 45–48, 50–51,
   163

N

Native Instruments, 129
   Absynth, 130
   FM7, 36, 72, 133
   Reaktor, 62, 64, 74, 135, 144
Noise, 17, 57–58
   gates, 179
   pink, 57
   white, 57, 105
   zipper, 141
Notch filters. *See* Band-reject filters
Note number, 151
NRPNs (non-registered parameter
   numbers), 154–55
Nyquist frequency, 22

O

Oberheim
  OB-8, 31
  Xpander, 46
Offsets, 47
Operating systems, 33–35
Oscillators. *See also* LFOs; Waveforms
  analog, 54–56, 58–64
  anti-aliased, 56–57
  audio rate modulation and, 71–73
  definition of, 53
  noise and, 57–58
  programming techniques for, 58–64
  sample playback, 65–71
Oscillator sync, 60, 61
Overdrive, 90, 171–72
Overtones, 17

P

Pages, 40–42
Parameters
  changing, 42–43
  definition of, 32
  displaying, 40–42
Partials, 17–18
Parts, 46
Pass-band, 83
Patches. *See* Presets
Phase
  cancellation, 26–29, 161
  in LFOs, 112–13
  -shifting, 170
Ping-pong delay, 168
Pink noise, 57
Pitch
  -bend, 61–62, 150–51, 156
  envelopes, 62–63
  modulating, 61, 62–63
  random, 64–65
  -shifting, 173
Play mode, 44
Pointers, 46
Polarity, 28–29
Poly aftertouch, 150
Polyphonic synths
  filters in, 90–91

monophonic vs., 45
PPG Wave 2.2, 70–71
Predelay, 166
Presets (patches)
  classifying, 39
  definition of, 36
  editing, 46, 49
Program change messages, 49–50, 153
Programs. *See* Presets
Propellerhead Reason, 71, 135
Pulse wave, 54–56, 103–4
Pulse width, 55–56

Q

Q, 88
Quantizers, 147

R

RAM
  definition of, 37
  organizing, 50
  use of, 37–39
Ramp-up, 110
Random "waveforms," 104–6
Reflections, early, 166
Refresh rate, 140
Release. *See* ADSRs
Rendering, 22
Resonance, 88–90
Response curves
  filter, 80–82, 84, 86, 87, 89
  velocity, 147–48
Reverb, 160, 164–67
Reverse reverb, 167
Reverse staccato, 136–37
Ring modulation, 73
Ring modulators, 181–82
Roland D-50, 36, 65, 71, 157
Rolloff slope, 85–87
ROM, 37–39
Rotary speaker effects, 170–71
RPNs (registered parameter
    numbers), 154–55

S

Sample

-and-hold, 104–6
definition of, 21–22
playback, 39, 65–71
start point, 69
word, 40
Samplers, 39
Sampling rate, 21–22
Sawtooth wave, 54–55, 103, 104
Secondary modulation, 107, 145–46
Sends, 160
Sequencer mode, 45
Sequential Circuits
    Prophet-5, 31
    Prophet-VS, 133–34
Serge Modular, 135–36
Shapes. *See* Envelopes
Shelving bands, 176, 177
Sidebands, 95
Signals
    analog vs. digital, 139–40
    audio, 155–56, 163–64
    clock, 155
    dry vs. wet, 161–62, 182–83
    granularity of, 141
    processing, 146–47
    resolution of, 140–41
    routing, 95–98, 143–45, 156,
        160–63
    types of, for modulation, 149–55
Signal-to-noise ratio (s/n ratio), 24
Sine wave. *See also* Waveforms
    definition of, 17, 54–55
    LFOs and, 102, 103
    phase of, 26–29
Single-cycle waves, 70–71
Single mode, 44
Slapback echo, 167
Soft keys, 41–42
Softsynths, 8–10
Software updates and upgrades,
    34–35
Song mode, 45
Sound
    acoustics vs. psychoacoustics, 13
    amplitude of, 15–16, 18–19
    frequency of, 16–18

loudness of, 15, 18
physical modeling of, 74–75
production of, 14–15
sensitivity to, 7–8
speed of, 15
waves, 14–16
Sound Quest Midi Quest, 4, 5
Speech, 85, 179–81
Spring reverbs, 157, 158
Square wave, 54–56, 103–4
Staccato, reverse, 136–37
Stairstepping, 141
State-variable filters, 83–84
Status bytes, 6
Steinberg Xphraze, 71, 134
Stereo delay, 168
Stop-band, 83
String sounds, 58
Sustain. *See* ADSRs
Synchronization
    LFO, 114
    oscillator, 60, 61
    timing, 60
Synthesis
    additive, 73–74
    granular, 74
    physical modeling, 74–75
Synthesizers
    analog vs. digital, 32–33
    batteries for, 37
    capabilities of, 1
    definition of, 1, 2
    hardware vs. software, 8–10
    history of, 1–2
    knobs for, 31–32, 139
    monophonic vs. polyphonic, 45
    owner manuals for, 3
    performance technique for, 2
    purchasing, 34
    researching, on the Internet, 10
    samplers vs., 39
Sys-ex data, 4, 155
System messages, 7

T
Temperaments, 63

Tempo, matching, 113, 114
Timbre
    definition of, 18
    effects, 115
Timing sync, 60
Transducers, 19–20
Tremolo, 101
Triangle wave, 54–55, 102–3
Triggering, single vs. multiple,
    127–28
Trigger modes, 110–12
Triggers, 119
Trills, 107, 114–15
Tuning tables, 63–64

U
U&I Software Metasynth, 73–74
Unison mode, 44
Update rate, 140
Updates, 34–35
Upgrades, 35
Ussachevsky, Vladimir, 120

V
VCAs (voltage-controlled amplifiers),
    145
Velocity
    cross-switching, 68–69
    modulation, 94
    note-off, 149
    note-on, 149
    response curves, 147–48
Vibrato, 72, 101, 109
VirSyn
    Cube, 73, 134
    Tera, 84
Vocoders, 179–81
Voice

allocation, 47–48
channels, 47
count, 9
definition of, 36
reserve, 47
Vowel sounds, 85

W
Waldorf
    Q, 97
    Wave 2.V, 71
Waveform memory, 39–40
Waveforms
    aliasing and, 56–57
    amplitude of, 15, 18–19
    analog, 54–56
    combining, 73–74, 76
    discovering, in factory patches,
        76–77
    found in LFOs, 102–6
    frequency of, 16–18, 54
    listening to, 75–76
    phase of, 26–29, 112–13
    single-cycle, 70–71
    swapping, 77
Wave sequencing, 71
White noise, 57, 105

Y
Yamaha, 5, 36, 47, 72, 126, 127
    DX7, 31, 36–37, 72, 157
    TX802, 46, 64
    TX81Z, 36–37
    VL-1, 75

Z
Zero, division by, 146
Zipper noise, 141